John B Bagshawe

The Catechism and Holy Scripture

John B Bagshawe

The Catechism and Holy Scripture

ISBN/EAN: 9783742861238

Manufactured in Europe, USA, Canada, Australia, Japa

Cover: Foto ©ninafisch / pixelio.de

Manufactured and distributed by brebook publishing software (www.brebook.com)

John B Bagshawe

The Catechism and Holy Scripture

THE CATECHISM AND HOLY SCRIPTURE,

WITH AN

APPENDIX AND NOTES.

BY THE

REV. J. B. BAGSHAWE, D.D.,

S. ELIZABETH'S, RICHMOND, SURREY.

BEING A

SECOND EDITION OF
"THE CATECHISM ILLUSTRATED."

R. WASHBOURNE,
18 PATERNOSTER ROW, LONDON.
1885.
(All Rights Reserved.)

Nihil obstat.

✠ GULIELMUS EP. AMYCLANUS,
Censor Deputatus.

Imprimatur.

HENRICUS EDUARDUS,
Card. Archiep. Westmon.

"THE CATECHISM AND HOLY SCRIPTURE" appears to me to be a very valuable exposition of the Catechism, by proof and interpretation from Holy Scripture. It lays a solid foundation for the doctrines of faith in a way most useful, not only to the taught, but to the teacher. I hope it may be largely used in our schools of every grade.

It will also be most useful for the instruction of those who are seeking to know the Catholic Faith, being even more full and detailed than Bossuet's Exposition; and as such I warmly commend it.

HENRY EDWARD,
Cardinal Archbishop of Westminster.

Easter, 1885.

PREFACE

TO THE

FIRST EDITION.

THIS compilation is intended to assist our children in acquiring a better knowledge of the Holy Scripture. The Catholic Church has always loved the Written Word of God. In the ages of persecution her children thought it their duty to preserve the Holy Scripture from profanation, if necessary, at the risk of their lives. Many martyrs suffered death rather than let their sacred books fall into pagan hands. When the bishops later on were able publicly to meet in Council, they placed the book of the Holy Scriptures on a throne in the midst of them. In the public offices of the Church those marks of respect to the book of the Gospels were introduced which we see used in our own days. When evil times arrived, and the old framework of society was broken up, it was nothing but the constant care of the Church which preserved to us the Holy Scriptures. In the middle ages—emphatically the ages of faith—men thought it an honour to spend their lives in copying them. They deemed no amount of time and labour too great to spend in enriching and beautifying those volumes which contained the Word of God. As they had these volumes in their hands, so did they also bear them in their hearts. Night and day you might have heard the praises of God sung in the words of Holy Scripture in a hundred monasteries. Every monk was supposed to know by heart the whole Psalter, and to carry out most literally the precept given by God to the Jews, "And these words, which I command thee this day, shall be in thy heart; and thou shalt tell them to thy children, and thou shalt meditate upon them sitting in thy house, and walking on thy journey, sleeping and rising" (Deut. vi. 6). Every one, who was educated at all, was familiar with the language of the Scriptures, so that the very words and phrases of Scripture had insinuated themselves into every kind of writing on indifferent subjects. Dr. Maitland, in the life-like account he gives of those times, tells us that the only way to understand the meaning of middle-age writers in difficult places is by referring to the language used in the Bible.

This shows us what is the instinct of the Catholic Church about the Holy Scriptures. The time did indeed come when restrictions were found necessary. When every artisan began to think it his business to find a faith for himself—and a confusion of tongues was the consequence; when men were "carried away by every wind of doctrine," and the "unlearned and unstable" had come upon those things "hard to be understood" which, S. Peter tells us, they "wrest to their own destruction" (2 S. Pet. iii. 16); then, indeed, the Church found it necessary, in some degree, to keep the Bible from the hands of those who were using it in such a manner as to profane the Holy Word of God and to endanger their own souls. The Church, therefore, made certain wise regulations about reading the Scriptures, intended to direct us how to make them, as the Apostle says, "profitable to teach, to reprove, to correct, to instruct in justice: that the man of God may be perfect, furnished to every good work" (2 Tim. iii. 16); at the same time commanding and exhorting her children to apply themselves earnestly, under proper guidance, to the study of them.—*Conc. Trid. Sess.* 5. c. 1 *de Refor.* Almost in our own times we find Pope Pius VI. declaring that the faithful should be "excited to the reading of the Holy Scriptures: for these are the most abundant sources, which ought to be left open to every one, to draw from them purity of morals, and of doctrine, to eradicate the errors which are so widely disseminated in these corrupt times;" and praising those who had put them before the faithful "in the language of their country," and in a manner "suitable to everyone's capacity."—*Letter of Pope Pius VI. to the Archbishop of Florence.*

It appears to me that the present is especially a time when Catholics are bound to have a proper knowledge of the Holy Scriptures and to display a great devotion towards them. The distinguishing heresy of the day is an attack on Revelation generally, and in particular on the Inspiration of the Bible, which ought to bring out a proportionate spirit of loyalty towards it in the Church. On the other hand, the danger to be apprehended to Faith, from an extensive use of the Bible, seems in a great measure to have died out with the decay of the principle of private judgment exercised on Scripture. This principle itself has been weighed in the balance and found wanting. All the evil that it could do has long since been done. The errors to which it gave rise have long since been confuted, so that it now seems more than ever a duty incumbent upon all Catholics to make themselves familiar with the Word of God, and to draw as plentifully as possible from those fountains which the Spirit of God has opened to them.

Of course, it is not to be supposed that any adequate knowledge of Holy Scripture can be acquired by reading a small collection of texts; but still I think that children would get a foundation for this kind of knowledge, and a taste for it, by looking for and learning a certain number of striking passages, and becoming acquainted with their application to the different doctrines taught by the Church.

The primary object of this book is not controversial, but devotional; that is, not to make our children sharp controversialists, but to store their minds with some of the grand thoughts and beautiful expressions which occur in the Inspired Writings, so that the truths of religion may not be to them naked forms of words, but may be associated with beautiful and devotional thoughts likely to come back to them in times of trial. I say the *primary* object because, of course, the principal texts, which will be useful to those who are called upon to give an account of their Faith, will be found in their places.

I have called the book the "Catechism *Illustrated*," because it does not attempt or profess to *prove* the Catholic Faith from Scripture. To do so would be entirely contrary to the spirit of the Church. Every Catholic knows that the doctrines of the Catholic Church are independent of Scripture; that is to say, that the Church teaches from the plenitude of the power committed to her; that she did so from the beginning, before the New Testament was written—centuries, indeed, before the Bible was collected into its present form; and that she would have done so in precisely the same manner had they never been written. For example, every Catholic knows that the Faith of the Church about the Holy Eucharist would have been precisely what it is, had it pleased God that not one of the passages relating to it ever had been written; and, therefore, that these passages, however clear they may be, cannot properly be referred to as the ground of the Church's teaching.

A Catholic looks upon the Church and the Holy Scriptures as two distinct and independent sources of religious knowledge, both coming from God—the one illustrating and explaining indeed, but not the mere echo of the other, dependent on it for authority.

I have also indulged in the hope that this book may be useful to Protestants. I believe the Catechism to be one of the best possible books of controversy, to those; at least, who are inquiring with a real desire to find the truth. It is impossible for anyone to have a reasonably accurate knowledge of the Catholic Faith without being brought nearer to it, especially when put in the way of seeing how closely it agrees, not with half a dozen isolated passages, but with the whole teaching and spirit of the Scriptures.

I must observe that, as the object of the book is not *con-*

troversy, but *illustration*, it will sometimes happen that texts are chosen which would not be legitimate in strict controversy; that is, texts the words of which admit of a different explanation from the one suggested, or which, from the context, appear to have been originally used in a different sense. I have subjoined a few words on the canon of Scripture; and also a list of the different books given in the Catholic and Protestant Bible, with a view to assisting such Protestants as may wish to verify any of the passages quoted.

I must conclude by asking the indulgence of the reader for the many omissions which he will certainly find in this little book; and by hoping that it may please God to make it a means of increasing the knowledge and love of His Holy Word, and of leading souls to that Faith taught by His Church.

RICHMOND,
Feast of SS. Peter and Paul, 1870.

PREFACE

TO THE

SECOND EDITION.

In publishing this second edition of the "Catechism Illustrated," I have called it by a new name, because the original title led people to suppose that the book was a Catechism illustrated by pictures, or a "Pictorial Catechism," and, indeed, at the present day, the word "Illustrated" is most commonly used in this sense. Those who wanted pictures would naturally be disappointed to find that my book did not contain any, and, on the other hand, those who did not care about pictures would be likely to avoid the book. I have, therefore, called the new edition, "The Catechism and Holy Scripture," which, it is believed, will more clearly express the character and objects of the work.

In this edition the texts of Scripture have been arranged so as to correspond with the new Version of the Catechism lately issued by the English Bishops. Besides the changes of the wording and arrangement which have been made in the new Catechism, a few questions and answers have been added for the more exact explanation of the Catholic Faith; it has, therefore, been necessary to introduce a number of new texts for their illustration. In other respects the book is unchanged.

It is obvious that a book of this kind is calculated to be of great use, and I desire it to be more widely known and circulated. All converts should make a careful study of the words of the Catechism, for in no other way can they get so accurate and complete an idea of the Faith. If they learn it in the concise way in which it is taught to Catholic children, they will get to know the Catholic Doctrine as a whole, and not fall into the mistake of studying those parts in which they are specially interested, and passing over others. A catechism, accompanied, as this is, by a series of Scripture texts, enforcing the words of the Catechism and throwing a light on their significance, cannot fail to be a very great assistance in the study.

It is most desirable, moreover, that our own people should get a better knowledge of the Scriptures. It would be a great advantage to all our children, if they were familiar with, at any rate, the most striking passages which bear on the doctrines and practices of a Christian life. This applies specially to children of the upper classes. We not unfrequently find young people who have been carefully educated in other things, and yet who have very little knowledge of the Holy Scriptures. They appear, indeed, hardly to have heard even of the most beautiful and striking passages that illustrate and enforce the teaching of the Church. This seems to show a great defect in the way in which they learned their religion. Some plan should be adopted to secure at least a reasonable acquaintance with the Holy Scriptures; for if the children have not this, they will be placed at a great disadvantage in after life, and will also be deprived of a great means of devotion.

Those whose duty it will hereafter be to teach religion to others, such as students at the training colleges, ought, it seems to me, to take special care to acquire a good knowledge of Holy Scripture. Of course, a knowledge of isolated passages is not a knowledge of Scripture—that can only be gained by continuous reading—but an acquaintance with the most striking texts would be a beginning, and would be likely to give a taste for Scripture reading, especially if children were encouraged to find out the passages in the places in which they occur. I have given the quotations at tolerable length, so that they may be useful for spiritual reading.

Let me call attention to the "Index of Texts" in the Appendix. I have there given a list of the most striking passages on each subject, with a word or two of each text—as a kind of key-note—and a reference to its place, both in the book, and in the Holy Scripture.

At the end of the introduction is a complete catalogue of the books of Scripture as they stand in the Vulgate, and *also* as they are to be found in the Church of England version; and in the Appendix there are a few passages from the Fathers, on disputed points, taken from Waterworth's "Faith of Catholics."

J. B. B.

S. Elizabeth's, Richmond,
Easter, 1885.

INTRODUCTION.

ON THE CANON OF SCRIPTURE.

The canon of Scripture received by the Catholic Church is that laid down by the Council of Trent. The word 'canon' means *rule*, and here it is used to signify the catalogue of works which the Church receives as inspired by God. Let us consider (1) the process by which such a canon of Scripture was arrived at; (2) the authority by which it became binding on the consciences of Christians; (3) what this canon actually is.

The Scriptures were written, not as one whole, but in the shape of a number of different treatises, which, so far from making parts of a whole, were written by different authors, at different times, addressed to different people, and for widely varying objects. Many books were addressed to small bodies, and, in the first instance, were not *intended* for all mankind. For example, most of St. Paul's epistles were written to the people of some particular city, for some special purpose, and were intended to be read only by the Christians residing there, and perhaps by those of the neighbouring towns. It must, therefore, have been many years before all the different parts of the Scripture could have been even known to Christians generally, and many more years before the Christian world could have been able to form any decided opinion on their genuineness and authority. We find, accordingly, in the early Church, a great uncertainty about the Scriptures. Portions of the New Testament were almost unknown in some countries, whilst apocryphal writings of all descriptions, highly coloured accounts of our Lord's life and miracles, and of the teaching of His Apostles, sprang up everywhere and appeared to carry with them more or less authority. How was all this confusion to end? It was obviously beyond the power of any individual, however learned and holy he might be, to pronounce in such a case as this. It could only end by the intervention of an authority having a right to speak in the Name of God. Nothing less than a Divine authority could venture to pronounce on the Divine Inspiration of God's Word. Accordingly, in due time, that is, when the knowledge of Scripture was sufficiently diffused, the Church did pronounce, and that decision has been final. In the year of our Lord 397 the Council of Carthage, following the tradition of the Church, and the teaching of other Councils which had preceded it, published a rule or canon of Scripture which has been the canon of the Christian Church ever since. The Council of Trent did little more than re-enact the same canon.

About three hundred years ago, when this canon had been for eleven centuries acknowledged by all Christians, Protestants thought fit to reconsider it, and to leave out some books both of the Old and New Testament. On what principle they did so is not very apparent. As they had rejected the idea of a Church teaching with authority from God,—the one principle on which Christians had hitherto received the Bible,—it is not easy to see how they could find a firm basis for a decision on the Holy Scriptures; and, accordingly, we are not much surprised to find that they could not agree amongst themselves, and that the Lutherans adopted one canon and the Calvinists another. The unfortunate result, however, is that, to the present day, Protestants, on the faith of the judgment of certain private individuals at the time of the Reformation, reject some portions of the Word of God. I have thought it desirable, therefore, to give a list of the books comprised in the canon of Scripture, showing the different names by which they are sometimes known, and marking those omitted by Protestants.

In the Anglican version the Psalms are divided and numbered in a manner which slightly differs from that in use in the Catholic Church.

In each version there are 150 Psalms. The two versions correspond until the ninth Psalm; but the ninth Psalm of the Vulgate includes the ninth and tenth of the English version. The consequence of this is that from Psalm ix. to Psalm cxiii. the number given to each Psalm in the English version is *one above* that given in the Vulgate. Thus the Miserere, Psalm l., is called in the English version, Psalm li. Psalm cxiii. of the Vulgate contains Psalm cxiv. and cxv. of the Anglican version, whilst, on the other hand, Psalms cxiv. and cxv. of the Vulgate are both comprised in Psalm cxvi. of the other version. Psalm cxvii., therefore, of the English version corresponds to Psalm cxvi. of the Vulgate; and so the Psalms in the former continue to be one higher in number till Psalm cxlvii. of the English version, which includes Psalms cxlvi. and cxlvii. of the Vulgate, so that Psalms cxlviii., cxlix., and cl. correspond in the two versions.

There is also a slight difference in the numbering of the verses in some of the Psalms. It may be added that there is more variation in the translations of the Psalms than in those of most other parts of Scripture; probably on account of their highly poetical nature, and on account of the devotional use made of them in the Church for so many centuries. It may be well to observe that a great many of the Scripture names are written and pronounced in two different ways—one taken from the Latin form of the Hebrew name, the other from the original. For the former it may be said that it is the form which has been almost exclusively used in the Christian Church for eighteen centuries; for the latter, that it is supposed more nearly to approach the name as actually used. In what degree either pronunciation resembles that in use in the time (say) of King David, may be rather a matter of speculation.

LIST OF BOOKS OF SCRIPTURE.

Old Testament.

	The Vulgate, or Catholic Version.			The Anglican Version.
Pentateuch	Genesis	otherwise called	...	Genesis.
	Exodus	,, ,,	...	Exodus.
	Leviticus	,, ,,	...	Leviticus.
	Numbers	,, ,,	...	Numbers.
	Deuteronomy	,, ,,	...	Deuteronomy.
	Josue	,, ,,	...	Joshua.
	Judges	,, ,,	...	Judges.
	Ruth	,, ,,	...	Ruth.
	1 Kings	,, ,,	...	1 Samuel.
	2 Kings	,, ,,	...	2 Samuel.
	3 Kings	,, ,,	...	1 Kings.
	4 Kings	,, ,,	...	2 Kings.
	1 Paralipomenon	,, ,,	...	1 Chronicles.
	2 Paralipomenon	,, ,,	...	2 Chronicles.
	1 Esdras	,, ,,	...	Ezra.
	2 Esdras	,, ,,	...	Nehemiah.
	Tobias	,, ,,	...	omitted.
	Judith	,, ,,	...	omitted.
	Esther	,, ,,	...	Esther.
	Job	,, ,,	...	Job.
	Psalms	,, ,,	...	Psalms.
	Proverbs	,, ,,	...	Proverbs.
	Ecclesiastes, *abbrev.* Eccl.	,,	...	Ecclesiastes.
	Canticle of Canticles	,,	...	Song of Solomon.
	Wisdom	,, ,,	...	omitted.
	Ecclesiasticus, *abbrev.* Ecclus.		...	omitted.
Greater Prophets	Isaias	,, ,,	...	Isaiah.
	Jeremias	,, ,,	...	Jeremiah.
	Lamentations	,, ,,	...	Lamentations.
	Baruch	,, ,,	...	omitted.
	Ezechiel	,, ,,	...	Ezekiel.
	Daniel	,, ,,	...	Daniel.

Introduction.

	The Vulgate, or Catholic Version.			The Anglican Version.
Lesser Prophets.	Osee	otherwise called	...	Hosea.
	Joel	,, ,,	...	Joel.
	Amos	,, ,,	...	Amos.
	Abdias	,, ,,	...	Obadiah.
	Jonas	,, ,,	...	Jonah.
	Micheas	,, ,,	...	Micah.
	Nahum	,, ,,	...	Nahum.
	Habacuc	,, ,,	...	Habakkuk.
	Sophonias	,, ,,	...	Zephaniah.
	Aggeus	,, ,,	...	Haggai.
	Zacharias	,, ,,	...	Zechariah.
	Malachias	,, ,,	...	Malachi.
	1 Machabees	,, ,,	...	omitted.
	2 Machabees	,, ,,	...	omitted.

New Testament.

Gospels.
- S. Matthew.
- S. Mark.
- S. Luke.
- S. John.

Acts of the Apostles.
S. Paul to the Romans.
,,   1 Corinthians.
,,   2 Corinthians.
,,   Galatians.
,,   Ephesians.
,,   Philippians.
,,   Colossians.
,,   1 Thessalonians.
,,   2 Thessalonians.
,,   1 Timothy.
,,   2 Timothy.
,,   Titus.
,,   Philemon.
,,   Hebrews.

S. James.
1 S. Peter.
2 S. Peter.
1 S. John.
2 S. John.
3 S. John.
S. Jude.
Apocalypse, otherwise called Revelation.

THE CATECHISM AND HOLY SCRIPTURE.

FAITH.

CHAPTER I.

1. Q. Who made you?
A. God made me.

God created man of the earth, and made him after His own image (*Ecclus*. xvii. 1).

Know ye that the Lord He is God: He made us, and not we ourselves. We are His people and the sheep of His pasture (*Ps*. xcix. 3).

2. Q. Why did God make you?
A. God made me to know Him, love Him, and serve Him in this world, and to be happy with Him for ever in the next.

Now this is eternal life: that they may know Thee, the only true God, and Jesus Christ, whom Thou hast sent (*S. John* xvii. 3).

My son, give Me thy heart: and let thy eyes keep My ways (*Prov*. xxiii. 26).

For what have I in heaven? and besides Thee what do I desire upon earth? For Thee my flesh and my heart hath fainted away: Thou art the God of my heart, and the God that is my portion for ever (*Ps*. lxxii. 25).

By Thy ordinance the day goeth on: for all things serve Thee (*Ps.* cxviii. 91).

Serve ye the Lord with fear: and rejoice unto Him with trembling (*Ps.* ii. 11).

Fear not, Abram, I am thy protector, and thy reward exceeding great (*Gen.* xv. 1).

One thing I have asked of the Lord, this will I seek after; that I may dwell in the house of the Lord all the days of my life; that I may see the delight of the Lord, and visit His temple (*Ps.* xxvi. 4).

3. Q. To whose image and likeness did God make you?

A. God made me to His own image and likeness.

And He said: Let us make man to our image and likeness (*Gen.* i. 26).

4. Q. Is this likeness to God in your body, or in your soul?

A. This likeness to God is chiefly in my soul.

Stripping yourselves of the old man with his deeds, and putting on the new, him who is renewed unto knowledge, according to the image of Him that created him (*Col.* iii. 9).

5. Q. How is your soul like to God?

A. My soul is like to God because it is a spirit, and is immortal.

God is a Spirit, and they that adore Him, must adore Him in spirit and in truth (*S. John* iv. 24).

Now the Lord is a Spirit. And where the Spirit of the Lord is, there is liberty (2 *Cor.* iii. 17).

6. Q. What do you mean when you say that your soul is immortal?

A. When I say that my soul is immortal, I mean that my soul can never die.

7. Q. Of which must you take most care, of your body or of your soul?

A. I must take most care of my soul; for Christ has said, "What doth it profit a man if he gain the whole world, and suffer the loss of his own soul?" (*S. Matt.* xvi. 26.)

And fear ye not them that kill the body, and are not able to kill the soul: but rather fear Him that can destroy both soul and body into hell (*S. Matt.* x. 28).

Seek ye therefore first the kingdom of God, and His justice, and all these things shall be added unto you (*S. Matt.* vi. 33).

For whosoever will save his life, shall lose it; for he that shall lose his life for My sake, shall save it. For what doth it profit a man, if he gain the whole world, and lose himself, and cast away himself? (*S. Luke* ix. 24.)

The kingdom of heaven is like unto a treasure hidden in a field; which a man having found, hideth, and for joy thereof goeth, and selleth all that he hath, and buyeth that field. Again the kingdom of heaven is like to a merchant seeking good pearls: who when he had found one pearl of great price, went his way, and sold all that he had, and bought it (*S. Matt.* xiii. 44).

Lay not up to yourselves treasures on earth: where the rust and moth consume, and where thieves break through and steal. But lay up to yourselves treasures in heaven: where neither rust nor moth doth consume, and where thieves do not break through, nor steal (*S. Matt.* vi. 19).

And He spoke a similitude to them, saying: The land of a certain rich man brought forth plenty of fruits. And he thought within himself, saying: What shall I do, because I have no room where to bestow my fruits? And he said: This will I do: I will pull down my barns, and will build greater: and into them will I gather all things that are grown to me, and my goods. And I will say to my soul: Soul, thou hast much goods laid up for many years; take thy rest, eat, drink, make good cheer. But God said to him: Thou fool, this night do they require thy soul of thee; and whose shall those things be which thou hast provided? So is he that layeth up treasure for himself, and is not rich towards God (*S. Luke* xii. 16).

8. Q. What must you do to save your soul?

A. To save my soul I must worship God by Faith, Hope, and Charity; that is, I must believe in Him, I must hope in Him, and I must love Him with my whole heart.

O the depth of the riches of the wisdom and of the knowledge of God! How incomprehensible are His judgments, and how unsearchable His ways! (*Rom.* xi. 23.)

For the weapons of our warfare are not carnal, but mighty to God unto the pulling down of fortifications, destroying counsels, and every height that exalteth itself against the knowledge of God, and bringing into captivity every understanding unto the obedience of Christ (2 *Cor.* x. 5).

For we are saved by hope. But hope that is seen, is not hope. For what a man seeth, why doth he hope for? But if we hope for that which we see not, we wait for it with patience (*Rom.* viii. 24).

In Thee, O Lord, have I hoped, let me never be confounded (*Ps.* xxx. 2).

Who then shall separate us from the love of Christ? shall tribulation? or distress? or famine? or nakedness? or danger? or persecution? or the sword? (*Rom.* viii. 35.)

If then you obey My commandments, which I command you this day, that you love the Lord your God, and serve Him with all your heart, and with all your soul: He will give to your land the early rain and the latter rain, that you may gather in your corn, and your wine, and your oil (*Deut.* xi. 13).

CHAPTER II.

9. Q. What is faith?
A. Faith is a supernatural gift of God, which enables us to believe without doubting whatever God has revealed.

For whatsoever is born of God, overcometh the world: and this is the victory which overcometh the world, our faith. Who is he that overcometh the world, but he that believeth that Jesus is the Son of God? (1 *S. John* v. 4.)

But let him ask in faith, nothing wavering. For he that wavereth is like a wave of the sea, which is moved and carried about by the wind (*S. James* i. 6).

See, here is water, what doth hinder me from being baptized? And Philip said: If thou believest with all thy heart thou mayst. And he answering, said: I believe that Jesus Christ is the Son of God (*Acts* viii. 36).

10. Q. Why must you believe whatever God has revealed?
A. I must believe whatever God has revealed, because God is the very truth, and can neither deceive nor be deceived.

God is not as a man, that He should lie, nor as the son of man, that He should be changed. Hath He said then, and will He not do? hath He spoken, and will He not fulfil? (*Num.* xxiii. 19.)

For His mercy is confirmed upon us: and the truth of the Lord remaineth for ever (*Ps.* cxvi. 2).

As for my God, His way is undefiled: the words of the Lord are fire-tried: He is the protector

11. Q. How are you to know what God has revealed?

A. I am to know what God has revealed by the testimony, teaching, and authority of the Catholic Church.

of all that trust in Him (*Ps.* xvii. 31).

And the Lord said to me: Thou hast seen well: for I will watch over my word to perform it (*Jer.* i. 12).

Heaven and earth shall pass away, but My words shall not pass (*S. Mark* xiii. 31).

Necessity of Revelation.

And Jesus answering, said to him: Blessed art thou, Simon Barjona: because flesh and blood hath not revealed it to thee, but My Father who is in heaven (*S. Matt.* xvi. 17).

At that time Jesus answered and said: I confess to Thee, O Father, Lord of heaven and earth, because Thou hast hid these things from the wise and prudent, and hast revealed them to little ones (*S. Matt.* xi. 25).

And no one knoweth the Son, but the Father: neither doth any one know the Father, but the Son, and he to whom it shall please the Son to reveal Him (*S. Matt.* xi. 27).

Testimony of the Church.

But you shall receive the power of the Holy Ghost coming upon you, and you shall be witnesses unto me in Jerusalem, and in all Judea, and Samaria, and even to the uttermost part of the earth (*Acts* i. 8).

This Jesus hath God raised again, whereof all we are witnesses (*Acts* ii. 33).

Authority of the Church.

He that heareth you, heareth Me : and he that despiseth you, despiseth Me. And he that despiseth Me, despiseth Him that sent Me (*S. Luke* x. 16).

12. Q. Who gave the Catholic Church divine authority to teach?

A. Jesus Christ gave the Catholic Church divine authority to teach, when He said : "Go ye and teach all nations" (*S. Matt.* xxviii. 19).

All power is given to Me in heaven and in earth : Go ye, therefore, and teach all nations : baptizing them in the Name of the Father, and of the Son, and of the Holy Ghost. Teaching them to observe all things whatsoever I have commanded you : and behold I am with you all days, even to the consummation of the world (*S. Matt.* xxviii. 18).

Go ye into the whole world and preach the Gospel to every creature. He that believeth and is baptized shall be saved; but he that believeth not shall be condemned (*S. Mark* xvi. 15).

13. Q. What are the chief things which God has revealed?

A. The chief things which God has revealed are contained in the Apostles' Creed.

14. Q. Say the Apostles' Creed.

A. I believe in God, the Father Almighty, Creator of heaven and earth;—and in Jesus Christ, His only Son, our Lord;—who was conceived by the Holy Ghost, born of the Virgin Mary;—suffered under Pontius Pilate, was crucified, dead, and buried;—He descended into hell; the third day He rose again from the dead;— He ascended into heaven; sitteth at the right hand of God the Father Almighty;—from thence He shall come to judge the living and the dead.—I believe in the Holy Ghost;— the Holy Catholic Church; the Communion of Saints;—the forgiveness of sins;—the resurrection of the body;—and life everlasting. Amen.

15. Q. How is the Apostles' Creed divided?

A. The Apostles' Creed is divided into twelve parts or articles.

FIRST ARTICLE OF THE CREED.

16. Q. What is the first article of the Creed?

A. The first article of the Creed is: "I believe in God, the Father Almighty, Creator of heaven and earth."

17. Q. What is God?

A. God is the supreme Spirit, who alone exists of Himself, and is infinite in all perfections.

For this cause I bow my knees to the Father of our Lord Jesus Christ, of whom all paternity in heaven and earth is named (*Eph.* iii. 14).

Blessed be God and the Father of our Lord Jesus Christ, the Father of mercies and the God of all consolation (2 *Cor.* i. 3).

Self-existence of God.

Moses said to God: Lo, I shall go to the children of Israel, and say to them: The God of your fathers hath sent me to you. If they should say to me: What is His name? what shall I say to them? God said to Moses: I AM WHO AM. He said: Thus shalt thou say to the children of Israel: HE WHO IS, hath sent me to you (*Exod.* iii. 13).

For as the Father hath life in Himself; so He hath given to the Son also to have life in Himself (*S. John* v. 26).

Abraham your father rejoiced that he might see My day: he saw it, and was glad. The Jews therefore said to Him: Thou art not yet fifty years old, and hast Thou seen Abraham? Jesus said to them: Amen, amen, I say to you, before Abraham was made, I am (*S. John* viii. 56).

Majesty of God.

Behold the Lord God shall come with strength, and His arm shall rule: behold His reward is with Him and His work is before Him. He shall feed His flock like a shepherd: He shall gather together the lambs with His arm, and shall take them up in His bosom, and He Himself shall carry them that are with young. Who hath measured the waters in the hollow of His hand, and weighed the heavens with His palm? Who hath poised with three fingers the bulk of the earth, and weighed the mountains in scales, and the hills in a balance? Who hath forwarded the spirit of the Lord? or who hath been His counsellor, and hath taught Him? With whom hath He consulted, and who hath instructed Him, and taught Him the path of justice, and taught Him knowledge, and showed Him the way of understanding? Behold the gentiles are as a drop of a bucket, and are counted as the smallest grain of a balance: behold the islands are as a little dust. And Libanus shall not be enough to burn, nor the beasts thereof sufficient for a burnt-offering. All nations are before Him as if they had no being at all, and are counted to Him as nothing, and vanity (*Isa.* xl. 10).

For great power always belonged to Thee alone: and who shall resist the strength of Thy arm? For the whole world before Thee is as the least grain of the balance, and as a drop of the morning dew, that falleth down upon the earth (*Wisd.* xi. 22).

He that liveth for ever created all things together. God only shall be justified, and He remaineth an invincible king for ever. Who is able to declare His works? For who shall search out His glorious acts? And who shall show forth the power of His majesty? or who shall be able to declare His mercy? (*Ecclus.* xviii. 1.)

For who shall say to Thee: What hast Thou done? or who shall withstand Thy judgment? or who shall come before Thee to be a revenger of wicked men? or who shall accuse Thee, if the nations perish, which Thou hast made? (*Wisd.* xii. 12.)

Goodness of God.

And behold one came and said to Him: Good Master, what good shall I do that I may have life everlasting? Who said to him: Why askest thou Me concerning good? One is good, God (*S. Matt.* xix. 16).

But Thou, our God, art gracious

and true, patient, and ordering all things in mercy. For if we sin, we are Thine, knowing Thy greatness: and if we sin not, we know that we are counted with Thee. For to know Thee is perfect justice: and to know Thy justice, and Thy power, is the root of immortality (*Wisd.* xv. 1).

What is man that Thou art mindful of him? or the son of man that Thou visitest him? (*Ps.* viii. 5.)

18. Q. Why is God called Almighty?

A. God is called "Almighty" because He can do all things: "With God all things are possible" (*S. Matt.* xix. 26).

Because no word shall be impossible with God (*S. Luke* i. 37).

He said to them: The things that are impossible with men, are possible with God (*S. Luke* xviii. 27).

19. Q. Why is God called Creator of heaven and earth?

God is called "Creator of heaven and earth," because He made heaven and earth, and all things, out of nothing, by His word.

By the word of the Lord the heavens were established, and all the power of them by the spirit of His mouth (*Ps.* xxxii. 6).

For He spoke and they were made: He commanded and they were created (*Ps.* xxxii. 9).

Thou art worthy, O Lord our God, to receive glory, and honour, and power: because Thou hast created all things, and for Thy will they were, and have been created (*Apoc.* iv. 11).

And: Thou in the beginning,

O Lord, didst found the earth: and the works of Thy hands are the heavens. They shall perish, but Thou shalt continue: and they shall all grow old as a garment. And as a vesture shalt Thou change them, and they shall be changed: but Thou art the self-same, and Thy years shall not fail (*Heb.* i. 10).

Thus saith the Lord: Heaven is My throne, and the earth My footstool: what is this house that you will build to Me? and what is this place of My rest? My hand made all these things, and all these things were made, saith the Lord. But to whom shall I have respect, but to him that is poor and little, and of a contrite spirit, and that trembleth at My words? (*Isa.* lxvi. 1.)

Where wast thou when I laid the foundations of the earth? tell Me if thou hast understanding. Who hath laid the measures thereof, if thou knowest? or who hath stretched the line upon it? Upon what are its bases grounded? or who laid the corner-stone thereof, when the morning stars praised Me together, and all the sons of God made a joyful melody? Who shut up the sea with doors, when it broke forth as issuing out of the womb: when I made a cloud the garment thereof, and wrapped it in a mist as in swaddling bands? I set My bounds around it, and made it bars and doors; and I said: Hitherto thou shalt come, and shalt go no further, and here thou shalt break thy swelling waves (*Job* xxxviii. 4).

God the Preserver.

How great are Thy works, O Lord! Thou hast made all things in wisdom: the earth is filled with Thy riches. So is this great sea, which stretcheth wide its arms: there are creeping things without number, creatures little and great. There the ships shall go: this sea-dragon which Thou hast formed to play therein. All expect of Thee that Thou give them food in season. What Thou givest to them they shall gather up: when Thou openest Thy hand, they shall all be filled with good. But if Thou turn away Thy face, they shall be troubled: Thou shalt take away their breath, and they shall fail, and shall return to their dust. Thou shalt send forth Thy spirit, and they shall be created: and Thou shalt renew the face of the earth (*Ps.* ciii. 24).

Are not two sparrows sold for a farthing? and not one of them shall fall on the ground without your Father. But the very hairs of your head are all numbered. Fear not therefore: better are

20. Q. Had God any beginning?
A. God had no beginning: He always was, He is, and He always will be.

you than many sparrows (*S. Matt.* x. 30).

I am alpha and omega, the beginning and the end, saith the Lord God, who is, and who was, and who is to come, the Almighty (*Apoc.* i. 8).

But of this one thing be not ignorant, my beloved, that one day with the Lord, is as a thousand years, and a thousand years as one day (2 *S. Peter* iii. 8).

For a thousand years in Thy sight are as yesterday, which is past. And as a watch in the night, as things that are counted nothing, shall their years be (*Ps.* lxxxix. 4.)

Before the mountains were made, or the earth and the world was formed: from eternity and to eternity Thou art God (*Ps.* lxxxix. 2).

The number of the days of men at the most are a hundred years: as a drop of water of the sea are they esteemed: and as a pebble of the sand, so are a few years compared to eternity (*Ecclus.* xviii. 8).

21. Q. Where is God?
A. God is everywhere.

Whither shall I go from Thy spirit? or whither shall I flee from Thy face? If I ascend into heaven, Thou art there: if I descend into hell, Thou art present. If I take my wings early in the morning, and dwell in the

22. Q. Does God know and see all things?
A. God knows and sees all things, even our most secret thoughts.

uttermost parts of the sea: even there also shall Thy hand lead me, and Thy right hand shall hold me. And I said: Perhaps darkness shall cover me: and night shall be my light in my pleasures. But darkness shall not be dark to Thee, and night shall be light as the day: the darkness thereof, and the light thereof are alike to Thee (*Ps.* cxxxviii. 7).

For in Him we live and move and are (*Acts* xvii. 28).

O the depth of the riches of the wisdom and of the knowledge of God! How incomprehensible are His judgments, and how unsearchable His ways! For who hath known the mind of the Lord? or who hath been His counsellor? (*Rom.* xi. 33.)

But thou when thou shalt pray, enter into thy chamber, and having shut the door, pray to thy Father in secret: and thy Father who seeth in secret will repay thee (*S. Matt.* vi. 6).

Say not: I shall be hidden from God, and who shall remember me from on high? In such a multitude I shall not be known: for what is my soul in such an immense creation? (*Ecclus.* xvi. 16.)

23. Q. Has God any body?
A. God has no body: He is a spirit.

God is a Spirit, and they that adore Him, must adore Him in spirit and in truth (*S. John* iv. 24).

24. Q. Is there only one God?

A. There is only one God.

See ye that I alone am, and there is no other God besides Me: I will kill, and I will make to live; I will strike, and I will heal, and there is none that can deliver out of My hand. I will lift My hand to heaven, and I will say: I live for ever. If I shall whet My sword as the lightning, and My hand take hold on judgment: I will render vengeance to My enemies, and repay them that hate me (*Deut.* xxxii. 39).

Who shall come before Thee to be a revenger of wicked men? Or who shall accuse Thee if the nations perish which Thou hast made?

For there is no other God but Thou, who hast care of all, that Thou shouldst show that Thou dost not give judgment unjustly (*Wisd.* xii. 13).

25. Q. Are there three Persons in God?

A. There are three Persons in God: God the Father, God the Son, and God the Holy Ghost.

26. Q. Are these three Persons three Gods?

A. These three Persons are not three Gods: the Father, the Son, and the Holy Ghost are all one and the same God.

27. Q. What is the

For there are three who give testimony in heaven, the Father, the Word, and the Holy Ghost. And these three are One (1 *S. John* v. 7).

mystery of the three Persons in one God called?

A. The mystery of the three Persons in one God is called the mystery of the Blessed Trinity.

28. Q. What do you mean by a mystery?

A. By a mystery I mean a truth which is above reason, but revealed by God.

29. Q. Is there any likeness to the Blessed Trinity in your soul?

A. There is this likeness to the Blessed Trinity in my soul, that as in one God there are three Persons, so in my one soul there are three powers.

30. Q. Which are the three powers of your soul?

A. The three powers of my soul are my memory, my understanding, and my will.

THE SECOND ARTICLE.

31. Q. What is the second article of the Creed?

A. The second article of the Creed is: "And in Jesus Christ, His only Son, our Lord."

Who being in the form of God, thought it not robbery to be equal with God: but debased Himself, taking the form of a servant, being made in the likeness of men, and in habit found as a man (*Phil.* ii. 6).

32. Q. Who is Jesus Christ?
A. Jesus Christ is God the Son, made man for us.

33. Q. Is Jesus Christ truly God?
A. Jesus Christ is truly God.

34. Q. Why is Jesus Christ truly God?
A. Jesus Christ is truly God because He has one and the same nature with God the Father.

And the Word was made flesh, and dwelt among us (and we saw His glory, the glory as it were of the only begotten of the Father) full of grace and truth (*S. John* i. 14).

And Jesus being baptized, forthwith came out of the water: and lo! the heavens were opened to him: and he saw the Spirit of God descending as a dove, and coming upon Him. And behold a voice from heaven, saying: This is My beloved Son, in whom I am well pleased (*S. Matt.* iii. 16).

Simon Peter answered and said: Thou art Christ the Son of the living God (*S. Matt.* xvi. 16).

Jesus saith to him: So long a time have I been with you, and have you not known Me? Philip, he that seeth Me, seeth the Father also (*S. John* xiv. 9).

Who being the brightness of His glory, and the figure of His substance, and upholding all things by the word of His power, making purgation of sins, sitteth on the right hand of the Majesty on high (*Heb.* i. 3).

And to the angels indeed He

saith: He that maketh His angels spirits, and His ministers a flame of fire. But to the Son: Thy throne, O God, is for ever and ever: a sceptre of justice is the sceptre of Thy kingdom (*Heb.* i. 7).

For what the law could not do in that it was weak through the flesh: God sending His Son in the likeness of sinful flesh, and of sin, hath condemned sin in the flesh (*Rom.* viii. 3).

Nathanael answered Him, and said: Rabbi, Thou art the Son of God, Thou art the King of Israel (*S. John* i. 49).

And the eunuch said: See, here is water, what doth hinder me from being baptized? And Philip said: If thou believest with all thy heart thou mayest. And he, answering, said: I believe that Jesus is the Son of God (*Acts* viii. 36).

Then rising up, He commanded the winds and the sea, and there came a great calm. But the men wondered, saying: What manner of man is this, for the winds and the sea obey Him? And when he was come on the other side of the water, into the country of the Gerasens, there met Him two that were possessed with devils, coming out of the sepulchres, exceeding fierce, so that none could pass by that way. And behold they cried out, saying: What have we to do with Thee, Jesus, Son of God? art Thou come hither to torment us before the time? (*S. Matt.* viii. 26.)

And I saw heaven opened, and behold a white horse: and He that sat upon him, was called Faithful and True, and with justice doth He judge and fight. And His eyes were as a flame of fire, and on His head were many diadems, and He had a name written, which no man knoweth but Himself. And He was clothed with a garment sprinkled with blood: and His name is called: The Word of God. And the armies that are in heaven followed Him on white horses, clothed in fine linen white and clean. And out of His mouth proceedeth a sharp two-edged sword: that with it He may strike the nations. And He shall rule them with a rod of iron: and he treadeth the wine-press of the fierceness of the wrath of God the Almighty. And He hath on His garment, and on His thigh written: King of Kings and Lord of Lords (*Apoc.* xix. 11).

35. Q. Was Jesus Christ always God?
A. Jesus Christ was always God, born of the Father from all eternity.

In the beginning was the Word, and the Word was with God, and the Word was God. The same was in the beginning with God. All things were made

36. Q. Which Person of the Blessed Trinity is Jesus Christ?

A. Jesus Christ is the Second Person of the Blessed Trinity.

37. Q. Is Jesus Christ truly man?

A. Jesus Christ is truly man.

by Him: and without Him was made nothing that was made (*S. John* i. 1).

The Jews therefore said to Him: Thou art not yet fifty years old, and hast Thou seen Abraham? Jesus said to them: Amen, amen, I say to you, before Abraham was made, I am (*S. John* viii. 57).

Jesus Christ yesterday, and to-day, and the same for ever (*Heb.* xiii. 8).

For we have not a high priest who cannot have compassion on our infirmities: but one tempted in all things like as we are, without sin (*Heb.* iv. 15).

And when He had fasted forty days and forty nights, afterwards he was hungry (*S. Matt.* iv. 2).

But they being troubled and frighted, supposed that they saw a spirit. And He said to them: Why are you troubled, and why do thoughts arise in your hearts? See My hands and feet, that it is I Myself; handle, and see: for a spirit hath not flesh and bones, as you see Me to have. And when He had said this, He showed them His hands and feet. But while they yet believed not, and wondered for joy, He said: Have you here anything to eat? And they

38. Q. Why is Jesus Christ truly man?
A. Jesus Christ is truly man because He has the nature of man, having a body and soul like ours.

39. Q. Was Jesus Christ always man?
A. Jesus Christ was not always man: He has been man only from the time of His Incarnation.

40. Q. What do you mean by the Incarnation?
A. I mean by the Incarnation that God the Son took to Himself the nature of man: "the Word was made flesh" (*S. John* i. 14).

41. Q. How many natures are there in Jesus Christ?
A. There are two

offered Him a piece of a broiled fish and a honey-comb (*S. Luke* xxiv. 37).

And this shall be a sign unto you. You shall find the infant wrapped in swaddling clothes, and laid in a manger (*S. Luke* ii. 12).

Then He saith to them: My soul is sorrowful even unto death: stay you here, and watch with Me (*S. Matt.* xxvi. 38).

But when the fulness of the time was come, God sent His Son, made of a woman, made under the law: that He might redeem them who were under the law; that we might receive the adoption of sons (*Gal.* iv. 4).

Behold thou shalt conceive in thy womb, and shalt bring forth a son: and thou shalt call His name Jesus. He shall be great, and shall be called the Son of the Most High, and the Lord God shall give unto Him the throne of David His father; and He shall reign in the house of Jacob for ever, and of His Kingdom there shall be no end (*S. Luke* i. 31).

And about the ninth hour Jesus cried with a loud voice, saying: Eli, Eli, lamma sabacthani? that is, My God, my God,

natures in Jesus Christ, the nature of God and the nature of man.

42. Q. Is there only one Person in Jesus Christ?

A. There is only one Person in Jesus Christ, which is the Person of God the Son.

43. Q. Why was God the Son made man?

A. God the Son was made man to redeem us from sin and hell, and to teach us the way to heaven.

why hast Thou forsaken me? (*S. Matt.* xxvii. 46.)

I and the Father are one. The Jews then took up stones to stone Him. Jesus answered them: Many good works I have shewed you from My Father; for which of those works do you stone me? The Jews answered Him: For a good work we stone Thee not, but for blasphemy; and because that Thou being a man, makest Thyself God (*S. John* x. 30).

Who His ownself bore our sins in His body upon the tree: that we being dead to sins, should live to justice: by whose stripes you were healed (1 *S. Peter* ii. 24).

But when the fulness of the time was come, God sent His Son, made of a woman, made under the law: that He might redeem them who were under the law; that we might receive the adoption of sons (*Gal.* iv. 4).

Looking for the blessed hope and coming of the glory of the great God and our Saviour Jesus Christ, who gave Himself for us, that He might redeem us from all iniquity, and might cleanse to Himself a people acceptable, a pursuer of good works (*Titus* ii. 13).

44. Q. What does the holy name Jesus mean?
A. The holy name JESUS means Saviour. (*S. Matt.* i. 21.)

Knowing that you were not redeemed with corruptible things as gold or silver, from your vain conversation of the tradition of your fathers, but with the precious Blood of Christ, as of a lamb unspotted and undefiled (1 *S. Peter* i. 18).

And she shall bring forth a Son: and thou shalt call His name Jesus. For He shall save His people from their sins (*S. Matt.* i. 21).

For which cause God also hath exalted Him, and hath given Him a name which is above all names: that in the Name of Jesus every knee should bow, of those that are in heaven, on earth, and under the earth: and that every tongue should confess that the Lord Jesus Christ is in the glory of God the Father (*Phil.* ii. 9).

But I will rejoice in the Lord: and I will joy in God my Jesus (*Hab.* iii. 18).

Be it known to you all, and to all the people of Israel, that by the Name of our Lord Jesus Christ of Nazareth, whom you crucified, whom God hath raised from the dead, even by Him this man standeth here before you whole. This is the stone which was rejected by you the builders; which is become the head of the corner. Neither is their salvation in any

45. Q. What does the name Christ mean?
A. The name CHRIST means Anointed.

other. For there is no other Name under heaven given to men, whereby we must be saved (*Acts* iv. 10).

Seventy weeks are shortened upon Thy people, and upon Thy holy city, that transgression may be finished, and sin may have an end, and iniquity may be abolished; and everlasting justice may be brought; and vision and prophecy may be fulfilled; and the Saint of Saints may be anointed (*Dan.* ix. 24).

And He went into the synagogue, according to His custom on the Sabbath day; and He rose up to read. And the book of Isaias the prophet was delivered unto Him. And as He unfolded the book, He found the place where it is written: the Spirit of the Lord is upon Me: wherefore He hath anointed Me, to preach the Gospel to the poor; He hath sent Me, to heal the contrite of heart, to preach deliverance to the captives and sight to the blind, to set at liberty them that are bruised, to preach the acceptable year of the Lord, and the day of reward. And when He had folded the book, He restored it to the minister and sat down. And the eyes of all in the synagogue were fixed on Him. And He began to say to them: This day is fulfilled the Scripture in your ears. And all gave testimony to Him, and they wondered at the words of grace that proceeded from His mouth (*S. Luke* iv. 16).

God sent the word to the children of Israel, preaching peace by Jesus Christ (He is Lord of all). You know the word which has been published through all Judea, for it began from Galilee, after the baptism which John preached; Jesus of Nazareth, how God anointed Him with the Holy Ghost, and with power: who went about doing good and healing all that were oppressed by the devil, for God was with Him (*Acts* x. 36).

46. Q. Where is Jesus Christ?

A. Jesus Christ is everywhere, as God. As God made man, He is in heaven, and in the Blessed Sacrament of the Altar.

And the Lord Jesus, after He had spoken to them, was taken up into heaven and sitteth on the right hand of God (*S. Mark* xvi. 19).

But Stephen, being full of the Holy Ghost, looking up stedfastly to heaven, saw the glory of God, and Jesus standing on the right hand of God. And he said: Behold I see the heaven opened, and the Son of Man standing on the right hand of God (*Acts* viii. 55).

Behold I am with you all days, even to the consummation of the world (*S. Matt.* xxviii. 20).

THE THIRD ARTICLE.

47. Q. What is the third article of the Creed?

A. The third article of the Creed is, "Who was conceived by the Holy Ghost, born of the Virgin Mary."

48. Q. What does the third article mean?

A. The third article means that God the Son took a Body and Soul like ours, in the womb of the Blessed Virgin Mary, by the power of the Holy Ghost.

The Holy Ghost shall come upon thee, and the power of the Most High shall overshadow thee. And therefore also the Holy which shall be born of thee shall be called the Son of God (*S. Luke* i. 35).

Prophecies of the Incarnation.

I will put enmities between thee and the woman, and thy seed and her seed: she shall crush thy head, and thou shalt lie in wait for her heel (*Gen.* iii. 15).

And in thy seed shall all the nations of the earth be blessed, because thou hast obeyed My voice (*Gen.* xxii. 18).

And I will multiply thy seed like the stars of heaven: and I will give to thy posterity all these countries: and in thy seed shall all the nations of the earth be blessed (*Gen.* xxvi. 4).

The sceptre shall not be taken away from Juda, nor a ruler from his thigh, till He come that is to be sent, and He shall be the expectation of nations (*Gen.* xlix. 10).

The blessings of thy father are strengthened with the blessings of his fathers: until the desire of the everlasting hills should come (*Gen.* xlix. 26).

A star shall rise out of Jacob

and a sceptre shall spring up from Israel (*Num.* xxiv. 17).

And there shall come forth a rod out of the root of Jesse, and a flower shall rise up out of his root. And the Spirit of the Lord shall rest upon him: the spirit of wisdom, and of understanding, the spirit of counsel, and of fortitude, the spirit of knowledge, and of godliness (*Isa.* xi. 1).

Therefore the Lord Himself shall give you a sign. Behold a virgin shall conceive, and bear a Son, and His name shall be called Emmanuel (*Isa.* vii. 14).

For a child is born to us, and a Son is given to us, and the government is upon His shoulder: and His name shall be called, Wonderful, Counsellor, God, the Mighty, the Father of the world to come, the Prince of Peace (*Isa.* ix. 6).

Know thou therefore, and take notice: that from the going forth of the word, to build up Jerusalem again, unto Christ the Prince, there shall be seven weeks, and sixty-two weeks: and the street shall be built again, and the walls in straitness of times. And after sixty-two weeks Christ shall be slain: and the people that shall deny Him shall not be His. And a people with their leader that shall come, shall destroy the city and the sanctuary: and the end thereof shall be waste, and after the end of the war the appointed desolation. And He shall confirm the covenant with many, in one week : and in the half of the week the victim and the sacrifice shall fail : and there shall be in the temple the abomination of desolation : and the desolation shall continue even to the consummation, and to the end (*Dan.* ix. 25).

Behold I send My Angel, and He shall prepare the way before My face. And presently the Lord, whom you seek, and the Angel of the testament, whom you desire, shall come to His temple. Behold He cometh, saith the Lord of Hosts (*Mal.* iii. 1).

And thou, Bethlehem Ephrata, art a little one among the thousands of Juda : out of thee shall He come forth unto Me that is to be the ruler in Israel, and His going forth is from the beginning, from the days of eternity (*Micheas* v. 2).

49. Q. Had Jesus Christ any Father on earth ?

A. Jesus Christ had no Father on earth : St. Joseph was only his Guardian or Foster-Father.

But while he thought on these things, behold the angel of the Lord appeared to him, in his sleep, saying : Joseph, son of David, fear not to take unto thee Mary thy wife, for that which is conceived in her is of the Holy Ghost, and she shall bring forth a Son, and thou shalt call His name Jesus. For He shall save His people from their sins (*S. Matt.* i. 20).

And the Holy Ghost descended in a bodily shape as a dove upon Him: and a voice came from heaven: Thou art My beloved Son, in Thee I am well pleased. And Jesus Himself was beginning about the age of thirty years, being (as it was supposed) the son of Joseph (*S. Luke* iii. 22).

50. Q. Where was our Saviour born?
A. Our Saviour was born in a stable at Bethlehem.

And it came to pass, after the angels departed from them into heaven, the shepherds said one to another: Let us go over to Bethlehem, and let us see this word that is come to pass, which the Lord hath showed to us. And they came with haste: and they found Mary and Joseph, and the Infant lying in a manger (*S. Luke* ii. 15).

51. Q. On what day was our Saviour born?
A. Our Saviour was born on Christmas Day.

And the angel said to them: Fear not; for behold I bring you good tidings of great joy, that shall be to all the people: for this day is born to you a Saviour, who is Christ the Lord, in the city of David (*S. Luke* ii. 10).

Prophecies of the Passion.— Words of our Lord.

THE FOURTH ARTICLE.

52. Q. What is the fourth article of the Creed?

Behold we go up to Jerusalem, and the Son of Man shall be betrayed to the chief priests and

The fourth article of the Creed is "Suffered under Pontius Pilate, was crucified, dead, and buried."

the scribes, and they shall condemn Him to death, and shall deliver Him to the gentiles to be mocked, and scourged, and crucified, and the third day he shall rise again (*S. Matt.* xx. 18).

The Son of Man indeed goeth, as is written of Him: but woe to that man, by whom the Son of Man shall be betrayed: it were better for him, if that man had not been born (*S. Matt.* xxvi. 24).

For she in pouring this ointment upon My body, hath done it for My burial (*S. Matt.* xxvi. 12).

And I, if I be lifted up from the earth, will draw all things to Myself. (Now this He said, signifying what death He should die.) (*S. John* xii. 32.)

Other Prophecies.

But He was wounded for our iniquities, He was bruised for our sins: the chastisement of our peace was upon Him, and by His bruises we are healed (*Isa.* liii. 5).

He was offered because it was His own will, and He opened not His mouth: He shall be led as a sheep to the slaughter, and shall be dumb as a lamb before His shearer, and He shall not open His mouth (*Isa.* liii. 7).

53. Q. What were the chief sufferings of Christ?

A. The chief sufferings of Christ were—*first*, His agony and His sweat of blood in the Garden; *secondly*, His being scourged at the pillar, and crowned with thorns; and *thirdly*, His carrying His cross, His crucifixion, and His death between two thieves.

They have dug My hands and feet: they have numbered all My bones (*Ps.* xxi. 17).

For I am ready for scourges: and My sorrow is continually before Me (*Ps.* xxxvii. 18).

And they gave Me gall for My food, and in My thirst they gave Me vinegar to drink (*Ps.* lxviii. 22).

And taking with Him Peter and the two sons of Zebedee, He began to grow sorrowful and to be sad. Then He saith to them: My soul is sorrowful even unto death: stay you here, and watch with me. And going a little further, He fell upon his face, praying, and saying: My Father, if it be possible, let this chalice pass from me. Nevertheless not as I will, but as Thou wilt (*S. Matt.* xxvi. 37).

And there appeared to Him an Angel from heaven strengthening Him. And being in an agony, He prayed the longer. And His sweat became as drops of blood trickling down upon the ground (*S. Luke* xxii. 43).

Then he released to them Barabbas, and having scourged Jesus, delivered Him unto them to be crucified. Then the soldiers of the governor, taking Jesus into the hall, gathered together unto Him the whole band: and stripping Him, they put a scarlet cloak about Him. And platting a crown of thorns, they put it upon His head, and a reed in His right hand. And bowing the knee before Him, they mocked Him, saying: Hail, King of the Jews (*S. Matt.* xxvii. 26).

And bearing His own cross He went forth to that place which is called Calvary, but in Hebrew Golgotha (*S. John* xix. 17).

And they put over His head His cause written: This is Jesus the King of the Jews. Then were crucified with him two thieves: one on the right hand, and one on the left (*S. Matt.* xxvii. 37).

And Jesus again crying with a loud voice, yielded up the ghost. And behold the veil of the temple was rent in two from the top even to the bottom, and the earth quaked, and the rocks were rent. And the graves were opened: and many bodies of the saints that had slept, arose (*S. Matt.* xxvii. 50).

54. Q. What are the chief sufferings of our Lord called?

A. The chief sufferings of our Lord are called the Passion of Jesus Christ.

But we see Jesus, who was made a little lower than the angels, for the suffering of death (*propter passionem mortis*) crowned with glory and honour (*Heb.* ii. 9).

55. Q. Why did our Saviour suffer?
A. Our Saviour suffered to atone for our sins, and to purchase for us eternal life.

For the wickedness of My people have I struck Him (*Isa.* liii. 8).

Now once at the end of ages, He hath appeared for the destruction of sin, by the sacrifice of Himself (*Heb.* ix. 26).

So also Christ was offered once to take away the sins of many (*Heb.* ix. 28).

56. Q. Why is Jesus Christ called our Redeemer?
A. Jesus Christ is called our Redeemer because His Precious Blood is the price by which we were ransomed.

And they sang a new canticle, saying: Thou art worthy, O Lord, to take the book and open the seals thereof: because Thou wast slain, and hast redeemed us to God in Thy blood out of every tribe and tongue and people and nation (*Apoc.* v. 9).

57. Q. On what day did our Saviour die?
A. Our Saviour died on Good Friday.

Then the Jews (because it was the parasceve) that the bodies might not remain upon the cross on the Sabbath-day (for that was a great Sabbath-day), besought Pilate that their legs might be broken, and that they might be taken away (*S. John* xix. 31).

58. Q. Where did our Saviour die?
A. Our Saviour died on Mount Calvary.

And they came to the place that is called Golgotha, which is the place of Calvary (*S. Matt.* xxvii. 33).

59. Q. Why do we make the sign of the cross?

And then shall appear the sign of the Son of Man in heaven (*S. Matt.* xxiv. 30).

A. We make the sign of the cross*—*first*, to put us in mind of the Blessed Trinity; and *secondly*, to remind us that God the Son died for us on the cross.

60. Q. In making the sign of the cross, how are we reminded of the Blessed Trinity?

A. In making the sign of the cross we are reminded of the Blessed Trinity by the words, "In the name of the Father, and of the Son, and of the Holy Ghost."

61. Q. In making the sign of the cross how are we reminded that Christ died for us on the cross?

A. In making the sign of the cross we are reminded that Christ died for us on the cross by the very form of the cross, which we make upon ourselves.

Hurt not the earth, nor the sea, nor the trees, till we sign the servants of our God in their foreheads (*Apoc.* vii. 3).

But God forbid that I should glory, save in the cross of our Lord Jesus Christ; by whom the world is crucified to me, and I to the world (*Gal.* vi. 14).

THE FIFTH ARTICLE.

62. Q. What is the fifth article of the Creed?

A. The fifth article of

In which also coming He preached to those spirits that were in prison (1 *S. Pet.* iii. 19).

* See Note A, Testimony of the Fathers to the ancient use of the Sign of the Cross.

the Creed is, "He descended into hell; the third day He rose again from the dead."

63. Q. What do you mean by the words, "He descended into hell"?
A. By the words, "He descended into hell," I mean that, as soon as Christ was dead, His blessed Soul went down into that part of hell called Limbo.

64. Q. What do you mean by Limbo?
A. By Limbo I mean a place of rest, where the souls of the just who died before Christ were detained.

65. Q. Why were the souls of the just detained in Limbo?
A. The souls of the just were detained in Limbo because they could not go up to the Kingdom of Heaven till Christ had opened it for them.

66. Q. What do you mean by the words, "The

Wherefore He saith: Ascending on high He led captivity captive; He gave gifts to men. Now that He ascended, what is it, but because He also descended first into the lower parts of the earth? (*Eph.* iv. 8.)

And it came to pass that the beggar died, and was carried by the Angels into Abraham's bosom (*S. Luke* xvi. 22).

I will break in pieces the gates of brass, and will burst the bars of iron (*Isa.* xlv. 2).
And He is the head of the body, the Church, who is the beginning, the first-born from the dead (*Col.* i. 18).

Prophecy of the Resurrection.
For as Jonas was in the whale's belly three days and three nights:

third day He rose again from the dead"?

A. By the words, "The third day He rose again from the dead," I mean that, after Christ had been dead and buried part of three days, He raised His blessed Body to life again on the third day.

so shall the Son of Man be in the heart of the earth three days and three nights (*S. Matt.* xii. 40).

Jesus answered, and said to them: Destroy this temple, and in three days I will raise it up. The Jews then said: Six and forty years was this temple in building, and wilt thou raise it up in three days? But He spoke of the temple of His body. When therefore He was risen again from the dead, His disciples remembered that He had said this, and they believed the scripture, and the word that Jesus had said (*S. John* ii. 19).

History of the Resurrection.

And in the end of the Sabbath, when it began to dawn towards the first day of the week, came Mary Magdalene and the other Mary to see the sepulchre. And behold there was a great earthquake. For an Angel of the Lord descended from heaven: and coming, rolled back the stone, and sat upon it: and his countenance was as lightning, and his raiment as snow. And for fear of him, the guards were struck with terror, and became as dead men. And the Angel answering, said to the women: Fear not you: for I know that you seek Jesus who was crucified. He is not here, for He is risen, as He said. Come, and see the place where the Lord was laid (*S. Matt.* xxviii. 1).

They say to her: Woman, why weepest thou? She saith to them: Because they have taken away my Lord: and I know not where they have laid Him. When she had thus said, she turned herself back, and saw Jesus standing; and she knew not that it was Jesus (*S. John* xx. 13).

But when the morning was come, Jesus stood on the shore: yet the disciples knew not that it was Jesus (*S. John* xxi. 4).

And it came to pass, that while they talked and reasoned with themselves, Jesus Himself also drawing near went with them. But their eyes were held that they should not know Him (*S. Luke* xxiv. 15).

Then He said to them: O foolish, and slow of heart to believe in all things which the prophets have spoken. Ought not Christ to have suffered these things, and so to enter into His glory? (*S. Luke* xxiv. 25.)

Importance of Christ's Resurrection.

And if Christ be not risen again, then is our preaching vain, and your faith is a' vain (1 *Cor.* xv. 14).

67. Q. On what day did Christ rise again from the dead?
A. Christ rose again from the dead on Easter Sunday.

But now Christ is risen from the dead, the first-fruits of them that sleep (1 *Cor.* xv. 20).

And when the sabbath was past, Mary Magdalen and Mary the mother of James and Salome bought sweet spices, that coming they might anoint Jesus. And very early in the morning, the first day of the week, they came to the sepulchre, the sun being now risen. And they said one to another: Who shall roll us back the stone from the door of the sepulchre? And looking, they saw the stone rolled back. For it was very great. And entering into the sepulchre, they saw a young man sitting on the right side, clothed with a white robe: and they were astonished. Who saith to them: Be not affrighted; ye seek Jesus of Nazareth, who was crucified: He is risen, He is not here, behold the place where they laid Him (*S. Mark* xvi. 1).

THE SIXTH ARTICLE.

68. Q. What is the sixth article of the Creed?
A. The sixth article of the Creed is "He ascended into heaven; sitteth at the right hand of God the Father Almighty."

And when He had said these things, while they looked on, He was raised up: and a cloud received Him out of their sight (*Acts* i. 9).

And the Lord Jesus, after He had spoken to them, was taken up into heaven, and sitteth on

69. Q. What do you mean by the words, "He ascended into heaven"?

A. By the words, "He ascended into heaven," I mean that our Saviour went up Body and Soul into heaven on Ascension Day, forty days after His resurrection.

70. Q. What do you mean by the words, "Sitteth at the right hand of God the Father Almighty"?

A. By the words, "Sitteth at the right hand of God the Father Almighty," I do not mean that God the Father has hands, for He is a spirit; but I mean that Christ, as God, is equal to the Father; and, as man, is in the highest place in heaven.

THE SEVENTH ARTICLE.

71. Q. What is the seventh article of the Creed?

the right hand of God (*S. Mark* xvi. 19).

Lift up your gates, O ye princes, and be ye lifted up, O eternal gates: and the King of Glory shall enter in. Who is this King of Glory? the Lord who is strong and mighty: the Lord mighty in battle. Lift up your gates, O ye princes, and be ye lifted up, O eternal gates: and the King of Glory shall enter in. Who is this King of Glory? the Lord of hosts, He is the King of Glory (*Ps.* xxiii. 7).

For He must reign, until He hath put all enemies under His feet (1 *Cor.* xv. 25).

Therefore, if you be risen with Christ, seek the things that are above, where Christ is sitting at the right hand of God: mind the things that are above, not the things that are upon the earth (*Col.* iii. 1).

Ye men of Galilee, why stand you looking up to heaven? This Jesus who is taken up from you

A. The seventh article of the Creed is, "From thence He shall come to judge the living and the dead."

72. Q. When will Christ come again?

A. Christ will come again from heaven at the last day, to judge all mankind.

into heaven, shall so come as you have seen Him going into heaven (*Acts* i. 11).

For as lightning cometh out of the east, and appeareth even into the west: so also shall the coming of the Son of Man be (*S. Matt.* xxiv. 27).

And all nations shall be gathered together before Him, and He shall separate them one from another, as the shepherd separateth the sheep from the goats (*S. Matt.* xxv. 32).

Behold, He cometh with the clouds, and every eye shall see Him, and they also that pierced Him. And all the tribes of the earth shall bewail themselves because of Him. Even so. Amen (*Apoc.* i. 7).

73. Q. What are the things Christ will judge?

A. Christ will judge our thoughts, words, works, and omissions.

But I say unto you, that every idle word that men shall speak, they shall render an account for it in the day of judgment (*S. Matt.* xii. 36).

And I saw the dead, great and small, standing in the presence of the throne, and the books were opened: and another book was opened, which is the book of life: and the dead were judged by those things which were written in the books, according to their works (*Apoc.* xx. 12).

74. Q. What will Christ say to the wicked?

A. Christ will say to the wicked, "Depart from Me, ye cursed, into everlasting fire, which was prepared for the devil and his angels" (*Matt.* xxv. 41).

Many will say to Me in that day: Lord, Lord, have we not prophesied in Thy name, and cast out devils in Thy name, and done many miracles in Thy name? And then will I profess unto them, I never knew you: depart from Me, you that work iniquity (*S. Matt.* vii. 22).

And he cried, and said: Father Abraham, have mercy on me, and send Lazarus that he may dip the tip of his finger in water, to cool my tongue, for I am tormented in this flame (*S. Luke* xvi. 24).

And whosoever was not found written in the book of life, was cast into the pool of fire (*Apoc.* xx. 15).

But the fearful, and unbelieving, and the abominable, and murderers, and whoremongers, and sorcerers, and idolaters, and all liars, they shall have their portion in the pool burning with fire and brimstone, which is the second death (*Apoc.* xxi. 8).

And the smoke of their torment shall ascend up for ever and ever: neither have they rest day nor night, who have adored the beast, and his image, and whosoever receiveth the character of his name (*Apoc.* xiv. 11).

And they shall go out, and see the carcases of the men that have transgressed against Me: their worm shall not die, and their fire shall not be quenched: and they shall be a loathsome sight to all flesh (*Isa.* lxvi. 24).

For Topheth is prepared from yesterday, prepared by the king, deep, and wide. The nourishments thereof are fire and much wood: the breath of the Lord as a torrent of brimstone kindling it (*Isa.* xxx. 33).

75. Q. What will Christ say to the just?
A. Christ will say to the just, "Come, ye blessed of My Father, possess ye the kingdom prepared for you" (*S. Matt.* xxv. 34).

And everyone that hath left house, or brethren, or sisters, or father, or mother, or wife, or children, or lands for My name's sake: shall receive an hundred fold, and shall possess life everlasting (*S. Matt.* xix. 29).

But, as it is written: That eye hath not seen, nor ear heard, neither hath it entered into the heart of man, what things God hath prepared for them that love Him (1 *Cor.* ii. 9).

And God shall wipe away all tears from their eyes: and death shall be no more, nor mourning, nor crying, nor sorrow shall be any more, for the former things are passed away (*Apoc.* xxi. 4).

And He took me up in spirit to a great and high mountain: and He shewed me the holy city Jerusalem coming down out of heaven from God, having the glory of God, and the light thereof was like to a precious stone, as to the jasper-stone, even as crystal (*Apoc.* xxi. 10).

And the city hath no need of the sun, nor of the moon to shine in it. For the glory of God hath enlightened it, and the Lamb is the lamp thereof (*Apoc.* xxi. 23).

76. Q. Will everyone be judged at death, as well as at the last day?

A. Everyone will be judged at death as well as at the last day: "It is appointed unto men once to die; and after this, the judgment" (*Heb.* ix. 27).

THE EIGHTH ARTICLE.

77. Q. What is the eighth article of the Creed?

A. The eighth article of the Creed is "I believe in the Holy Ghost."

78. Q. Who is the Holy Ghost?

A. The Holy Ghost is the Third Person of the Blessed Trinity.

Going therefore teach ye all nations: baptizing them in the name of the Father, and of the Son, and of the Holy Ghost (*S. Matt.* xxviii. 19).

The grace of our Lord Jesus Christ, and the charity of God, and the communication of the Holy Ghost be with you all. Amen (2 *Cor.* xiii. 13).

And the Holy Ghost descended in a bodily shape as a dove upon Him: and a voice came from heaven: Thou art My beloved Son, in Thee I am well pleased (*S. Luke* iii. 22).

And He said to them: Have

you received the Holy Ghost since ye believed? But they said to Him: We have not so much as heard whether there be a Holy Ghost. And He said: In what then were you baptized? Who said: In John's baptism. Then Paul said, John baptized the people with the baptism of penance, saying: That they should believe in Him who was to come after him, that is to say, in Jesus. Having heard these things they were baptized in the name of the Lord Jesus. And when Paul had imposed his hands on them, the Holy Ghost came upon them, and they spoke with tongues and prophesied (*Acts* xix. 2).

79. Q. From whom doth the Holy Ghost proceed?
A. The Holy Ghost proceeds from the Father and the Son.

But when the Paraclete cometh, whom I will send you from the Father, the Spirit of truth, who proceedeth from the Father, He shall give testimony of Me (*S. John* xv. 26).

But when He, the Spirit of truth, is come, He will teach you all truth. For He shall not speak of Himself: but what things soever He shall hear, He shall speak, and the things that are to come He shall shew you. He shall glorify Me; because He shall receive of Mine, and shall show it to you (*S. John* xvi. 13).

80. Q. Is the Holy Ghost equal to the Father and to the Son?
A. The Holy Ghost is equal to the Father and to the Son, for He is the same Lord and God as they are.

And because you are sons, God hath sent the Spirit of His Son into your hearts, crying: Abba, Father (*Gal.* iv. 6).

And I will ask the Father, and He shall give you another Paraclete, that He may abide with you for ever (*S. John* xiv. 16).

But Peter said: Ananias, why hath Satan tempted thy heart, that thou shouldst lie to the Holy Ghost, and by fraud keep part of the price of the land? Whilst it remained, did it not remain to thee? and after it was sold, was it not in thy power? Why hast thou conceived this thing in thy heart? Thou hast not lied to men, but to God (*Acts* v. 3).

81. Q. When did the Holy Ghost come down on the Apostles?
A. The Holy Ghost came down on the Apostles on Whit-Sunday, in the form of "parted tongues as it were of fire" (*Acts* ii. 3).

And when the days of the pentecost were accomplished, they were all together in one place: and suddenly there came a sound from heaven, as of a mighty wind coming, and it filled the whole house where they were sitting. And there appeared to them parted tongues as it were of fire, and it sat upon every one of them: and they were all filled with the Holy Ghost, and they began to speak with divers tongues, according as the Holy Ghost gave them to speak (*Acts* ii. 1).

82. Q. Why did the Holy Ghost come down on the Apostles?

A. The Holy Ghost came down on the Apostles to confirm their faith, to sanctify them, and to enable them to found the Church.

But you shall receive the power of the Holy Ghost coming upon you, and you shall be witnesses unto Me in Jerusalem, and in all Judea, and Samaria, and even to the uttermost part of the earth (*Acts* i. 8).

But the Paraclete, the Holy Ghost, whom the Father will send in My name, He will teach you all things, and bring all things to your mind, whatsoever I shall have said to you (*S. John* xiv. 26).

For it is not you that speak, but the Spirit of your Father that speaketh in you (*S. Matt.* x. 20).

But all these things one and the same Spirit worketh, dividing to everyone according as He will (1 *Cor.* xii. 11).

Christ the Head of the whole Church, comprising Church Militant, Church Suffering, and Church Glorious.

THE NINTH ARTICLE.

83. Q. What is the ninth article of the Creed?

A. The ninth article of the Creed is "The Holy Catholic Church; the Communion of Saints."

84. Q. What is the Catholic Church?

A. The Catholic

But you are come to Mount Sion, and to the city of the living God, the Heavenly Jerusalem, and to the company of many thousands of Angels, and to the Church of the first-born, who are written in the heavens, and to God the Judge of all, and to the spirits of the just made perfect, and to Jesus the Mediator of the New Testament, and to

Church is the union of all the faithful under one head.

85. Q. Who is the Head of the Catholic Church?
A. The Head of the Catholic Church is Jesus Christ our Lord.

the sprinkling of blood which speaketh better than that of Abel (*Heb.* xii. 22).

And He hath subjected all things under His feet: and hath made Him head over all the Church, which is His body (*Eph.* i. 22).

Giving thanks to God the Father, who hath made us worthy to be partakers of the lot of the Saints in light, who hath delivered us from the power of darkness, and hath translated us into the Kingdom of the Son of His love (*Col.* i. 12).

And He is the head of the body, the Church, who is the beginning, the first-born from the dead: that in all things He may hold the primacy (*Col.* i. 18).

Prophecies of the Church.

And in the last days the mountain of the House of the Lord shall be prepared on the top of mountains, and it shall be exalted above the hills, and all nations shall flow unto it. And many people shall go, and say: Come and let us go up to the mountain of the Lord, and to the house of the God of Jacob, and He will teach us His ways, and we will walk in His paths: for the law shall come forth from Sion, and

The Catechism and Holy Scripture. 51

the word of the Lord from Jerusalem (*Isa.* ii. 2).

Thus thou sawest, till a stone was cut out of a mountain without hands: and it struck the statue upon the feet thereof that were of iron and of clay, and broke them in pieces (*Dan.* ii. 34).

But in the days of those kingdoms the God of Heaven will set up a kingdom that shall never be destroyed, and His kingdom shall not be delivered up to another people, and it shall break in pieces, and shall consume all these kingdoms, and itself shall stand for ever (*Dan.* ii. 44).

Supremacy of St. Peter.*

86. Q. Has the Church a visible Head on earth?

A. The Church has a visible Head on earth— the Bishop of Rome, who is the Vicar of Christ.

87. Q. Why is the Bishop of Rome the Head of the Church?

A. The Bishop of Rome is the Head of the Church because he is the Successor of St. Peter, whom Christ appointed to be the Head of the Church.

He saith unto them, But whom say ye that I am? And Simon Peter answered and said, Thou art the Christ, the Son of the living God. And Jesus answered and said unto him, Blessed art thou, Simon Barjona: for flesh and blood hath not revealed it unto thee, but My Father who is in Heaven. And I say also unto thee, That thou art Peter, and upon this rock I will build My Church; and the gates of hell shall not prevail against it. And I will give unto thee the keys of the Kingdom of Heaven; and whatsoever thou shalt bind on

* See note B, on the Supremacy of the Pope in the Early Church.

88. Q. How do you know that Christ appointed St. Peter to be the Head of the Church?

A. I know that Christ appointed St. Peter to be the Head of the Church because Christ said to him: "Thou art Peter, and upon this rock I will build My Church, and the gates of hell shall not prevail against it. And to thee I will give the keys of the kingdom of heaven" (*S. Matt.* xvi. 18, 19).

89. Q. What is the Bishop of Rome called?

A. The Bishop of Rome is called the Pope, which word signifies Father.

90. Q. Is the Pope the spiritual Father of all Christians?

A. The Pope is the spiritual Father of all Christians.

91. Q. Is the Pope the Shepherd and Teacher of all Christians?

A. The Pope is the Shepherd and Teacher of all Christians, because Christ made St. Peter the Shepherd of the whole flock when He earth shall be bound in Heaven, and whatsoever thou shalt loose on earth shall be loosed in Heaven (*S. Matt.* xvi. 15).

When therefore they had dined, Jesus saith to Simon Peter: Simon son of John, lovest thou Me more than these? He saith to Him: Yea, Lord, Thou knowest that I love Thee. He saith to him: Feed My lambs. He saith to him again: Simon son of John, lovest thou Me? He saith to Him: Yea, Lord, Thou knowest that I love Thee. He saith to him: Feed My lambs. He said to him, the third time: Simon son of John, lovest thou Me? Peter was grieved, because He said to him the third time, Lovest thou Me? And he said to Him: Lord, Thou knowest all things: Thou knowest that I love Thee. He said to him: Feed My sheep (*S. John* xxi. 15).

And the Lord said: Simon, Simon, behold Satan hath desired to have you, that he may sift you as wheat. But I have prayed for thee that thy faith fail not: and thou being once converted confirm thy brethren (*S. Luke* xxii. 31).

said, "Feed My lambs, feed My sheep." He also prayed that his "faith" might never fail, and commanded him to "confirm" his brethren (*S. John* xxi. 15, 16, 17; *S. Luke* xxii. 32).

92. Q. Is the Pope infallible?

A. The Pope is infallible.

93. Q. What do you mean when you say that the Pope is infallible?

A. When I say that the Pope is infallible, I mean that the Pope cannot err when, as Shepherd and Teacher of all Christians, he defines a doctrine, concerning faith or morals, to be held by the whole Church.

94. Q. Has the Church of Christ any marks by which we may know her?

A. The Church of Christ has four marks by which we may know her: she is One—she is Holy—she is Catholic—she is Apostolic.

The Church Visible.

And other sheep I have, that are not of this fold: them also I must bring, and they shall hear My voice, and there shall be one fold and one Shepherd (*S. John* x. 16).

Then shall the Kingdom of Heaven be like to ten virgins, who taking their lamps went out to meet the bridegroom and the bride. And five of them were foolish, and five wise. But the five foolish, having taken their lamps, did not take oil with them. But the wise took oil in their vessels with the lamps (*S. Matt.* xxv. 1).

Again, the Kingdom of Heaven is like to a net cast into the sea, and gathering together of all kind of fishes (*S. Matt.* xiii. 47).

One body and one Spirit: as you are called in one hope of your calling (*Eph.* iv. 4).

The Church an organized Body —not a mere collection of individuals.

And He gave some apostles, and some prophets, and other some evangelists, and other some pastors and doctors. For the perfecting of the Saints, for the work of the ministry, for the edifying of the body of Christ (*Eph.* iv. 11).

Now you are the body of Christ, and members of member. And God indeed hath set some in the Church, first apostles, secondly prophets, thirdly doctors; after that miracles, then the graces of healings, helps, governments, kinds of tongues, interpretations of speeches (1 *Cor.* xii. 27).

Take heed to yourselves, and to the whole flock, wherein the Holy Ghost hath placed you bishops, to rule the Church of

God, which He hath purchased with His own Blood. I know that after my departure ravening wolves will enter in among you, not sparing the flock. And of your own selves shall arise men speaking perverse things, to draw away disciples after them. Therefore watch, keeping in memory, that for three years I ceased not with tears to admonish every one of you night and day (*Acts* xx. 28).

Feed the flock of God which is among you, taking care of it not by constraint, but willingly, according to God: not for filthy lucre's sake, but voluntarily. Neither as lording it over the clergy, but being made a pattern of the flock from the heart (1 *S. Pet.* v. 2).

But if a man know not how to rule his own house, how shall he take care of the Church of God? (1 *Tim.* iii. 5.)

Let no man despise thy youth: but be thou an example of the faithful, in word, in conversation, in charity, in faith, in chastity. Till I come, attend unto reading, to exhortation, and to doctrine. Neglect not the grace that is in thee, which was given thee by prophecy, with imposition of the hands of the priesthood (1 *Tim.* iv. 12).

Obey your prelates, and be

95. Q. How is the Church One?

A. The Church is One because all her members agree in one Faith, have all the same Sacrifice and Sacraments, and are all united under one Head.

subject to them. For they watch as being to render an account of your souls (*Heb.* xiii. 17).

We are of God. He that knoweth God heareth us. He that is not of God heareth us not. By this we know the spirit of truth, and the spirit of error (1 *S. John* iv. 6).

And One, Holy Catholic, and Apostolic Church.—Nicene Creed.

Holy Father, keep them in Thy name, whom Thou hast given Me: that they may be one, as We also are (*S. John* xvii. 11).

Careful to keep the unity of the Spirit in the bond of peace. One body and one Spirit: as you are called in one hope of your calling. One Lord, one faith, one baptism. One God and Father of all, who is above all, and through all, and in us all (*Eph.* iv. 3).

For we, being many, are one bread, one body, all that partake of one bread (1 *Cor.* x. 17).

For as the body is one, and hath many members; and all the members of the body, whereas they are many, yet are one body: so also is Christ. For in one Spirit were we all baptized into one body, whether Jews, or gentiles, whether bond or free: and in one Spirit we have all been made to drink. For the body also is not one member, but many (1 *Cor.* xii. 12).

For as in one body we have many members, but all the members have not the same office: so we being many, are one body in Christ, and every one members one of another. And having different gifts, according to the grace that is given us (*Rom.* xii. 4).

96. Q. How is the Church Holy?
A. The Church is Holy because she teaches a holy doctrine, offers to all the means of holiness, and is distinguished by the eminent holiness of so many thousands of her children.

As He chose us in Him before the foundation of the world, that we should be holy and unspotted in His sight in charity (*Eph.* i. 4).

That He might present it to Himself a glorious Church, not having spot or wrinkle, or any such thing, but that it should be holy and without blemish (*Eph.* v. 27).

But you are a chosen generation, a kingly priesthood, a holy nation, a purchased people: that you may declare His virtues, who hath called you out of darkness into His marvellous light (1 *S. Pet.* ii. 9).

Holiness becometh Thy house, O Lord, unto length of days (*Ps.* xcii. 5).

97. Q. What does the word Catholic mean?
A. The word Catholic means Universal.

And He said to them: Go ye into the whole world and preach the gospel to every creature (*S. Mark* xvi. 15).

98. Q. How is the Church Catholic or Universal?

A. The Church is Catholic or Universal because she subsists in all ages, teaches all nations, and is the one Ark of Salvation for all.

For there is no distinction of the Jew and the Greek: for the same is Lord over all, rich unto all that call upon Him (*Rom.* x. 12).

Their sound hath gone forth into all the earth, and their words unto the ends of the whole world (*Rom.* x. 18).

And Peter opening his mouth, said: In very deed I perceive that God is not a respecter of persons. But in every nation, he that feareth Him, and worketh justice, is acceptable to Him (*Acts* x. 34).

Arise, be enlightened, O Jerusalem: for thy light is come, and the glory of the Lord is risen upon thee. For behold darkness shall cover the earth, and a mist the people: but the Lord shall arise upon thee, and His glory shall be seen upon thee. And the gentiles shall walk in thy light, and kings in the brightness of thy rising. Lift up thy eyes round about, and see: all these are gathered together, they are come to thee: thy sons shall come from afar, and thy daughters shall rise up at thy side. Then shalt thou see, and abound, and thy heart shall wonder and be enlarged, when the multitude of the sea shall be converted to thee, the strength of the gentiles shall come to thee (*Isa.* lx. 1).

99. Q. How is the Church Apostolic?

A. The Church is Apostolic, because she holds the doctrines and traditions of the Apostles, and because, through the unbroken succession of her Pastors, she derives her Orders and her Mission from them.

After this, I saw a great multitude, which no man could number, of all nations, and tribes, and peoples, and tongues: standing before the throne, and in sight of the Lamb, clothed with white robes, and palms in their hands (*Apoc.* vii. 9).

He said therefore to them again: Peace be to you. As the Father hath sent Me, I also send you (*S. John* xx. 21).

And He saith to them: Come ye after Me, and I will make you to be fishers of men (*S. Matt.* iv. 19).

How then shall they call on Him, in whom they have not believed? Or how shall they believe Him, of whom they have not heard? And how shall they hear without a preacher? And how shall they preach unless they be sent, as it is written: How beautiful are the feet of them that preach the gospel of peace, of them that bring glad tidings of good things! (*Rom.* x. 15.)

And they were persevering in the doctrine of the apostles, and in the communication of the breaking of bread, and in prayers (*Acts* ii. 42).

And Jesus coming spoke to them, saying: All power is given to Me in heaven and in earth.

100. Q. Can the Church err in what she teaches?

A. The Church cannot err in what she teaches as to faith or morals, for she is our infallible guide in both.

101. Q. How do you know that the Church cannot err in what she teaches?

A. I know that the Church cannot err in what she teaches, because Christ promised that the gates of hell shall never prevail against His Church; that the Holy Ghost shall teach her all things; and that He Himself will be with her all days, even to the consummation of the world (*S. Matt.* xvi. 18; *S. John* xiv. 16-26; *S. Matt.* xxviii. 20).

Going therefore teach ye all nations: baptizing them in the name of the Father, and of the Son, and of the Holy Ghost, teaching them to observe all things whatsoever I have commanded you: and behold I am with you all days, even to the consummation of the world (*S. Matt.* xxviii. 18).

And I say to thee: That thou art Peter; and upon this rock I will build My church, and the gates of hell shall not prevail against it (*S. Matt.* xvi. 18).

But into whatsoever city you enter, and they receive you not, going forth into the streets thereof, say: Even the very dust of your city that cleaveth to us we wipe off against you. You know this, that the kingdom of God is at hand. I say to you, it shall be more tolerable at that day for Sodom, than for that city (*S. Luke* x. 10).

He that heareth you, heareth Me: and he that despiseth you, despiseth Me. And he that despiseth Me, despiseth Him that sent Me (*S. Luke* x. 16).

And if he will not hear them: tell the Church. And if he will not hear the Church, let him be to thee as the heathen and publican (*S. Matt.* xviii. 17).

That thou mayest know how thou oughtest to behave thyself

102. Q. What do you mean by the Communion of Saints?

A. By the Communion of Saints I mean that all the members of the Church, in heaven, on earth, and in purgatory, are in communion with each other, as being one body in Jesus Christ.

103. Q. How are the faithful on earth in communion with each other?

A. The faithful on earth are in communion with each other by professing the same faith, obeying the same authority, and assisting each other with their prayers and good works.

in the house of God, which is the Church of the living God, the pillar and ground of the truth (1 *Tim.* iii. 15).

Mutual and Intercessory Prayer.

Peter therefore was kept in prison. But prayer was made without ceasing by the Church unto God for him (*Acts* xii. 5).

We give thanks to God always for you all; making a remembrance of you in our prayers without ceasing (1 *Thess.* i. 2).

Pray one for another, that you may be saved. For the continual prayer of a just man availeth much (*S. James* v. 16).

When Moses lifted up his hands, Israel overcame; but if he let them down a little, Amalec overcame (*Exod.* xvii. 11).

And again the Lord said to Moses: I see that this people is stiff-necked. Let Me alone, that My wrath may be kindled against them, and that I may destroy them, and I will make of thee a great nation. But Moses besought the Lord his God, saying: Why, O Lord, is Thy indignation enkindled against Thy people, whom Thou hast brought out of the land of Egypt, with great power, and with a mighty hand? Let not the Egyptians say, I beseech Thee: He craftily brought them out, that he might kill them in the mountains, and destroy them from the earth ; let Thy anger cease, and be appeased upon the wickedness of Thy people. Remember Abraham, Isaac, and Israel, Thy servants, to whom Thou sworest by Thy ownself, saying : I will multiply your seed as the stars of heaven : and this whole land that I have spoken of, I will give to your seed, and you shall possess it for ever. And the Lord was appeased from doing the evil which He had spoken against His people (*Exod.* xxxii. 9).

They forgot God, who saved them, who had done great things in Egypt, wondrous works in the land of Cham : terrible things in the Red Sea. And He said that He would destroy them : had not Moses His chosen stood before Him in the breach : to turn away His wrath, lest He should destroy them (*Ps.* cv. 21).

And the Lord said to Moses : Get ye out from the midst of this multitude, this moment will I destroy them. And as they were lying on the ground, Moses said to Aaron : Take the censer, and putting fire in it from the altar, put incense upon it, and go quickly to the people to pray for them : for already wrath is gone out from the Lord, and the plague rageth. When Aaron had

104. Q. How are we in communion with the Saints in heaven?

A. We are in communion with the Saints in heaven by honouring them as the glorified members of the Church; and also by our praying to them, and by their praying for us.

done this, and had run to the midst of the multitude which the burning fire was now destroying, he offered the incense: and standing between the dead and the living, he prayed for the people, and the plague ceased (*Num.* xvi. 44).

So I say to you, there shall be joy before the Angels of God upon one sinner doing penance (*S. Luke* xv. 10).

And when he had opened the fifth seal, I saw under the altar the souls of them that were slain for the word of God, and for the testimony which they held. And they cried with a loud voice, saying: How long, O Lord holy and true, dost Thou not judge and revenge our blood on them that dwell on the earth?

And white robes were given to every one of them one: and it was said to them, that they should rest yet for a little time, till their fellow-servants, and their brethren, who are to be slain, even as they, should be filled up (*Apoc.* vi. 9).

And another Angel came, and stood before the altar, having a golden censer: and there was given to him much incense, that he should offer of the prayers of all Saints upon the golden altar, which is before the throne of

God. And the smoke of the incense of the prayers of the Saints ascended up before God, from the hand of the Angel (*Apoc.* viii. 3).

When thou didst pray with tears, and didst bury the dead, and didst leave thy dinner, and hide the dead by day in thy house, and bury them by night, I offered thy prayer to the Lord (*Tobias* xii. 12).

Then Onias answering, said: This is a lover of his brethren, and of the people of Israel: this is he that prayeth much for the people, and for all the holy city, Jeremias the prophet of God (2 *Macc.* xv. 14).

105. Q. How are we in communion with the souls in Purgatory?

A. We are in communion with the souls in Purgatory by helping them with our prayers and good works: "It is a holy and wholesome thought to pray for the dead, that they may be loosed from sins" (2 *Macc.* xii. 46).

106. Q. What is Purgatory?

A. Purgatory is a place where souls suffer for a time after death on account of their sins.

Be at agreement with thy adversary betimes, whilst thou art in the way with him: lest perhaps the adversary deliver thee to the judge, and the judge deliver thee to the officer, and thou be cast into prison. Amen I say to thee, thou shalt not go out from thence till thou repay the last farthing (*S. Matt.* v. 25).

Now if any man build upon this foundation, gold, silver, precious stones, wood, hay, stubble: Every man's work shall be manifest: for the day of the Lord shall declare it, because it shall be revealed in fire: and the fire shall try every man's work, of what sort it is. If any man's

107. Q. What souls go to Purgatory?

A. Those souls go to Purgatory that depart this life in *venial* sin; or that have not fully paid the debt of *temporal* punishment due to those sins of which the guilt has been forgiven.

108. Q. What is temporal punishment?

A. Temporal punishment is punishment which will have an end, either in this world, or in the world to come.

109. Q. How do you prove that there is a Purgatory?

A. I prove that there is a Purgatory from the constant teaching of the Church; and from the doctrine of Holy Scripture, which declares that God will render to every man according to his works; that nothing defiled shall enter heaven; and that some will be saved, "yet so as by fire" (*S. Matt.* xvi. 27; *Apoc.* xxi. 27; 1 *Cor.* iii. 15).

work abide, which he hath built thereupon, he shall receive a reward. If any man's work burn, he shall suffer loss: but he himself shall be saved, yet so as by fire (1 *Cor.* iii. 12).

And they found under the coats of the slain some of the donaries of the idols of Jamnia, which the law forbiddeth to the Jews, so that all plainly saw that for this cause they were slain. Then they all blessed the just judgment of the Lord, who had discovered the things that were hidden. And so, betaking themselves to prayers, they besought Him that the sin which had been committed might be forgotten. But the most valiant Judas exhorted the people to keep themselves from sin, forasmuch as they saw, before their eyes, what had happened because of the sins of those that were slain, and, making a gathering, he sent twelve thousand drachmas of silver to Jerusalem for sacrifice to be offered for the sins of the dead, thinking well and religiously concerning the Resurrection. For if he had not hoped that they that were slain should rise again, it would have seemed superfluous and vain to pray for the dead. And because he considered that they who had fallen asleep with godliness, had great grace laid up for them. It is therefore a holy and wholesome thought to pray for the dead, that they may be loosed from sins (2 *Macc.* xii. 40).

THE TENTH ARTICLE.

110. Q. What is the tenth article of the Creed?

A. The tenth article of the Creed is "The forgiveness of sins."

111. Q. What do you mean by "The forgiveness of sins"?

A. By "The forgiveness of sins," I mean that Christ has left the power of *forgiving sins* to the Pastors of His Church (*S. John* xx. 23).

For all have sinned; and do need the glory of God (*Rom.* iii. 23).

If we say that we have no sin; we deceive ourselves, and the truth is not in us. If we confess our sins; He is faithful and just, to forgive us our sins and to cleanse us from all iniquity (1 *S. John* i. 8).

For in many things we all offend (*S. James* iii. 2).

For this is My blood of the New Testament: which shall be shed for many unto remission of sins (*S. Matt.* xxvi. 28).

In whom we have redemption through His blood, the remission of sins (*Col.* i. 14).

Be it known therefore to you, men brethren, that through Him forgiveness of sins is preached to you: and from all the things, from which you could not be justified by the law of Moses (*Acts* xiii. 38).

My little children, these things I write to you that you may not sin. But if any man sin, we have an advocate with the Father, Jesus Christ the just. And He is the propitiation for our sins:

112. Q. By what means are sins forgiven?
A. Sins are forgiven principally by the Sacraments of Baptism and Penance.

113. Q. What is sin?
A. Sin is an offence against God, by any thought, word, deed, or omission, against the law of God.

114. Q. How many kinds of sin are there?
A. There are two kinds of sin, original sin and actual sin.

115. Q. What is original sin?
A. Original sin is that guilt and stain of sin which we inherit from Adam, who was the origin and head of all mankind.

and not for ours only, but also for those of the whole world (1 *S. John* ii. 1).

Original Sin.

Wherefore as by one man sin entered into this world, and by sin death: and so death passed upon all men in whom all have sinned (*Rom.* v. 12).

Therefore as by the offence of one, unto all men to condemnation: so also by the justice of one, unto all men to justification of life. For as by the disobedience of one man, many were made sinners: so also by the obedience of one, many shall be made just (*Rom.* v. 18).

For by a man came death, and by a man the resurrection of the dead. And as in Adam all die, so also in Christ all shall be made alive (1 *Cor.* xv. 21).

Actual Sin.

The soul that sinneth, the same shall die: the son shall not bear the iniquity of the father, and the father shall not bear the iniquity of the son: the justice of the just shall be upon him, and the wickedness of the wicked shall be upon him. But if the wicked do penance for all his sins, which he hath committed, and keep all My commandments, and do judgment, and justice, living he shall live, and shall not die (*Ezechiel* xviii. 20).

Thy own wickedness shall reprove thee, and thy apostacy shall rebuke thee. Know thou, and see that it is an evil and a bitter thing for thee, to have left the Lord thy God, and that My fear is not with thee, saith the Lord the God of Hosts. Of old time thou hast broken My yoke, thou hast burst My bands, and thou saidst: I will not serve (*Jer.* ii. 19).

Sins of Thought.

But I say to you, that whosoever shall look on a woman to lust after her, hath already committed adultery with her in his heart (*S. Matt.* v. 28).

For from the heart come forth evil thoughts, murders, adulteries, fornications, thefts, false testimonies, blasphemies. These are the things that defile a man (*S. Matt.* xv. 19).

Sins of Word.

If any man offend not in word: the same is a perfect man (*S. James* iii. 2).

But I say unto you, that every idle word that men shall speak, they shall render an account for it in the day of judgment. For

The Catechism and Holy Scripture.

116. Q. What was the sin committed by Adam?
A. The sin committed by Adam was the sin of disobedience when he ate the forbidden fruit.

117. Q. Have all mankind contracted the guilt and stain of original sin?
A. All mankind have contracted the guilt and stain of original sin, except the Blessed Virgin, who, through the merits of her Divine Son, was conceived without the least guilt or stain of original sin.

118. Q. What is this privilege of the Blessed Virgin called?

by thy words thou shalt be justified, and by thy words thou shalt be condemned (*S. Matt.* xii. 36).

And to Adam He said: Because thou hast hearkened to the voice of thy wife, and hast eaten of the tree whereof I commanded thee that thou shouldst not eat, cursed is the earth in thy work; with labour and toil shalt thou eat thereof all the days of thy life. Thorns and thistles shall it bring forth to thee; and thou shalt eat the herbs of the earth. In the sweat of thy face shalt thou eat bread till thou return to the earth, out of which thou wast taken: for dust thou art, and unto dust thou shalt return (*Gen.* iii. 17).

And the Angel being come in, said unto her: Hail, full of grace, the Lord is with thee: Blessed art thou among women (*S. Luke* i. 28).

And a great sign appeared in Heaven: A woman clothed with the sun and the moon under her feet, and on her head a crown of twelve stars (*Apoc.* xii. 1).

Thou art all fair, O my love, and there is not a spot in thee (*Canticles* iv. 7).

A. This privilege of the Blessed Virgin is called the Immaculate Conception.

119. Q. What is actual sin?
A. Actual sin is every sin which we ourselves commit.

120. Q. How is actual sin divided?
A. Actual sin is divided into mortal sin and venial sin.

121. Q. What is mortal sin?
A. Mortal sin is a grievous offence against God.

122. Q. Why is it called mortal sin?
A. It is called mortal sin because it kills the soul and deserves hell.

Be not deceived, God is not mocked. For what things a man shall sow, those also shall he reap. For he that soweth in his flesh, of the flesh also shall reap corruption. But he that soweth in the spirit, of the spirit shall reap life everlasting (*Gal.* vi. 7).

For there is no respect of persons with God. For whosoever have sinned without the law, shall perish without the law: and whosoever have sinned in the law, shall be judged by the law (*Rom.* ii. 11).

For the wages of sin, is death. But the grace of God, life everlasting in Jesus Christ our Lord (*Rom.* vi. 23).

And they violated Me among My people, for a handful of barley, and a piece of bread (*Ezechiel* xiii. 19).

Behold all souls are Mine: as the soul of the father, so also the soul of the son is Mine: the soul that sinneth, the same shall die (*Ezechiel* xviii. 4).

123. Q. How does mortal sin kill the soul?
A. Mortal sin kills the soul by depriving it of

And at midnight there was a cry made: Behold the bridegroom cometh, go ye forth to meet him. Then all those virgins

sanctifying grace, which is the supernatural life of the soul.

124. Q. Is it a great evil to fall into mortal sin?
A. It is the greatest of all evils to fall into mortal sin.

125. Q. Where will they go who die in mortal sin?
A. They who die in mortal sin will go to hell for all eternity.

126. Q. What is venial sin?

arose and trimmed their lamps. And the foolish said to the wise: Give us of your oil, for our lamps are gone out. The wise answered, saying: Lest perhaps there be not enough for us and for you, go you rather to them that sell, and buy for yourselves. Now, whilst they went to buy, the bridegroom came, and they that were ready went in with him to the marriage, and the door was shut. But at last came also the other virgins, saying: Lord, Lord, open to us. But He answering, said: Amen, amen, I know you not. Watch ye, therefore, for you know not the day nor the hour (*S. Matt.* xxv. 6).

Let your loins be girt, and lamps burning in your hands, and you yourselves like to men who wait for their Lord (*S. Luke* xii. 34).

And whatsoever was not found written in the Book of Life was cast into the pool of fire (*Apoc.* xx. 15).

And the smoke of their torments shall ascend up for ever and ever; neither have they rest day nor night, who have adored the beast and his image, and whosoever receiveth the character of his name (*Apoc.* xiv. 11).

For a just man shall fall seven times, and shall rise again: but

A. Venial sin is an offence which does not kill the soul, yet displeases God, and often leads to mortal sin.

127. Q. Why is it called venial sin?

A. It is called venial sin because it is more easily pardoned than mortal sin.

THE ELEVENTH ARTICLE.

128. Q. What is the eleventh article of the Creed?

A. The eleventh ar-

the wicked shall fall down into evil (*Prov.* xxiv. 16).

Shall man be justified in comparison of God, or shall a man be more pure than his Maker? Behold they that serve Him are not steadfast, and in His angels He found wickedness: how much more shall they that dwell in houses of clay, who have an earthly foundation, be consumed as with the moth? (*Job* iv. 17.)

What is man that he should be without spot, and he that is born of a woman that he should appear just? Behold among His saints none is unchangeable, and the heavens are not pure in His sight (*Job* xv. 14).

If we say that we have no sin; we deceive ourselves, and the truth is not in us (1 *S. John* i. 8).

And enter not into judgment with Thy servant: for in Thy sight no man living shall be justified (*Ps.* cxlii. 2).

And why seest thou the mote that is in thy brother's eye, and seest not the beam that is in thy own eye? (*S. Matt.* vii. 3.)

Amen, amen, I say unto you, that the hour cometh, and now is, when the dead shall hear the voice of the Son of God, and

ticle of the Creed is "The resurrection of the body."

129. Q. What do you mean by "The resurrection of the body"?

A. By "The resurrection of the body" I mean that we shall all rise again with the same bodies at the day of judgment.

THE TWELFTH ARTICLE.

130. Q. What is the twelfth article of the Creed?

they that hear shall live (*S. John* v. 25).

Jesus said to her: I am the resurrection and the life: he that believeth in Me, although he be dead, shall live (*S. John* xi. 25).

For if the dead rise not again, neither is Christ risen again. And if Christ be not risen again, your faith is vain, for you are yet in your sins. Then they also that are fallen asleep in Christ, are perished. If in this life only we have hope in Christ, we are of all men most miserable (1 *Cor.* xv. 16).

Behold I tell you a mystery. We shall indeed rise again: but we shall not all be changed. In a moment, in the twinkling of an eye, at the last trumpet: for the trumpet shall sound, and the dead shall rise again incorruptible: and we shall be changed. For this corruptible must put on incorruption; and this mortal must put on immortality (1 *Cor.* xv. 51).

For I know that my Redeemer liveth, and in the last day I shall rise out of the earth. And I shall be clothed again with my skin, and in my flesh I shall see my God (*Job* xix. 25).

Wonder not at this, for the hour cometh wherein all that are

A. The twelfth article of the Creed is "Life everlasting."

131. Q. What does "Life everlasting" mean?
A. "Life everlasting" means that the good shall live for ever in the glory and happiness of heaven.

132. Q. What is the glory and happiness of heaven?
A. The glory and happiness of heaven is to see, love, and enjoy God for ever.

133. Q. What does the Scripture say of the happiness of heaven?
A. The Scripture says of the happiness of heaven, "That eye hath not seen, nor ear heard, neither hath it entered into the heart of man, what things God hath prepared for them that love Him" (1 *Cor*. ii. 9).

in the graves shall hear the voice of the Son of God. And they that have done good things, shall come forth unto the resurrection of life; but they that have done evil, unto the resurrection of judgment (*S. John* v. 28).

And many of those that sleep in the dust of the earth, shall awake: some unto life everlasting, and others unto reproach, to see it always (*Dan*. xii. 2).

Blessed are they that wash their robes in the blood of the Lamb: that they may have a right to the tree of life, and may enter in by the gates into the city (*Apoc*. xxii. 14).

And he took me up in spirit to a great and high mountain, and he showed me the holy city Jerusalem coming down out of heaven from God, having the glory of God — and the light thereof was like to a precious stone ... And I saw no temple therein: for the Lord God Almighty is the temple thereof, and the Lamb. And the city hath no need of the sun nor of the moon to shine in it; for the glory of God hath enlightened it, and the Lamb is the lamp thereof (*Apoc*. xxi. 10).

And I heard a great voice from the throne, saying: Behold the tabernacle of God with men, and He shall dwell with them. And they shall be His people, and God Himself with them shall be their God. And God shall wipe away all tears from their eyes, and death shall be no more; nor murmuring, nor crying, nor sorrow shall be no more, for the former things are passed away. And He that sat on the throne, said: Behold, I make all things new (*Apoc.* xxi. 3).

134. Q. Shall not the wicked also live for ever?
A. The wicked also shall live, and be punished for ever in the fire of hell.

And the sea gave up the dead that were in it, and death and hell gave up their dead that were in them: and they were judged every one according to their works. And hell and death were cast into the pool of fire. This is the second death (*Apoc.* xx. 13).

HOPE.

CHAPTER III.

135. Q. Will Faith alone save us?

A. Faith alone will not save us without good works; we must also have Hope and Charity.

What Faith is.

Now faith is the substance of things to be hoped for, the evidence of things that appear not. For by this the ancients obtained a testimony. By faith we understand that the world was framed by the word of God; that from invisible things visible things might be made (*Heb.* xi. 1).

Necessity of Faith.

But without faith it is impossible to please God. For he that cometh to God, must believe that He is, and is a rewarder to them that seek Him (*Heb.* xi. 6).

But that in the law no man is justified with God, it is manifest: because the just man liveth by faith (*Gal.* iii. 11).

By whom also we have access through faith into this grace, wherein we stand, and glory in the hope of the glory of the sons of God (*Rom.* v. 2).

For whatsoever is born of God, overcometh the world: and this is the victory which overcometh the world, our faith (1 *S. John* v. 4).

Faith a virtue to be guarded by Prayer.

Having faith and a good conscience, which some rejecting have made shipwreck concerning the faith (1 *Tim.* i. 19).

And Jesus answering said to them: Amen I say to you, if you shall have faith, and stagger not, not only this of the fig-tree shall you do, but also if you shall say to this mountain, Take up and cast thyself into the sea, it shall be done (*S. Matt.* xxi. 21).

Dearly beloved, taking all care to write unto you concerning your common salvation, I was under a necessity to write unto you: to beseech you to contend earnestly for the faith once delivered to the saints (*S. Jude* 3).

And the apostles said to the Lord: Increase our faith (*S. Luke* xvii. 5).

And immediately the father of the boy crying out, with tears, said: I do believe, Lord: help my unbelief (*S. Mark* ix. 23).

Not sufficient of itself.

So faith also, if it have not works, is dead in itself. But some man will say: Thou hast faith, and I have works; shew me thy faith without works: and I will shew thee, by works, my faith. Thou believest that there is one God. Thou dost well: the devils also believe and tremble. But wilt thou know, O vain man, that faith without works is dead? (*S. James* ii. 17.)

And if I should have prophecy, and should know all mysteries, and all knowledge, and if I should have all faith, so that I could remove mountains, and have not charity, I am nothing (1 *Cor.* xiii. 2).

Many will say to me in that day: Lord, Lord, have we not prophesied in Thy name, and cast out devils in Thy name, and done many miracles in Thy name? And then will I profess unto them, I never knew you: depart from Me, you that work iniquity (*S. Matt.* vii. 22).

For in Christ Jesus neither circumcision availeth any thing, nor uncircumcision: but faith that worketh by charity (*Gal.* v. 6).

136. Q. What is Hope?

A. Hope is a supernatural gift of God, by which we firmly trust that God will give us eternal life, and all the means necessary to obtain it, if we do what He requires of us.

137. Q. Why must we hope in God?

And Moses indeed was faithful to all in his house as a servant, for a testimony of those things which were to be said: but Christ as the Son in His own house: which house we are, if we hold fast the confidence and glory of hope unto the end (*Heb.* iii. 5).

To Thee, O God, my God, I will give praise upon the harp:

A. We must hope in God, because He is infinitely good, infinitely powerful, and faithful to His promises.

138. Q. Can we do any good work of ourselves towards our salvation?
A. We can do no good work of ourselves towards our salvation; we need the help of God's grace.

why art Thou sad, O my soul? and why dost Thou disquiet me? Hope in God, for I will still give praise to Him; the salvation of my countenance, and my God (*Ps.* xlii. 5).

When His wrath shall be kindled in a short time, blessed are all they that trust in Him (*Ps.* ii. 13).

In Thee, O Lord, have I hoped, O never let me be confounded (*Ps.* xxx. 2).

Wherefore I give you to understand, that no man, speaking by the spirit of God, saith anathema to Jesus. And no man can say, the Lord Jesus, but by the Holy Ghost (1 *Cor.* xii. 3).

But by the grace of God, I am what I am: and His grace in me hath not been void, but I have laboured more abundantly than all they: yet not I, but the grace of God with me (1 *Cor.* xv. 10).

For it is God who worketh in you, both to will and to accomplish, according to His good will (*Phil.* ii. 13).

No man can come to Me, except the Father, who hath sent Me, draw him, and I will raise him up in the last day (*S. John* vi. 44).

I am the vine: you the branches: he that abideth in Me,

and I in him, the same beareth much fruit: for without Me you can do nothing (*S. John* xv. 5).

And we helping do exhort you, that you receive not the grace of God in vain (2 *Cor.* vi. 1).

Unless the Lord build the house, they labour in vain that build it. Unless the Lord keep the city, he watcheth in vain that keepeth it (*Ps.* cxxvi. 1).

I have planted, Apollo watered, but God gave the increase. Therefore neither he that planteth is any thing, nor he that watereth: but God that giveth the increase (1 *Cor.* iii. 6).

Being justified freely by His grace, through the redemption that is in Christ Jesus (*Rom.* iii. 24).

Wherefore, brethren, labour the more that by good works you may make sure your calling and election. For doing these things, you shall not sin at any time (2 *S. Pet.* i. 10).

Habitual or Sanctifying Grace.

And hope confoundeth not: because the charity of God is poured forth in our hearts, by the Holy Ghost who is given to us (*Rom.* v. 5).

Let your loins be girt, and lamps burning in your hands (*S. Luke* xii. 35).

And he saith to him: Friend,

139. Q. What is grace?

A. Grace is a supernatural gift of God, freely bestowed upon us for our sanctification and salvation.

how camest thou in hither not having a wedding garment? But he was silent. Then the king said to the waiters: Bind his hands and feet, and cast him into the exterior darkness: there shall be weeping and gnashing of teeth (*S. Matt.* xxii. 12).

Actual or Helping Grace.

Let no temptation take hold on you, but such as is human. And God is faithful, who will not suffer you to be tempted above that which you are able: but will make also with temptation issue, that you may be able to bear it (1 *Cor.* x. 13).

And He said to me: My grace is sufficient for thee: for power is made perfect in infirmity (2 *Cor.* xii. 9).

I can do all things in Him who strengtheneth me (*Phil.* iv. 13).

140. Q. How must we obtain God's grace?
A. We must obtain God's grace chiefly by prayer and the holy Sacraments.

For the continual prayer of a just man availeth much (*S. James* v. 16).

And I say to you, Ask, and it shall be given you: seek, and you shall find: knock, and it shall be opened to you (*S. Luke* xi. 9).

The Sacraments means of Grace and Refreshment for those within the Fold.

I am the door. By Me, if any man enter in, he shall be

PRAYER.

141. Q. What is prayer?

A. Prayer is the raising up of the mind and heart to God.

142. Q. How do we raise up our mind and heart to God?

A. We raise up our mind and heart to God by thinking of God; by adoring, praising, and thanking Him; and by begging of Him all blessings for soul and body.

143. Q. Do those pray well who, at their prayers, think neither of God nor of what they say?

A. Those who, at their prayers, think neither of God nor of what they say, do not pray well; but they offend God, if their distractions are wilful.

144. Q. Which is the best of all prayers?

A. The best of all

saved: and he shall go in, and go out, and shall find pastures (*S. John* x. 9).

But thou when thou shalt pray, enter into thy chamber, and having shut the door, pray to thy Father in secret: and thy Father who seeth in secret will repay thee (*S. Matt.* vi. 6).

Prayer is good with fasting and alms, more than to lay up treasures of gold (*Tobias* xii. 8).

Let nothing hinder thee from praying always, and be not afraid to be justified even to death: for the reward of God continueth for ever. Before prayer prepare thy soul: and be not as a man that tempteth God (*Ecclus.* xviii. 22).

You ask, and receive not: because you ask amiss (*S. James* iv. 3).

My heart grew hot within me: and in my meditation a fire shall flame out (*Ps.* xxxviii. 4).

With desolation is all the land made desolate: because there is none that considereth in the heart (*Jer.* xii. 11).

And when you are praying, speak not much, as the heathens. For they think that in their much

prayers is the "Our Father," or the Lord's Prayer.

145. Q. Who made the Lord's Prayer?

A. Jesus Christ Himself made the Lord's Prayer.

146. Q. Say the Lord's Prayer.

A. Our Father who art in heaven, hallowed be Thy name; Thy kingdom come; Thy will be done on earth as it is in heaven; give us this day our daily bread; and forgive us our trespasses, as we forgive them that trespass against us; and lead us not into temptation; but deliver us from evil. Amen.

147. Q. In the Lord's Prayer who is called "Our Father"?

A. In the Lord's Prayer God is called "Our Father."

148. Q. Why is God called "Our Father"?

speaking they may be heard. Be not you therefore like to them, for your Father knoweth what is needful for you before you ask Him. Thus therefore shall you pray: Our Father who art in heaven, hallowed be Thy name. Thy kingdom come. Thy will be done on earth as it is in Heaven. Give us this day our supersubstantial bread. And forgive us our debts, as we also forgive our debtors. And lead us not into temptation. But deliver us from evil. Amen (*S. Matt.* vi. 7).

And it came to pass, that as He was in a certain place praying, when He ceased, one of His disciples said to Him: Lord, teach us to pray, as John also taught his disciples. And He said to them: When you pray, say: Father, hallowed be Thy name. Thy kingdom come. Give us this day our daily bread, and forgive us our sins, as we also forgive everyone that is indebted to us (*S. Luke* xi. 1).

As a father hath compassion on his children, so hath the Lord compassion on them that fear Him: for He knoweth our frame. He remembereth that we are dust (*Ps.* cii. 13).

The son honoureth the father, and the servant his master: if

A. God is called "Our Father" because He is the Father of all Christians, whom He has made His children by Holy Baptism.

149. Q. Is God also the Father of all mankind?

A. God is also the Father of all mankind, because He made them all, and loves and preserves them all.

150. Q. Why do we say "Our" Father, and not "My" Father?

A. We say "Our" Father, and not "My" Father, because, being all brethren, we are to pray not for ourselves only, but also for all others.

151. Q. When we say, "Hallowed be Thy

then I be a father, where is My honour? and if I be a master, where is My fear? saith the Lord of hosts (*Mal.* i. 6).

And call no man your father upon the earth: for one is your Father, who is in heaven (*S. Matt.* xxiii. 9).

For you have not received the spirit of bondage again in fear: but you have received the spirit of adoption of sons, whereby we cry: Abba (Father). For the Spirit Himself giveth testimony to our spirit, that we are the sons of God. And if sons, heirs also: heirs indeed of God, and joint heirs with Christ (*Rom.* viii. 15).

But be not you called Rabbi. For one is your Master, and all you are brethren. And call none your father upon earth: for one is your Father who is in heaven (*S. Matt.* xxiii. 8).

For I wished myself to be an anathema from Christ, for my brethren, who are my kinsmen according to the flesh (*Rom.* ix. 3).

In this we have known the charity of God, because He hath laid down His life for us: and we ought to lay down our lives for the brethren (1 *S. John* iii. 16).

O Lord our God, how admirable is Thy name in the whole

name," what do we pray for?

A. When we say, "Hallowed be Thy name," we pray that God may be known, loved, and served by all His creatures.

152. Q. When we say, "Thy kingdom come," what do we pray for?

A. When we say, "Thy kingdom come," we pray that God may come and reign in the hearts of all by His grace in this world, and bring us all hereafter to His heavenly kingdom.

earth! For Thy magnificence is elevated above the heavens (*Ps.* viii. 2).

Praise the Lord, ye children: praise ye the name of the Lord. Blessed be the name of the Lord, from henceforth now and for ever. From the rising of the sun unto the going down of the same, the name of the Lord is worthy of praise (*Ps.* cxii. 1).

Not to us, O Lord, not to us; but to Thy name give glory (*Ps.* cxiii. 9).

Kingdom of God—Heaven.

And he said to Jesus: Lord, remember me when Thou shalt come into Thy kingdom. And Jesus said to Him: Amen I say to thee, this day thou shalt be with Me in Paradise (*S. Luke* xxiii. 42).

Then shall the just shine as the sun, in the kingdom of their Father (*S. Matt.* xiii. 43).

And immediately I was in the spirit: and behold there was a throne set in heaven, and upon the throne One sitting. And He that sat, was to the sight like the jasper and the sardine-stone: and there was a rainbow round about the throne, in sight like unto an emerald. And round about the throne were four-and-twenty seats: and upon the seats, four-and-twenty ancients sitting, clothed in white garments, and on their heads were crowns of gold. And from the throne proceeded lightnings and voices and thunders: and there were seven lamps burning before the throne, which are the seven spirits of God. And in the sight of the throne was as it were a sea of glass like to crystal: and in the midst of the throne and round about the throne were four living creatures full of eyes before and behind (*Apoc.* iv. 2).

And above the firmament that was over their heads, was the likeness of a throne, as the appearance of the sapphire-stone, and upon the likeness of the throne, was a likeness as of the appearance of a man above upon it. And I saw, as it were, the resemblance of amber, as the appearance of fire within it round about: from His loins and upward, and from His loins downward, I saw, as it were, the resemblance of fire shining round about. As the appearance of the rainbow when it is in a cloud on a rainy day: this was the appearance of the brightness round about (*Ezech.* i. 26).

And I dispose to you, as My Father hath disposed to Me, a kingdom: that you may eat and drink at My table in My kingdom: and may sit upon thrones judging the twelve tribes of Israel (*S. Luke* xxii. 29).

Kingdom of God, the Church.

Again, the kingdom of heaven is like to a net cast into the sea, and gathering together of all kind of fishes. Which, when it was filled, they drew out, and sitting by the shore, they chose out the good into vessels, but the bad they cast forth. So shall it be at the end of the world. The Angels shall go out, and shall separate the wicked from among the just (*S. Matt.* xiii. 47).

Another parable He proposed unto them, saying: The kingdom of heaven is like to a grain of mustard seed, which a man took and sowed in his field: which is the least indeed of all seeds: but when it is grown up, it is greater than all herbs, and becometh a tree, so that the birds of the air come, and dwell in the branches thereof (*S. Matt.* xiii. 31).

Kingdom of God's Grace within us.

Another parable He spoke to them: The kingdom of heaven is like to leaven, which a woman took and hid in three measures of meal, until the whole was leavened (*S. Matt.* xiii. 33).

153. Q. When we say, "Thy will be done on earth as it is in heaven," what do we pray for?

A. When we say, "Thy will be done on earth as it is in heaven," we pray that God may enable us, by His grace, to do His will in all things, as the Blessed do in heaven.

Neither shall they say: Behold here, or behold there. For lo, the kingdom of God is within you (*S. Luke* xvii. 21).

Then said I: Behold I come: in the head of the book it is written of Me: that I should do Thy will, O God (*Heb.* x. 7).

Jesus saith to them: My meat is to do the will of Him that sent Me, that I may perfect His work (*S. John* iv. 34).

And going a little further, He fell upon His face, praying, and saying: My Father, if it be possible, let this chalice pass from Me. Nevertheless, not as I will, but as Thou wilt (*S. Matt.* xxvi. 39).

So Samuel told him all the words and did not hide them from him. And he answered: It is the Lord: let Him do what is good in His sight (1 *Kings* iii. 18).

For it is better for us to die in battle, than to see the evils of our nation, and of the holies: nevertheless as it shall be the will of God in heaven, so be it done (1 *Macc.* iii. 60).

154. Q. When we say, "Give us this day our daily bread," what do we pray for?

A. When we say,

And the tempter coming, said to Him: If Thou be the Son of God, command that these stones be made bread. Who answered and said: It is written, Not in

"Give us this day our daily bread," we pray that God may give us daily all that is necessary for soul and body.

bread alone doth man live, but in every word that proceedeth from the mouth of God (*S. Matt.* iv. 3).

Consider the ravens, for they sow not, neither do they reap, neither have they store-house nor barn, and God feedeth them. How much are you more valuable than they? (*S. Luke* xii. 24.)

Who giveth to beasts their food: and to the young ravens that call upon Him (*Ps.* cxlvi. 9).

All expect of Thee that Thou give them food in season. When Thou givest to them they shall gather up: when Thou openest Thy hand, they shall all be filled with good (*Ps.* ciii. 27).

155. Q. When we say, "Forgive us our trespasses, as we forgive them that trespass against us," what do we pray for?

A. When we say, "Forgive us our trespasses, as we forgive them that trespass against us," we pray that God may forgive us our sins, as we forgive others the injuries they do to us.

Then his lord called him; and said to him: Thou wicked servant, I forgave thee all the debt, because thou besoughtest me: shouldst not thou then have had compassion also on thy fellow-servant, even as I had compassion on thee? And his Lord being angry, delivered him to the torturers until he should pay all the debt. So also shall My heavenly Father do to you, if you forgive not every one his brother from your hearts (*S. Matt.* xviii. 32).

If therefore thou offer thy gift at the altar, and there thou rememberest that thy brother hath

156. Q. When we say, "Lead us not into temptation," what do we pray for?
A. When we say, "Lead us not into temptation," we pray that God may give us grace not to yield to temptation.

157. Q. When we say, "Deliver us from evil," what do we pray for?
A. When we say, "Deliver us from evil," we pray that God may free us from all evil, both of soul and body.

anything against thee; leave there thy offering before the altar, and go first to be reconciled to thy brother: and then coming thou shalt offer thy gift (*S. Matt.* v. 23).

A hard heart shall fare evil at the last: and he that loveth danger shall perish in it (*Ecclus.* iii. 27).

Jesus said to him: It is written, again: Thou shall not tempt the Lord thy God (*S. Matt.* iv. 7).

Blessed is the man that endureth temptation; for when he hath been proved, he shall receive the crown of life, which God hath promised to them that love Him. Let no man, when he is tempted, say that he is tempted by God. For God is not a tempter of evils, and He tempteth no man. But every man is tempted by his own concupiscence, being drawn away and allured (*S. James* i. 12).

If I take my wings early in the morning, and dwell in the uttermost parts of the sea: even there also shall Thy hand lead me: and Thy right hand shall hold me (*Ps.* cxxxviii. 9).

He will overshadow thee with His shoulders: and under His wings thou shalt trust. His truth shall compass thee with a shield:

thou shalt not be afraid of the terror of the night. Of the arrow that flieth in the day, of the business that walketh about in the dark: of invasion, or of the noon-day devil. A thousand shall fall at thy side, and ten thousand at thy right hand: but it shall not come nigh thee (*Ps.* xc. 4).

Come to Me, all you that labour, and are burdened, and I will refresh you (*S. Matt.* xi. 28).

For though I should walk in the midst of the shadow of death, I will fear no evils, for Thou art with me (*Ps.* xxii. 4).

158. Q. Should we ask the Angels and Saints to pray for us?

A. We should ask the Angels and Saints to pray for us because they are our friends and brethren, and because their prayers have great power with God.

Are they not all ministering spirits, sent to minister for them, who shall receive the inheritance of salvation? (*Heb.* i. 14.)

Who have received the law by the disposition of Angels, and have not kept it (*Acts* vii. 53).

For He hath given His Angels charge over thee; to keep thee in all thy ways. In their hands they shall bear thee up: lest thou dash thy foot against a stone (*Ps.* xc. 11).

The Angel that delivereth me from all evils, bless these boys: and let my name be called upon them, and the names of my fathers Abraham and Isaac, and may they grow into a multitude upon the earth (*Gen.* xlviii. 16.)

159. Q. How can we show that the Angels and Saints know what passes on earth?
A. We can show that the Angels and Saints know what passes on earth from the words of Christ: "There shall be joy before the Angels of God on one sinner doing penance (*S. Luke* xv. 10).

160. Q. What is the chief prayer to the Blessed Virgin which the Church uses?
A. The chief prayer to the Blessed Virgin which the Church uses is the Hail Mary.

161. Q. Say the Hail Mary.
A. Hail Mary, full of grace; the Lord is with thee; Blessed art thou amongst women, and blessed is the fruit of thy womb, Jesus. Holy Mary, Mother of God, pray for us sinners, now, and at the hour of our death. Amen.

162. Q. Who made the first part of the Hail Mary?

See that you despise not one of these little ones: for I say to you, that their Angels in heaven always see the face of My Father who is in heaven (*S. Matt.* xviii. 10).

They that shall be accounted worthy of that world and of the resurrection from the dead, shall neither be married nor take wives: neither can they die any more, for they are equal to the Angels, and are the children of God, being children of the resurrection (*S. Luke* xx. 35).

And in the sixth month, the Angel Gabriel was sent from God into a city of Galilee, called Nazareth, to a virgin espoused to a man whose name was Joseph, of the house of David: and the virgin's name was Mary. And the Angel being come in, said unto her: Hail, full of grace, the Lord is with thee: Blessed art thou among women (*S. Luke* i. 26).

And it came to pass; that when Elizabeth heard the salutation of Mary, the infant leaped in her womb. And Elizabeth was filled with the Holy Ghost: and she cried out with a loud voice, and said: Blessed art thou among women, and blessed is the fruit of thy womb. And whence is this to me, that the mother of my Lord should come to me?

A. The Angel Gabriel and St. Elizabeth, inspired by the Holy Ghost, made the first part of the Hail Mary.

163. Q. Who made the second part of the Hail Mary?

A. The Church of God, guided by the Holy Ghost, made the second part of the Hail Mary.

164. Q. Why should we frequently say the Hail Mary?

A. We should frequently say the Hail Mary to put us in mind of the Incarnation of the Son of God; and to honour our Blessed Lady, the Mother of God.

165. Q. Have we another reason for often saying the Hail Mary?

A. We have another reason for often saying the Hail Mary—to ask our Blessed Lady to pray for us sinners at all times, but especially at the hour of our death.

166. Q. Why does the Catholic Church show great devotion to the Blessed Virgin?

For behold as soon as the voice of thy salutation sounded in my ears, the infant in my womb leaped for joy. And blessed art thou that hast believed, because those things shall be accomplished that were spoken to thee by the Lord (*S. Luke* i. 41).

Because He hath regarded the humility of His handmaid: for behold from henceforth all generations shall call me blessed (*S. Luke* i. 48).

And it came to pass as he spoke these things a certain woman from the crowd, lifting up her voice, said to Him: Blessed

A. The Catholic Church shows great devotion to the Blessed Virgin because she is the Immaculate Mother of God.

167. Q. How is the Blessed Virgin Mother of God?

A. The Blessed Virgin is Mother of God because Jesus Christ her Son, who was born of her as man, is not only man, but is also truly God.

is the womb that bore Thee, and the paps that gave Thee suck. But He said: Yea, rather blessed are they that hear the Word of God, and keep it (*S. Luke* xi. 27).

168. Q. Is the Blessed Virgin our Mother also?

A. The Blessed Virgin is our Mother also because, being the brethren of Jesus, we are the children of Mary.

Now there stood by the cross of Jesus, His mother and His mother's sister, Mary of Cleophas, and Mary Magdalen. When Jesus therefore had seen His mother and the disciple standing whom He loved, He saith to His mother: Woman, behold thy Son. After that He saith to the disciple: Behold thy mother. And from that hour the disciple took her to his own (*S. John* xix. 25).

CHARITY.

CHAPTER IV.

THE COMMANDMENTS OF GOD.

169. Q. What is Charity?

A. Charity is a supernatural gift of God by which we love God above all things, and our neighbour as ourselves for God's sake.

God is charity. By this hath the charity of God appeared towards us, because God hath sent His only begotten Son into the world that we may live by Him. In this is charity: not as though we had loved God, but because He hath first loved us, and sent His Son to be a propitiation for our sins. My dearest, if God hath so loved us, we ought also to love one another (1 *S. John* iv. 8).

Thou shalt love the Lord with thy whole heart, and with thy whole soul, and with thy whole mind, and with thy whole strength. This is the first commandment. And the second is like to it: Thou shalt love thy neighbour as thyself. There is no other commandment greater than these (*S. Mark* xii. 30).

170. Q. Why must we love God?

A. We must love God because He is infinitely good in Himself and infinitely good to us.

And behold one came and said to Him: Good Master, what good shall I do that I may have life everlasting? Who said to Him: Why askest thou Me concerning good? One is good,

171. Q. How do we show that we love God?
A. We show that we love God by keeping His commandments: for Christ says, "If you love Me, keep My commandments" (*S. John* xiv. 15).

172. Q. How many Commandments are there?
A. There are ten Commandments.

173. Q. Say the ten Commandments.
A. I am the Lord thy God, who brought thee out of the land of Egypt, and out of the house of bondage.
1. Thou shalt not have strange gods before Me.

God. But if thou wilt enter into life, keep the commandments (*S. Matt.* xix. 16).

How good is God to Israel, to them that are of a right heart! (*Ps.* lxxii. 1).

Give glory to the Lord for He is good, for His mercy endureth for ever (*Ps.* cv. 1).

Yea, I have loved thee with an everlasting love, therefore have I drawn thee, taking pity on thee (*Jer.* xxxi. 3).

In this we know that we love the children of God, when we love God and keep His commandments. For this is the charity of God, that we keep His commandments: and His commandments are not heavy (1 *S. John* v. 2).

And now the third day was come, and the morning appeared: and behold the thunders began to be heard, and lightning to flash, and a very thick cloud to cover the mount, and the noise of the trumpet sounded exceedingly loud, and the people that was in the camp feared.... And the Lord came down upon Mount Sinai, into the very top of the Mount; and He called Moses unto the top thereof. And when he was gone up thither, He

Thou shalt not make to thyself any graven thing, nor the likeness of anything that is in heaven above, or in the earth beneath, nor of those things that are in the waters under the earth. Thou shalt not adore them nor serve them.

2. Thou shalt not take the name of the Lord thy God in vain.

3. Remember that thou keep holy the Sabbath day.

4. Honour thy father and thy mother.

5. Thou shalt not kill.

6. Thou shalt not commit adultery.

7. Thou shalt not steal.

8. Thou shalt not bear false witness against thy neighbour.

9. Thou shalt not covet thy neighbour's wife.

10. Thou shalt not covet thy neighbour's goods.

174. Q. Who gave the ten Commandments?

A. God gave the ten Commandments to

said unto him: Go down and charge the people, lest they should have a mind to pass the limits to see the Lord, and a very great multitude of them should perish .... And the Lord spoke all these words: I am the Lord thy God who brought thee out of the land of Egypt, out of the house of bondage. Thou shalt not have strange Gods before Me. Thou shalt not make to thyself a graven thing, nor the likeness of anything that is in the heaven above, or in the earth beneath, nor of those things that are in the waters under the earth. Thou shalt not adore them nor serve them. I am the Lord thy God, mighty, jealous, visiting the iniquities of the fathers upon the children unto the third and fourth generation of them that hate Me, and showing mercy unto thousands to them that love Me and keep My commandments (*Exod.* xix. 16).

Do not think that I am come to destroy the Law, or the Prophets. I am not come to destroy, but to fulfil. For amen I say unto you,

Moses in the Old Law, and Christ confirmed them in the New.

till heaven and earth pass, one jot, or one tittle shall not pass from the Law, till all be fulfilled (*S. Matt.* v. 17).

Keep the precepts of the Lord thy God, and the testimonies and ceremonies which He hath commanded thee (*Deut.* vi. 17).

And He will be merciful to us, if we keep and do all His precepts before the Lord our God, as He hath commanded us (*Deut.* vi. 25).

Lay up these My words in your hearts and minds, and hang them for a sign on your hands, and place them between your eyes. Teach your children that they meditate on them, when thou sittest in thy house, and when thou walkest on the way, and when thou liest down and risest up. Thou shalt write them upon the posts and the doors of thy house (*Deut.* xi. 18).

And by this we know that we have known Him, if we keep His Commandments. He who saith that he knoweth Him, and keepeth not His Commandments, is a liar, and the truth is not in him: but he that keepeth His word, in him in very deed the charity of God is perfected: and by this we know that we are in Him (1 *S. John* ii. 3).

Now whosoever shall keep the whole law, but offend in one

point, is become guilty of all (*S. James* ii. 10).

Decline from evil and do good, and dwell for ever and ever (*Ps.* xxxvi. 27).

For My people have done two evils. They have forsaken Me, the fountain of living water, and have digged to themselves cisterns, broken cisterns, that can hold no water (*Jer.* ii. 13).

Hating that which is evil, cleaving to that which is good (*Rom.* xii. 9).

Turn away from evil and do good: seek after peace and pursue it. The eyes of the Lord are upon the just: and His ears unto their prayers. But the countenance of the Lord is against them that do evil things: to cut off the remembrance of them from the earth (*Ps.* xxxiii. 15).

I.

175. Q. What is the first Commandment?

A. The first Commandment is, "I am the Lord thy God, who brought thee out of the land of Egypt, and out of the house of bondage. Thou shalt not have strange gods before Me. Thou shalt not make to thyself any graven thing,

And one of them, a doctor of the Law, asked Him, tempting Him: Master, which is the great Commandment in the Law? Jesus said to him: Thou shalt love the Lord thy God with thy whole heart, and with thy whole soul, and with thy whole mind. This is the greatest and the first Commandment. And the second is like to this: Thou shalt love thy neighbour as thyself. On these

nor the likeness of anything that is in heaven above, or in the earth beneath, nor of those things that are in the waters under the earth. Thou shalt not adore them nor serve them."

two Commandments dependeth the whole Law and the Prophets (*S. Matt.* xxii. 35).

Beware thou never join in friendship with the inhabitants of that land, which may be thy ruin: but destroy their altars, break their statues, and cut down their groves. Adore not any strange god. The Lord His name is Jealous: He is a jealous God (*Exod.* xxxiv. 12).

Thou shalt fear the Lord thy God, and shalt serve Him only, and thou shalt swear by His name (*Deut.* vi. 13).

Thou hast made heaven and earth and all things. Thou art Lord of all, and there is none that can resist Thy majesty. Thou knowest all things, and Thou knowest that it was not out of pride or contempt or any desire of glory that I refused to worship the proud Aman . . . but I feared lest I should transfer the honour of my God to a man, and lest I should adore anyone except my God (*Esth.* xiii. 10).

176. Q. What are we commanded to do by the first Commandment?

A. By the first Commandment we are commanded to worship the one, true, and living

And now, Israel, what doth the Lord thy God require of thee, but that thou fear the Lord thy God, and walk in His ways, and love Him, and serve the Lord thy God, with all thy heart, and with all thy soul? (*Deut.* x. 12.)

God, by Faith, Hope, Charity, and Religion.

177. Q. What are the sins against Faith?

A. The sins against Faith are all false religions, wilful doubt, disbelief, or denial of any article of Faith, and also culpable ignorance of the doctrines of the Church.

But though we, or an angel from heaven, preach a gospel to you besides that which we have preached to you, let him be anathema. As we said before, so now I say again: If anyone preach to you a gospel, besides that which you have received, let him be anathema (*Gal.* i. 8).

That henceforth we be no more children tossed to and fro, and carried about with every wind of doctrine by the wickedness of men, by cunning craftiness by which they lie in wait to deceive (*Eph.* iv. 14).

Hold the form of sound words, which thou hast heard of me in faith, and in the love which is in Christ Jesus. Keep the good thing committed to thy trust by the Holy Ghost, who dwelleth in us (2 *Tim.* i. 13).

And the things which thou hast heard of me by many witnesses, the same commend to faithful men, who shall be fit to teach others also (2 *Tim.* ii. 2).

A man that is a heretic, after the first and second admonition, avoid: knowing that he, that is such an one, is subverted, and sinneth, being condemned by his own judgment (*Titus* iii. 10).

And Nadab and Abiu, the

178. Q. How do we expose ourselves to the danger of losing our Faith?

A. We expose ourselves to the danger of losing our Faith by neglecting our spiritual duties, reading bad books, going to non-Catholic schools, and taking part in the services or prayers of a false religion.

179. Q. What are the sins against Hope?

A. The sins against Hope are despair and presumption.

180. Q. What are the chief sins against Religion?

A. The chief sins against Religion are the worship of false gods or idols, and the giving to

sons of Aaron, taking their censers, put fire therein, and incense on it, offering before the Lord strange fire: which was not commanded them. And fire coming out from the Lord destroyed them, and they died before the Lord (*Levit.* x. 1).

He that loveth the danger shall perish in it (*Ecclus.* iii. 27).

Beware of false prophets who come to you in the clothing of sheep, but inwardly are ravening wolves (*S. Matt.* vii. 15).

If thou lose hope, being weary in the day of distress, thy strength shall be diminished (*Prov.* xxiv. 10).

Although He should kill me, I will trust in Him (*Job* xiii. 15).

For they have esteemed all the idols of the heathens for gods, which neither have the use of eyes to see, nor noses to draw breath, nor ears to hear, nor fingers of hands to handle, and as for their feet, they are slow to

any creature whatsoever the honour which belongs to God alone.

181. Q. Does the first Commandment forbid the making of images?

A. The first Commandment does not forbid the making of images, but the making of idols; that is, it forbids us to make images to be adored or honoured as gods.

walk. For man made them: and he that borroweth his own breath, fashioned them. For no man can make a god like to himself. For being mortal himself, he formeth a dead thing with his wicked hands. For he is better than they whom he worshippeth, because he indeed hath lived, though he were mortal, but they never. Moreover, they worship also the vilest creatures: but things without sense compared to these, are worse than they (*Wisd.* xv. 15).

Being therefore the offspring of God, we must not suppose the divinity to be like unto gold or silver, or stone, the graving of art and device of man (*Acts* xvii. 29).

He made also the propitiatory, that is, the oracle, of the purest gold, two cubits and a half in length, and a cubit and a half in breadth. Two cherubim also of beaten gold, which he set on the two sides of the propitiatory: one cherub in the top of one side, and the other cherub in the top of the other side: two cherubim at the two ends of the propitiatory, spreading their wings and covering the propitiatory, and looking one towards the other, and towards it (*Exod.* xxxvii. 6).

And all the walls of the temple round about he carved with divers figures and carvings: and he made in them cherubim and palm-trees, and divers representations as it were standing out, and coming forth from the wall (3 *Kings* vi. 29).

He made also a molten sea of ten cubits from brim to brim, round all about; the height of it was five cubits, and a line of thirty cubits compassed it round about. And a graven work under the brim of it compassed it, for ten cubits going about the sea: there were two rows cast of chamfered sculptures. And it stood upon twelve oxen, of which three looked towards the north, and three towards the west, and three towards the south, and three towards the east, and the sea was above upon them, and their hinder parts were all hid within (3 *Kings* vii. 23).

And the Lord said to him: Make a brazen serpent, and set it up for a sign: whosoever being struck shall look on it, shall live. Moses therefore made a brazen serpent, and set it up for a sign: which when they that were bitten looked upon, they were healed (*Num.* xxi. 8).

182. Q. Does the first Commandment forbid

The soul that shall go aside after magicians and soothsayers,

dealing with the devil and superstitious practices?

A. The first Commandment forbids all dealing with the devil and superstitious practices, such as consulting spiritualists and fortune-tellers, and trusting to charms, omens, dreams, and such like fooleries.

and shall commit fornication with them, I will set my face against that soul, and destroy it out of the midst of its people (*Levit.* xx. 6).

And an angel of the Lord spoke to Elias the Thesbite, saying: Arise, and go up to meet the messengers of the King of Samaria, and say to them: Is there not a God in Israel, that ye go to consult Beelzebub the god of Accaron? Wherefore thus saith the Lord: From the bed, on which thou art gone up, thou shalt not come down, but thou shalt surely die. And Elias went away. And the messengers turned back to Ochozias (4 *Kings* i. 3).

And Saul said to his servants: Seek me a woman that hath a divining spirit, and I will go to her, and inquire by her. And his servants said to him: There is a woman that hath a divining spirit at Endor. Then he disguised himself: and put on other clothes, and he went, and two men with him, and they came to the woman by night, and he said to her: Divine to me by thy divining spirit, and bring me up him whom I shall tell thee. And the woman said to him: Behold thou knowest all that Saul hath done, and how he hath rooted out the magicians and soothsayers from the land: why then dost thou lay a snare for my life, to cause me to be put to death? And Saul swore unto her by the Lord, saying: As the Lord liveth there shall no evil happen to thee for this thing. And the woman said to him: Whom shall I bring up to thee? And he said: Bring me up Samuel. And when the woman saw Samuel, she cried out with a loud voice, and said to Saul: Why hast thou deceived me? for thou art Saul. And the king said to her: Fear not: what hast thou seen? And the woman said to Saul: I saw gods ascending out of the earth. And he said to her: What form is he of? And she said: An old man cometh up, and he is covered with a mantle. And Saul understood that it was Samuel, and he bowed himself with his face to the ground, and adored. And Samuel said to Saul: Why hast thou disturbed my rest, that I should be brought up? And Saul said: I am in great distress: for the Philistines fight against me, and God is departed from me, and would not hear me, neither by the hand of prophets, nor by dreams: therefore I have called thee, that thou mayest shew me what I shall do. And Samuel said:

Why askest thou me, seeing the Lord has departed from thee, and is gone over to thy rival? For the Lord will do to thee as He spoke by me, and He will rend thy kingdom out of thy hand, and will give it to thy neighbour David (1 *Kings* xxviii. 7).

And many of them who had followed curious arts, brought together their books, and burnt them before all: and counting the price of them, they found the money to be fifty thousand pieces of silver (*Acts* xix. 19).

Deceitful divinations and lying omens and the dreams of evil doers, are vanity (*Ecclus.* xxxiv. 5).

For dreams have deceived many, and they have failed that put their trust in them (*Ecclus.* xxxiv. 7).

Sin of Sacrilege.

183. Q. Are all sins of sacrilege and simony also forbidden by the first Commandment?

A. All sins of sacrilege and simony are also forbidden by the first Commandment.

But the children of Israel transgressed the Commandment, and took to their own use of the anathema. For Achan the son of Charmi, the son of Zabdi, the son of Zare of the tribe of Juda, took something of the anathema: and the Lord was angry against the children of Israel (*Josue* vii. 1).

Then Saul said: Bring me the holocaust, and the peace-offerings. And he offered the holocaust. And when he had made

But Heliodorus executed that which he had resolved on, himself being present in the same place with his guard about the treasury. But the spirit of the Almighty God gave a great evidence of His presence, so that all that had presumed to obey him, falling down by the power of God, were struck with fainting and dread. For there appeared to them a horse with a terrible rider upon him, adorned with a very rich covering: and he ran fiercely and struck Heliodorus with his forefeet, and he that sat upon him seemed to have armour of gold. Moreover, there appeared two other young men beautiful and strong, bright and glorious, and in comely apparel: who stood by him, on either side, and scourged him without ceasing with many stripes. And Heliodorus suddenly fell to the ground, and they took him up covered with great darkness; and having put him into a litter, they carried him out (2 *Mach.* iii. 23).

Sin of Simony.

And when Simon saw that by the imposition of the hands of the Apostles the Holy Ghost was given, he offered them money, saying: Give me also this power, that on whomsoever I shall lay

The Catechism and Holy Scripture.

184. Q. Is it forbidden to give divine honour and worship to the Angels and Saints?

A. It is forbidden to give divine honour or worship to the Angels and Saints, for this belongs to God alone.

185. Q. What kind of honour or worship should we pay to the Angels and Saints?

A. We should pay to the Angels and Saints an inferior honour or worship, for this is due to them as the servants and special friends of God.

my hands he may receive the Holy Ghost. But Peter said to him: Keep thy money to thyself to perish with thee, because thou hast thought that the gift of God may be purchased with money (*Acts* viii. 18).

Then Jesus saith to him: Begone, Satan: for it is written, The Lord thy God shalt thou adore, and Him only shalt thou serve (*S. Matt.* iv. 10).

And I fell down before his feet, to adore him. And he saith to me: See thou do it not: I am thy fellow-servant, and of thy brethren who have the testimony of Jesus. Adore God (*Apoc.* xix. 10).

The just shall shine, and shall run to and fro like sparks among the reeds. They shall judge nations, and rule over people, and their Lord shall reign for ever (*Wisd.* iii. 7).

You are My friends; if you do the things that I command you. I will not now call you servants; for the servant knoweth not what his lord doth. But I have called you friends: because all things whatsoever I have heard of My Father, I have made known to you (*S. John* xv. 14).

Then Peter, answering, said to Him: Behold we have left all things, and have followed Thee:

what therefore shall we have? And Jesus said to them: Amen I say to you, that you, who have followed Me, in the regeneration, when the Son of Man shall sit on the seat of His majesty, you also shall sit on twelve seats judging the twelve tribes of Israel (*S. Matt.* xix. 27).

186. Q. What honour should we give to relics, crucifixes, and holy pictures?

A. We should give to relics, crucifixes, and holy pictures a relative honour, as they relate to Christ and His Saints, and are memorials of them.

And he took up the mantle of Elias, that fell from him: and going back, he stood upon the bank of the Jordan, and he struck the waters with the mantle of Elias, that had fallen from him: and they were not divided. And he said: Where is now the God of Elias? And he struck the waters, and they were divided, hither and thither, and Eliseus passed over (4 *Kings* ii. 13).

And Eliseus died, and they buried him. And the rovers from Moab came into the land the same year. And some that were burying a man, saw the rovers, and cast the body into the sepulchre of Eliseus. And when it had touched the bones of Eliseus, the man came to life, and stood upon his feet (4 *Kings* xiii. 20).

And behold, a woman who was troubled with an issue of blood twelve years, came behind Him, and touched the hem of His garment. For she said within herself: If I shall touch only His garment, I shall be healed. But Jesus turning and seeing her, said: Be of good heart, daughter, thy faith hath made thee whole. And the woman was made whole from that hour (*S. Matt.* ix. 20).

And they besought Him that they might touch but the hem of His garment. And as many as touched were made whole (*S. Matt.* xiv. 36).

And the multitude of men and women who believed in the Lord was more increased: insomuch that they brought forth the sick into the streets, and laid them on beds and couches, that when Peter came, his shadow at the least might overshadow any of them, and they might be delivered from their infirmities (*Acts* v. 14).

And God wrought by the hand of Paul more than common miracles. So that even there were brought from his body to the sick handkerchiefs and aprons, and the diseases departed from them, and the wicked spirits went out of them (*Acts* xix. 11).

187. Q. Do we pray to relics or images?
A. We do not pray to relics or images, for

The idols of the Gentiles are silver and gold, the works of the hands of men. They have mouths and speak not: they

they can neither see, nor hear, nor help us.

have eyes and see not. They have ears and hear not: they have noses and smell not. They have hands and feel not: they have feet and walk not: neither shall they cry out through their throat. Let them that make them become like unto them: and all such as trust in them (*Ps.* cxiii. 4, or cxiii. 12).

II.

188. Q. What is the second Commandment?

A. The second Commandment is, 'Thou shalt not take the Name of the Lord thy God in vain.'

189. Q. What are we commanded by the second Commandment?

A. By the second Commandment we are commanded to speak with reverence of God and all holy persons and things, and to keep our lawful oaths and vows.

Thou shalt not take the Name of the Lord thy God in vain: for the Lord will not hold him guiltless that shall take the Name of the Lord his God in vain (*Exod.* xx. 7).

And let not the naming of God be usual in thy mouth, and meddle not with the names of saints, for thou shalt not escape free from them (*Ecclus.* xxiii. 10).

If thou hast vowed anything to God, defer not to pay it: for an unfaithful and foolish promise displeaseth Him: but whatsoever thou hast vowed, pay it. And it is much better not to vow, than after a vow not to perform the things promised (*Eccles.* v. 3).

Vow ye, and pay to the Lord your God (*Ps.* lxxv. 12).

And he that blasphemeth the Name of the Lord, dying let him die: all the multitude shall stone him, whether he be a native or a stranger. He that blasphemeth the Name of the Lord, dying let him die (*Levit.* xxiv. 16).

Rash, unjust, and unnecessary Oaths.

190. Q. What does the second Commandment forbid?

A. The second Commandment forbids all false, rash, unjust, and unnecessary oaths; as also blaspheming, cursing, and profane words.

But I say to you not to swear at all, neither by heaven, for it is the throne of God: nor by the earth, for it is His footstool: nor by Jerusalem, for it is the city of the Great King: neither shalt thou swear by thy head, because thou canst not make one hair white or black. But let your speech be yea, yea: no, no: and that which is over and above these, is of evil (*S. Matt.* v. 34).

But above all things, my brethren, swear not, neither by heaven nor by the earth, nor by any other oath. But let your speech be, yea, yea: no, no: that you fall not under judgment (*S. James* v. 12).

And when day was come, some of the Jews gathered together, and bound themselves under a curse, saying, that they would neither eat, nor drink, till they killed Paul (*Acts* xxiii. 12).

191. Q. Is it ever lawful to swear or to take an oath?

A. It is lawful to swear, or to take an

But Jesus held His peace. And the high priest said to Him: I adjure Thee by the Living God that Thou tell us if Thou be the Christ, the Son of God? Jesus

oath, only when God's honour, or our own, or our neighbour's good requires it.

III.

192. Q. What is the third Commandment?

A. The third Commandment is, "Remember that thou keep holy the Sabbath-day."

193. Q. What are we commanded by the third Commandment?

A. By the third Commandment we are commanded to keep the Sunday holy.

194. Q. How are we to keep the Sunday holy?

A. We are to keep the Sunday holy by hearing Mass and resting from servile works.

195. Q. Why are we commanded to rest from servile works?

A. We are commanded to rest from servile works that we may have time and opportunity for prayer, going to the Sacraments, hearing instructions, and reading good books.

said to him: Thou hast said it (*S. Matt.* xxvi. 63).

But the king shall rejoice in God, and all they shall be praised that swear by him (*Ps.* lxii. 12).

Keep you My Sabbath: for it is holy unto you: he that shall profane it, shall be put to death: he that shall do any work in it, his soul shall perish out of the midst of his people. Six days shall you do work: in the seventh day is the Sabbath, the rest holy to the Lord. Everyone that shall do any work on this day, shall die. Let the children of Israel keep the Sabbath, and celebrate it in their generations. It is an everlasting covenant (*Exod.* xxxi. 14).

For the Son of Man is Lord even of the Sabbath (*S. Matt.* xii. 8).

And on the first day of the week, when we were assembled to break bread, Paul discoursed with them, being to depart on the morrow (*Acts* xx. 7).

And he said to them: The Sabbath was made for man, and not man for the Sabbath. Therefore the Son of Man is Lord of the Sabbath also (*S. Mark* ii. 27).

Spirit of the Christian Sabbath.

And the ruler of the synagogue (being angry that Jesus had

healed on the Sabbath), answering said to the multitude: Six days there are wherein you ought to work. In them therefore come, and be healed; and not on the Sabbath-day. And the Lord answering him, said: Ye hypocrites, doth not everyone of you on the Sabbath-day loose his ox or his ass from the manger, and lead them to water? And ought not this daughter of Abraham, whom Satan hath bound, lo, these eighteen years, be loosed from this bond on the Sabbath-day? (*S. Luke* xiii. 14.)

And answering them, He said: Which of you shall have an ass or an ox fall into a pit; and will not immediately draw him out on the Sabbath-day? (*S. Luke* xiv. 5.)

Or have ye not read in the Law, that on the Sabbath-days the priests in the temple break the Sabbath, and are without blame? (*S. Matt.* xii. 5.)

IV.

196. Q. What is the fourth Commandment?

A. The fourth Commandment is, "Honour thy father and thy mother."

Honour thy father and thy mother, that thou mayest be long-lived upon the land which the Lord thy God will give thee (*Exod.* xx. 12).

Children, obey your parents in the Lord, for this is just. Honour thy father and thy mother, which is the first Commandment with a

197. Q. What are we commanded by the fourth Commandment?

A. By the fourth Commandment we are commanded to love, reverence, and obey our parents in all that is not sin.

promise: that it may be well with thee, and thou mayest be long-lived upon earth (*Eph.* vi. 1).

And he that honoureth his mother, is as one that layeth up a treasure. He that honoureth his father, shall have joy in his own children, and in the day of his prayer he shall be heard. He that honoureth his father, shall enjoy a long life: and he that obeyeth the father, shall be a comfort to his mother (*Ecclus.* iii. 5).

Children, obey your parents, in all things: for this is well pleasing to the Lord (*Col.* iii. 20).

Obedience to Pastors.

198. Q. Are we commanded to obey our parents only?

A. We are commanded to obey, not only our parents, but also our bishops and pastors, the civil authorities, and our lawful superiors.

He that heareth you heareth Me; and he that despiseth you despiseth Me; and he that despiseth Me despiseth Him that sent Me (*S. Luke* x. 16).

Obey your prelates, and be subject to them. For they watch as being to render an account of your souls: that they may do this with joy, and not with grief. For this is not expedient for you (*Heb.* xiii. 17).

Obedience to Rulers and Masters.

Be ye subject therefore to every human creature for God's

sake: whether it be to the king as excelling: or to governors as sent by Him for the punishment of evil doers, and for the praise of the good: for so is the will of God, that by doing well you may put to silence the ignorance of foolish men: as free, and not as making liberty a cloak for malice, but as the servants of God. Honour all men. Love the brotherhood. Fear God. Honour the king (1 S. Pet. ii. 13).

Servants, be subject to your masters with all fear, not only to the good and gentle, but also to the froward (1 S. Pet. ii. 18).

Servants, be obedient to them that are your lords according to the flesh, with fear and trembling, in the simplicity of your heart as to Christ: not serving to the eye, as it were pleasing men, but as the servants of Christ, doing the will of God from the heart, with a good will serving, as to the Lord, and not to men. Knowing that whatsoever good thing any man shall do, the same shall he receive from the Lord, whether he be bond, or free (*Eph.* vi. 5).

199. Q. Are we bound to assist our parents in their wants?

A. We are bound to assist our parents in their

Harken to thy father that begot thee, and despise not thy mother when she is old. The eye that mocketh at his father, and that despiseth the labour of

wants, both spiritual and temporal.

200. Q. Are we bound in justice to contribute to the support of our pastors?
A. We are bound in justice to contribute to the support of our pastors; for St. Paul says, 'The Lord ordained that they who preach the Gospel should live by the Gospel' (1 *Cor.* ix. 14).

his mother in bearing him, let the ravens of the brooks pick it out, and the young eaglets devour it (*Prov.* xxx. 17).

Know you not that they who work in the holy place, eat the things that are of the holy place; and they that serve the altar, partake with the altar? So also the Lord ordained that they who preached the Gospel, should live by the Gospel (1 *Cor.* ix. 13).

If we have sown unto you spiritual things, is it a great matter if we reap your carnal things? (1 *Cor.* ix. 11.)

Who serveth as a soldier at any time, at his own charges? Who planteth a vineyard, and eateth not of the fruit thereof? Who feedeth a flock, and eateth not of the milk of the flock? (1 *Cor.* ix. 7.)

And in the same house remain, eating and drinking such things as they have. For the labourer is worthy of his hire. Remove not from house to house. And into what city soever you enter, and they receive you, eat such things as are set before you (*S. Luke* x. 7).

201. Q. What is the duty of parents towards their children?
A. The duty of parents

And you fathers, provoke not your children to anger: but bring them up in the discipline and correction of the Lord (*Eph.* vi. 4).

towards their children is to provide for them, to instruct and correct them, and to give them a good Catholic education.

202. Q. What is the duty of masters, mistresses, and other superiors?

A. The duty of masters, mistresses, and other superiors is to take proper care of those under their charge, and to enable them to practise their religious duties.

203. Q. What does the fourth Commandment forbid?

A. The fourth Commandment forbids all contempt, stubbornness, and disobedience to our parents and lawful superiors.

And you masters, do the same things to them, forbearing threatenings: knowing, that the Lord both of them and you is in heaven: and there is no respect of persons with Him (*Eph.* vi. 9).

Masters, do to your servants that which is just and equal, knowing that you also have a Master in heaven (*Col.* iv. 1).

For I have foretold unto him, that I will judge his house for ever, for iniquity, because he knew that his sons did wickedly, and did not chastise them (1 *Kings* iii. 13).

A foolish son is the anger of the father: and the sorrow of the mother that bore him (*Prov.* xvii. 25).

A son ill-taught is the confusion of the father: and a foolish daughter shall be to his loss (*Ecclus.* xxii. 3).

If a man have a stubborn and unruly son, who will not hear the commandments of his father or mother, and being corrected, slighteth obedience: they shall take him and bring him to the ancients of his city, and to the gate of judgment, and shall say to them: This our son is rebellious and stubborn, he slighteth hearing our admonitions, he giveth himself to revelling, and to debauchery and banquetings:

the people of the city shall stone him: and he shall die, that you may take away the evil out of the midst of you, and all Israel hearing it may be afraid (*Deut.* xxi. 18).

He that curseth his father and mother, his lamp shall be put out in the midst of darkness (*Prov.* xx. 20).

204. Q. Is it sinful to belong to a Secret Society?

A. It is sinful to belong to any Secret Society that plots against the Church or State, or to any Society that by reason of its secrecy is condemned by the Church; for St. Paul says: "Let every soul be subject to the higher powers; he that resisteth the power resisteth the ordinance of God; and they that resist purchase to themselves damnation" (*Rom.* xiii. 1, 2).

V.

205. Q. What is the fifth Commandment?

A. The fifth Commandment is, "Thou shalt not kill."

And the Lord said to Cain: Where is thy brother Abel? And he answered, I know not: am I my brother's keeper? And He said to him: What hast thou done? the voice of thy brother's

206. Q. What does the fifth Commandment forbid?
A. The fifth Commandment forbids all wilful murder, fighting, quarrelling, and injurious words; and also scandal and bad example.

207. Q. Does the fifth Commandment forbid anger?
A. The fifth Commandment forbids anger, and, still more, hatred and revenge.

blood crieth to Me from the earth. Now, therefore, cursed shalt thou be upon the earth, which hath opened her mouth and received the blood of thy brother at thy hand (*Gen.* iv. 9).

Whosoever shall shed man's blood, his blood shall be shed: for man was made to the image of God (*Gen.* ix. 6).

He that striketh, and killeth a man, dying let him die (*Levit.* xxiv. 17).

As the vapour of a chimney, and the smoke of the fire goeth up before the fire: so also injurious words, and reproaches, and threats, before blood (*Ecclus.* xxii. 30).

Be angry, and sin not. Let not the sun go down upon your anger. Give not place to the devil (*Eph.* iv. 26).

You know, my dearest brethren. And let every man be swift to hear, but slow to speak, and slow to anger. For the anger of man worketh not the justice of God (*S. James* i. 19).

Whosoever hateth his brother, is a murderer. And you know that no murderer hath eternal life abiding in himself (1 *S. John* iii. 15).

If it be possible, as much as is in you, having peace with all men. Not revenging yourselves, my dearly beloved; but give place unto wrath, for it is written: Revenge to Me: I will repay, saith the Lord. But if thy enemy be hungry, give him to eat: if he thirst, give him to drink. For, doing this, thou shalt heap coals of fire upon his head. Be not overcome by evil, but overcome evil by good (*Rom.* xii. 18).

He that seeketh to revenge himself, shall find vengeance from the Lord, and He will surely keep his sins in remembrance (*Ecclus.* xxviii. 1).

Then his lord called him; and said to him: Thou wicked servant, I forgave thee all the debt, because thou besoughtest me: shouldst not thou then have had compassion also on thy fellow-servant, even as I had compassion on thee? And his lord being angry, delivered him to the torturers until he should pay all the debt. So also shall My heavenly Father do to you, if you forgive not every one his brother from your hearts (*S. Matt.* xviii. 32).

If therefore thou offer thy gift at the altar, and there thou rememeber that thy brother hath anything against thee; leave there thy offering before the altar, and go first to be reconciled to thy brother: and then

208. Q. Why are scandal and bad example forbidden by the fifth Commandment?

A. Scandal and bad example are forbidden by the fifth Commandment, because they lead to the injury and spiritual death of our neighbour's soul.

coming thou shalt offer thy gift (*S. Matt.* v. 23).

Thou shalt not hate thy brother in thy heart, but reprove him openly, lest thou incur sin through him. Seek not revenge, nor be mindful of the injury of thy citizens. Thou shalt love thy friend as thyself. I am the Lord (*Levit.* xix. 17).

But he that shall scandalize one of these little ones that believe in Me, it were better for him that a millstone should be hanged about his neck, and that he should be drowned in the depth of the sea. Woe to the world because of scandals. For it must needs be that scandals come : but nevertheless woe to that man by whom the scandal cometh (*S. Matt.* xviii. 6).

And if thy right eye scandalize thee, pluck it out and cast it from thee. For it is expedient for thee that one of thy members should perish, rather than thy whole body be cast into hell. And if thy right hand scandalize thee, cut it off, and cast it from thee ; for it is expedient for thee that one of thy members should perish, rather than that thy whole body go into hell (*S. Matt.* v. 29).

And through thy knowledge shall the weak brother perish,

VI.

209. Q. What is the sixth Commandment?

A. The sixth Commandment is, "Thou shalt not commit adultery."

210. Q. What does the sixth Commandment forbid?

A. The sixth Commandment forbids all sins of impurity with another's wife or husband.

211. Q. Does the sixth Commandment forbid whatever is contrary to holy purity?

A. The sixth Commandment forbids whatever is contrary to holy purity in looks, words, or actions.

212. Q. Are immodest plays and dances forbidden by the sixth Commandment?

for whom Christ hath died? Now when you sin thus against the brethren, and wound their weak conscience, you sin against Christ. Wherefore if meat scandalize my brother, I will never eat flesh, lest I should scandalize my brother (1 *Cor.* viii. 11).

If any man commit adultery with the wife of another, and defile his neighbour's wife, let them be put to death, both the adulterer and the adulteress (*Levit.* xx. 10).

Mortify therefore your members which are upon the earth, fornication, uncleanness, lust, evil concupiscence, and covetousness, which is the service of idols. For which things the wrath of God cometh upon the children of unbelief (*Col.* iii. 5).

But fornication and all uncleanness, or covetousness, let it not so much as be named among you, as becometh saints. Or obscenity, or foolish talking, or scurrility, which is to no purpose: but rather giving of thanks (*Eph.* v. 3).

I made a covenant with my eyes, that I would not so much as think upon a virgin. For what part should God from above have in me, and what inheritance

A. Immodest plays and dances are forbidden by the sixth Commandment, and it is sinful to look at them.

213. Q. Does the sixth Commandment forbid immodest songs, books, and pictures?

A. The sixth Commandment forbids immodest songs, books, and pictures, because they are most dangerous to the soul, and lead to mortal sin.

the Almighty from on high? (*Job.* xxxi. 1).

Gaze not upon a maiden, lest her beauty be a stumbling-block to thee (*Ecclus.* ix. 5).

For from the heart come forth evil thoughts, murders, adulteries, fornications, thefts, false testimonies, blasphemies. These are the things that defile a man (*S. Matt.* xv. 19).

Blessed are the clean of heart: for they shall see God (*S. Matt.* v. 8).

O how beautiful is the chaste generation with glory: for the memory thereof is immortal: because it is known both with God and with men. When it is present, they imitate it: and they desire it when it hath withdrawn itself, and it triumpheth crowned for ever, winning the reward of undefiled conflicts (*Wisd.* iv. 1).

Be not deceived; God is not mocked: for whatsoever a man soweth, that shall he also reap. For he that soweth to his flesh shall of the flesh reap corruption; but he that soweth to the Spirit shall of the Spirit reap life everlasting (*Gal.* vi. 7).

VII.

214. Q. What is the seventh Commandment?

A. The seventh Commandment is, "Thou shalt not steal."

He that stole, let him now steal no more, but rather let him labour working with his hands the thing which is good, that he may have something to give to

215. Q. What does the seventh Commandment forbid?

A. The seventh Commandment forbids all unjust taking away, or keeping what belongs to another.

him that suffereth need (*Eph.* iv. 28).

But let none of you suffer as a murderer, or a thief, or a railer, or a coveter of other men's things. But if as a Christian, let him not be ashamed, but let him glorify God in this name (1 *S. Pet.* iv. 15).

Render therefore to all men their dues. Tribute, to whom tribute is due: custom to whom custom: fear to whom fear: honour to whom honour (*Rom.* xiii. 7).

216. Q. Is all manner of cheating in buying and selling forbidden by the seventh Commandment?

A. All manner of cheating in buying and selling is forbidden by the seventh Commandment, and also every other way of wronging our neighbour.

A deceitful balance is an abomination before the Lord: and a just weight is His will (*Prov.* xi. 1).

Diverse weights are an abomination before the Lord: a deceitful balance is not good (*Prov.* xx. 23).

217. Q. Are we bound to restore ill-gotten goods?

A. We are bound to restore ill-gotten goods if we are able, or else the sin will not be forgiven; we must also pay our debts.

But Zacheus standing said to the Lord, Behold, Lord, the half of my goods I give to the poor: and if I have wronged any man of anything, I restore him fourfold. Jesus said to him: This day is salvation come to this house, because he also is a son of Abraham (*S. Luke* xix. 8).

218. Q. Is it dishonest in servants to waste their master's time or property?
A. It is dishonest in servants to waste their master's time or property, because it is wasting what is not their own.

There was a certain rich man who had a steward, and the same was accused unto him that he had wasted his goods. And he called him and said to him: How is it that I hear this of thee? Give an account of thy stewardship, for now thou canst be steward no longer (*S. Luke* xvi. 1).

VIII.

219. Q. What is the eighth Commandment?
A. The eighth Commandment is, "Thou shalt not bear false witness against thy neighbour."

220. Q. What does the eighth Commandment forbid?
A. The eighth Commandment forbids all false testimony, rash judgment, and lies.

And bringing two men, sons of the devil, they made them sit against him: and they, like men of the devil, bore witness against him before the people, saying: Naboth hath blasphemed God and the king: wherefore they brought him forth without the city, and stoned him to death. And they sent to Jezabel, saying: Naboth is stoned, and is dead . . . . Thus saith the Lord: In this place wherein the dogs have licked the blood of Naboth, they shall lick thy blood also (3 *Kings* xxi. 13).

Rash Judgment.

Who art thou that judgest another man's servant? To his own lord he standeth or falleth. And he shall stand; for God is able to make him stand (*Rom.* xiv. 4).

Judge not, and you shall not

be judged. Condemn not, and you shall not be condemned. Forgive, and you shall be forgiven (*S. Luke* vi. 37).

Lying.

There shall not enter into it anything defiled, or that worketh abomination and maketh a lie, but they that are written in the book of life of the Lamb (*Apoc.* xxi. 27).

A lie is a foul blot in a man, and yet it will be continually in the mouth of men without discipline. A thief is better than a man that is always lying: but both of them shall inherit destruction (*Ecclus*. xx. 26).

Lying lips are an abomination to the Lord: but they that deal faithfully please Him (*Prov*. xii. 22).

Hypocrisy.

And when great multitudes stood about Him, so that they trod one upon another, He began to say to His disciples: Beware ye of the leaven of the Pharisees, which is hypocrisy (*S. Luke* xii. 1).

There let us feast, not with the old leaven, nor with the leaven of malice and wickedness, but with the unleavened bread of sincerity and truth (1 *Cor*. v. 8).

221. Q. Are calumny and detraction forbidden by the eighth Commandment?

A. Calumny and detraction are forbidden by the eighth Commandment, and also tale-bearing, and any words which injure our neighbour's character.

222. Q. If you have injured your neighbour by speaking ill of him, what are you bound to do?

A. If I have injured my neighbour by speaking ill of him, I am bound to make him satisfaction by restoring his good name as far as I can.

Lying lips hide hatred: he that uttereth reproach is foolish. In the multitude of words there shall not want sin: but he that refraineth his lips is most wise (*Prov.* x. 18).

The man that in private detracted his neighbour, him did I persecute. With him that had a proud eye, and an unsatiable heart, I would not eat (*Ps.* c. 5).

IX.

223. Q. What is the ninth Commandment?

A. The ninth Commandment is, "Thou shalt not covet thy neighbour's wife."

224. Q. What does the ninth Commandment forbid?

A. The ninth Commandment forbids all wilful consent to impure thoughts and desires,

But every man is tempted by his own concupiscence, being drawn away and allured. Then when concupiscence hath conceived, it bringeth forth sin. But sin, when it is completed, begetteth death (*S. James* i. 14).

You have heard that it was said to them of old: Thou shalt not commit adultery. But I say to you, that whosoever shall look on a woman to lust after her, hath already committed adultery

and all wilful pleasure in the irregular motions of the flesh.

with her in his heart (*S. Matt.* v. 27).

225. Q. What sins commonly lead to the breaking of the sixth and ninth Commandments?
A. The sins that commonly lead to the breaking of the sixth and ninth Commandments are gluttony, drunkenness, and intemperance, and also idleness, bad company, and the neglect of prayer.

Behold, this was the iniquity of Sodom, thy sister, pride, fulness of bread, and abundance, and the idleness of her, and of her daughters, and they did not put forth their hand to the needy and to the poor (*Ezech.* xvi. 49).

X.

226. Q. What is the tenth Commandment?
A. The tenth Commandment is, "Thou shalt not covet thy neighbour's goods."

227. Q. What does the tenth Commandment forbid?
A. The tenth Commandment forbids all envious and covetous thoughts and unjust desires of our neighbours' goods and profits.

For all that is in the world is the concupiscence of the flesh, and the concupiscence of the eyes, and the pride of life, which is not of the Father, but is of the world. And the world passeth away, and the concupiscence thereof (1 *S. John* ii. 16).

CHAPTER V.

THE COMMANDMENTS OF THE CHURCH.

228. Q. Are we bound to obey the Church?

A. We are bound to obey the Church, because Christ has said to the pastors of the Church, "He that heareth you heareth Me; and he that despiseth you despiseth Me" (*S. Luke* x. 16).

229. Q. What are the chief Commandments of the Church?

A. The chief Commandments of the Church are:

1. To keep the Sundays and Holydays of Obligation holy, by hearing Mass and resting from servile works.
2. To keep the days of fasting and abstinence appointed by the Church.
3. To go to confession at least once a year.
4. To receive the Blessed Sacrament at least once a year, and that at Easter or thereabouts.
5. To contribute to

the support of our pastors.

6. Not to marry within certain degrees of kindred, nor to solemnize marriage at the forbidden times.

230. Q. What is the first Commandment of the Church?

A. The first Commandment of the Church is, "To keep the Sundays and Holydays of Obligation holy, by hearing Mass and resting from servile works.'

231. Q. Which are the Holydays of Obligation observed in England?

A. The Holydays of Obligation observed in England are Christmas Day, the Circumcision, the Epiphany, the Ascension, Corpus Christi, SS. Peter and Paul, the Assumption of our Lady, and All Saints.

232. Q. Is it a mortal sin to neglect to hear Mass on Sundays and Holydays of Obligation?

A. It is a mortal sin to neglect to hear Mass

Seven days shalt thou celebrate feasts to the Lord thy God, in the place which the Lord shall choose.... Three times a year shall all thy males appear before the Lord thy God, in the place which he shall choose; in the feast of unleavened bread, in the feast of weeks, and in the feast of tabernacles (*Deut.* xvi. 15).

Behold upon the mountains the feet of him that bringeth good tidings and that preacheth peace: O Judah, keep thy festivals and pay thy vows (*Nahum* i. 15).

on Sundays and Holydays of Obligation.

233. Q. Are parents, masters, and mistresses bound to provide that those under their charge shall hear Mass on Sundays and Holydays of Obligation?

A. Parents, masters, and mistresses are bound to provide that those under their charge shall hear Mass on Sundays and Holydays of Obligation.

234. Q. What is the second Commandment of the Church?

A. The second Commandment of the Church is, "To keep the days of fasting and abstinence appointed by the Church."

235. Q. What are fasting days?

A. Fasting days are days on which we are allowed to take but one meal, and are forbidden to eat flesh-meat without special leave.

236. Q. Which are the fasting days?

A. The fasting days are the forty days of

Then was Jesus led up by the spirit into the wilderness to be tempted by the devil. And when He had fasted forty days and forty nights, He was afterward hungry (*S. Matt.* iv. 1).

And when you fast, be not as the hypocrites, sad. For they disfigure their faces, that they may appear unto men to fast. Amen I say to you, they have received their reward. But thou, when thou fastest, anoint thy head, and wash thy face; that thou appear not to men to fast, but to thy Father Who is in secret: and thy Father Who seeth in secret, will repay thee (*S. Matt.* vi. 16).

And the disciples of John and the Pharisees used to fast: and

Lent; certain Vigils; the Ember days; and in England the Wednesdays and Fridays in Advent.

237. Q. What are days of abstinence?

A. Days of abstinence are days on which we are forbidden to eat flesh-meat, but are allowed the usual number of meals.

238. Q. Which are the days of abstinence?

A. The days of abstinence are all Fridays except the Friday on which Christmas Day may fall; and the Sundays in Lent, unless leave be given to eat meat on them.

they come and say to Him: Why do the disciples of John and of the Pharisees fast; but Thy disciples do not fast? And Jesus saith to them: Can the children of the marriage fast, as long as the bridegroom is with them? As long as they have the bridegroom with them, they cannot fast. But the days will come when the bridegroom shall be taken away from them: and then they shall fast in those days (*S. Mark* ii. 18).

But this kind is not cast out but by prayer and fasting (*S. Matt.* xvii. 20).

Now therefore saith the Lord: Be converted to Me with all your heart, in fasting, and in weeping, and in mourning. And rend your hearts, and not your garments, and turn to the Lord our God: for He is gracious and merciful, patient and rich in mercy, and ready to repent of the evil (*Joel* ii. 12).

Why have we fasted, and Thou hast not regarded: have we humbled our souls, and Thou hast not taken notice? Behold in the day of your fast your own will is found, and you exact of all your debtors (*Isa.* lviii. 3).

Then they fasting and praying, and imposing their hands upon them, sent them away (*Acts* xiii. 3).

Eleazar, one of the chief of the scribes, a man advanced in years, and of a comely countenance, was pressed to open his mouth to eat swine's flesh. But he, choosing rather a most glorious death than a hateful life, went forward voluntarily to the torment. And considering in what manner he was to come to it, patiently bearing, he determined not to do any unlawful things for the love of life (2 *Mach.* vi. 18).

239. Q. Why does the Church command us to fast and abstain?
A. The Church commands us to fast and abstain that so we may mortify the flesh and satisfy God for our sins.

And He said to all: If any man will come after Me, let him deny himself, and take up his cross daily, and follow Me (*S. Luke* ix. 23).

Strive to enter by the narrow gate: for many, I say unto you, shall seek to enter, and shall not be able (*S. Luke* xiii. 24).

And everyone that striveth for the mastery refraineth himself from all things: and they indeed that they may receive a corruptible crown; but we an incorruptible one. I therefore so run, not as at any uncertainty: I so fight, not as one beating the air: but I chastise my body, and bring it into subjection: lest perhaps, when I have preached to others, I myself should become a castaway (1 *Cor.* ix. 25).

And from the days of John the

Baptist until now, the kingdom of heaven suffereth violence, and the violent bear it away (*S. Matt.* xi. 12).

240. Q. What is the third Commandment of the Church?

A. The third Commandment of the Church is, "To go to confession at least once a year."

241. Q. How soon are children bound to go to confession?

A. Children are bound to go to confession as soon as they have come to the use of reason, and are capable of mortal sin.

242. Q. When are children generally supposed to come to the use of reason?

A. Children are generally supposed to come to the use of reason about the age of seven years.

243. Q. What is the fourth Commandment of the Church?

A. The fourth Commandment of the Church is, "To receive the Blessed Sacrament at least once a year, and that at Easter or thereabouts."

244. Q. How soon are Christians bound to receive the Blessed Sacrament?

A. Christians are bound to receive the Blessed Sacrament as soon as they are capable of being instructed in this sacred mystery.

245. Q. What is the fifth Commandment of the Church?

A. The fifth Commandment of the Church is, "To contribute to the support of our pastors."

246. Q. Is it a duty to contribute to the support of religion?

A. It is a duty to contribute to the support of religion according to our means, so that God may be duly honoured and worshipped, and the kingdom of His Church extended.

247. Q. What is the sixth Commandment of the Church?

A. The sixth Com-

And all the multitude of the children of Israel, going out from the presence of Moses, offered first-fruits to the Lord with a most ready and devout mind to make the work of the Tabernacle of the testimony. Whatever was necessary to the service, and to the holy vestments, both men and women gave bracelets and earrings, rings and tablets: every vessel of gold was set aside to be offered to the Lord .... and so they ceased from offering gifts, because the things that were offered did suffice, and were too much (*Exod.* xxv. 20).

mandment of the Church is, "Not to marry within certain degrees of kindred, nor to solemnize marriage at the forbidden times."

248. Q. Which are the times in which it is forbidden to solemnize marriage?

A. The times in which it is forbidden to solemnize marriage are from the first Sunday of Advent till after the Epiphany, and from Ash Wednesday till after Low Sunday.

THE SACRAMENTS.

CHAPTER VI.

249. Q. What is a Sacrament?

A. A Sacrament is an outward sign of inward grace, ordained by Jesus Christ, by which grace is given to our souls.

250. Q. Do the Sacraments always give grace?

A. The Sacraments always give grace to those who receive them worthily.

251. Q. Whence have the Sacraments the power of giving grace?

A. The Sacraments have the power of giving grace from the merits of Christ's Precious Blood, which they apply to our souls.

But if we walk in the light as He also is in the light: we have fellowship one with another, and the blood of Jesus Christ His Son cleanseth us from all sin (1 *S. John* i. 7).

And to Jesus the Mediator of the New Testament, and to the sprinkling of blood which speaketh better than that of Abel (*Heb.* xii. 24).

Wherefore Jesus also, that He might sanctify the people by His own blood, suffered without the gate. Let us go forth therefore to Him without the camp; bearing His reproach (*Heb.* xiii. 12).

252. Q. Ought we to have a great desire to receive the Sacraments?

A. We ought to have a great desire to receive the Sacraments, because they are the chief means of our salvation.

253. Q. Is a character given to the soul by any of the Sacraments?

A. A character is given to the soul by the Sacraments of Baptism, Confirmation, and Holy Order.

254. Q. What is a character?

A. A character is a mark or seal on the soul which cannot be effaced, and therefore the Sacrament conferring it may not be repeated.

These are they who are come out of great tribulation, and have washed their robes, and have made them white in the blood of the Lamb (*Apoc.* vii. 14).

And they sung a new canticle, saying: Thou art worthy, O Lord, to take the book, and to open the seals thereof: because Thou wast slain, and hast redeemed us to God, in Thy blood, out of every tribe, and tongue, and people, and nation (*Apoc.* v. 9).

Many waters cannot quench charity, neither can the floods drown it: if a man should give all the substance of his house for love, he shall despise it as nothing (*Cant.* viii. 7).

That we may be unto the praise of His glory, we who before hoped in Christ. In whom you also after you had heard the word of truth (the Gospel of your salvation), in whom also believing you were signed with the Holy Spirit of promise, Who is the pledge of our inheritance (*Eph.* i. 12).

Grieve not the Holy Spirit of God, whereby you are sealed unto the day of redemption (*Eph.* iv. 30).

The light of Thy countenance, O Lord, is signed upon us (*Ps.* iv. 7).

The Lord hath sworn, and he will not repent: Thou art a priest for ever according to the order of Melchisedech (*Ps.* cix. 4).

255. Q. How many Sacraments are there?
A. There are seven Sacraments: Baptism, Confirmation, Holy Eucharist, Penance, Extreme Unction, Holy Order, and Matrimony.

I.

256. Q. What is Baptism?
A. Baptism is a Sacrament which cleanses us from original sin, makes us Christians, children of God, and members of the Church.

Go ye, therefore, and teach all nations, baptizing them in the Name of the Father, and of the Son, and of the Holy Ghost (*S. Matt.* xxviii. 19).

And as they went on their way, they came to a certain water: and the eunuch said: See here is water, what doth hinder me from being baptized? And Philip said: If thou believest with all thy heart thou mayst. And he answering, said: I believe that Jesus Christ is the Son of God. And he commanded the chariot to stand still: and they went down into the water, both Philip and the eunuch, and he baptized him (*Acts* viii. 36).

One Lord, one faith, one baptism (*Eph.* iv. 5).

For as many of you as have

257. Q. Does Baptism also forgive actual sins?
A. Baptism also forgives actual sins, with all punishment due to them, when it is received in proper dispositions by those who have been guilty of actual sin.

258. Q. Who is the ordinary minister of Baptism?
A. The ordinary minister of Baptism is a priest; but anyone may baptize in case of necessity, when a priest cannot be had.

259. Q. How is Baptism given?
A. Baptism is given by pouring water on the head of the child, saying at the same time these words, " I baptize thee in the name of the Father, and of the Son, and of the Holy Ghost."

260. Q. What do we promise in Baptism?
A. We promise in Baptism to renounce the devil and all his works and pomps.

been baptized in Christ, have put on Christ (*Gal.* iii. 27).

Now when they had heard these things, they had compunction in their heart, and said to Peter, and to the rest of the Apostles: What shall we do, men and brethren? But Peter said to them: Do penance, and be baptized every one of you, in the Name of Jesus Christ, for the remission of your sins: and you shall receive the gift of the Holy Ghost (*Acts* ii. 37).

And now why tarriest thou? Rise up, and be baptized, and wash away thy sins, invoking His Name (*Acts* xxii. 16).

In which also coming, He preached to those spirits that were in prison: which had been some time incredulous, when they waited for the patience of God in the days of Noe, when the ark was a-building: wherein a few, that is, eight souls, were saved by water. Whereunto baptism being of the like form, now saveth you also: not the putting away of the filth of the flesh, but the examination of a good conscience towards God by the resurrection of Jesus Christ (1 *S. Pet.* iii. 19).

And he said to them: Have you received the Holy Ghost since ye believed? But they said to him: We have not so

261. Q. Is Baptism necessary for salvation?
A. Baptism is necessary for salvation, because Christ has said, "Unless a man be born again of water and the Holy Ghost, he cannot enter into the kingdom of God" (*S. John* iii. 5).

II.
262. Q. What is Confirmation?
A. Confirmation is a Sacrament by which we receive the Holy Ghost, in order to make us strong and perfect Christians and soldiers of Jesus Christ.

much as heard whether there be a Holy Ghost. And he said: In what, then, were you baptized? Who said: In John's baptism. Then Paul said: John baptized the people with the baptism of penance, saying: That they should believe in Him Who was to come after him, that is to say, in Jesus. Having heard these things, they were baptized in the Name of the Lord Jesus (*Acts* xix. 2).

He that believeth and is baptized, shall be saved: but he that believeth not, shall be condemned (*S. Mark* xvi. 16).|

And I will ask the Father, and He shall give you another Paraclete, that He may abide with you for ever (*S. John* xiv. 16).
But the Paraclete, the Holy Ghost, Whom the Father will send in My Name, He will teach you all things, and bring all things to your mind, whatsoever I shall have said to you (*S. John* xiv. 26).
And when the days of the

pentecost were accomplished, they were all together in one place: and suddenly there came a sound from heaven, as of a mighty wind coming, and it filled the whole house where they were sitting. And there appeared to them parted tongues as it were of fire, and it sat upon every one of them: and they were all filled with the Holy Ghost, and they began to speak with divers tongues, according as the Holy Ghost gave them to speak (*Acts* ii. 1).

Wherefore leaving the word of the beginning of Christ, let us go on to things more perfect, not laying again the foundation of penance from dead works, and of faith towards God, of the doctrine of baptisms, and imposition of hands, and of the resurrection of the dead, and of eternal judgment (*Heb.* vi. 1).

And the spirit of the Lord shall rest upon him: the spirit of wisdom, and of understanding, the spirit of counsel, and of fortitude, the spirit of knowledge, and of godliness. And he shall be filled with the spirit of the fear of the Lord. He shall not judge according to the sight of the eyes, nor reprove according to the hearing of the ears (*Isa.* xi. 2).

But the fruit of the Spirit is, charity, joy, peace, patience, be-

263. Q. Who is the ordinary minister of Confirmation?
A. The ordinary minister of Confirmation is a Bishop.

264. Q. How does the Bishop administer the Sacrament of Confirmation?
A. The Bishop administers the Sacrament of Confirmation by praying that the Holy Ghost may come down upon those who are to be confirmed; and by laying his hand on them, and making the sign of the cross with chrism on their foreheads; at the same time pronouncing certain words.

265. Q. What are the words used in Confirmation?

nignity, goodness, longanimity, mildness, faith, modesty, continency, chastity. Against such there is no law (*Gal.* v. 22).

Now when the Apostles who were in Jerusalem had heard that Samaria had received the word of God, they sent unto them Peter and John. Who when they were come, prayed for them, that they might receive the Holy Ghost. For He was not as yet come upon any of them: but they were only baptized in the Name of the Lord Jesus (*Acts* viii. 14).

Then they laid their hands upon them, and they received the Holy Ghost (*Acts* viii. 17).

Use of Holy Oil.

Thou shalt anoint Aaron and his sons, and shalt sanctify them, that they may do the office of priesthood unto Me. And thou shalt say to the children of Israel: This oil of unction shall be holy unto Me throughout your generations. The flesh of man shall not be anointed therewith, and you shall make none other of the same composition, because it is sanctified, and shall be holy unto you (*Exod.* xxx. 30).

A. The words used in Confirmation are these: "I sign thee with the sign of the cross, and I confirm thee with the chrism of salvation; in the name of the Father, and of the Son, and of the Holy Ghost. Amen."

III.

266. Q. What is the Sacrament of the Holy Eucharist?*

A. The Sacrament of the Holy Eucharist is the true Body and Blood of Jesus Christ, together with His Soul and Divinity, under the appearances of bread and wine.

267. Q. How are the bread and wine changed into the Body and Blood of Christ?

A. The bread and wine are changed into the Body and Blood of Christ by the power of God, to Whom nothing is impossible or difficult.

268. Q. When are the bread and wine changed into the Body and Blood of Christ?

Promise.

I am the living bread, which came down from heaven. If any man eat of this bread, he shall live for ever: and the bread that I will give, is My flesh for the life of the world. The Jews therefore strove among themselves, saying: How can this man give us His flesh to eat? Then Jesus said to them: Amen, amen, I say unto you: Except you eat the flesh of the Son of Man, and drink His blood, you shall not have life in you. He that eateth My flesh, and drinketh My blood, hath everlasting life: and I will raise him up in the last day. For My flesh is meat indeed: and My blood is drink indeed (*S. John* vi. 51).

Institution.

And whilst they were at supper, Jesus took bread, and blessed,

° See note C, on the Real Presence.

A. The bread and wine are changed into the Body and Blood of Christ when the words of consecration, ordained by Jesus Christ, are pronounced by the priest in the Holy Mass.

and broke; and gave to His disciples, and said: Take ye, and eat: this is My body. And taking the chalice He gave thanks: and gave to them, saying: Drink ye all of this. For this is My blood of the new testament which shall be shed for many unto remission of sins (*S. Matt.* xxvi. 26).

Subsequent References.

For I have received of the Lord that which also I delivered unto you, that the Lord Jesus, the same night in which He was betrayed, took bread, and giving thanks, broke, and said: Take ye and eat: this is My body which shall be delivered for you: this do for the commemoration of Me. In like manner also the chalice, after he had supped, saying: This chalice is the new testament in My blood: this do ye, as often as you shall drink, for the commemoration of Me. For as often as you shall eat this bread, and drink the chalice, you shall shew the death of the Lord until He come. Therefore whosoever shall eat this bread, or drink the chalice of the Lord unworthily, shall be guilty of the body and of the blood of the Lord (1 *Cor.* xi. 23).

The chalice of benediction, which we bless, is it not the

communion of the blood of Christ? And the bread, which we break, is it not the partaking of the body of the Lord? (1 Cor. x. 16.)

Miracles Illustrating the Miracle of Transubstantiation.

Jesus saith to them: Fill the water-pots with water. And they filled them up to the brim. And Jesus saith to them: Draw out now, and carry to the chief steward of the feast. And they carried it. And when the chief steward had tasted the water made wine, and knew not whence it was, but the waiters knew who had drawn the water (*S. John* ii. 7).

And Jesus took the loaves: and when He had given thanks, He distributed to them that were sat down. In like manner also of the fishes as much as they would. And when they were filled, He said to His disciples: Gather up the fragments that remain, lest they be lost. They gathered up therefore, and filled twelve baskets with the fragments of the five barley loaves, which remained over and above to them that had eaten (*S. John* vi. 11).

Institution of the Holy Eucharist.

And taking bread, He gave thanks, and brake: and gave to

them, saying: This is My body which is given for you. Do this for a commemoration of Me. In like manner the chalice also, after He had supped, saying: This is the chalice, the new testament in My blood, which shall be shed for you (*S. Luke* xxii. 19).

Figures of the Holy Eucharist.

And He said: Behold Adam is become as one of us, knowing good and evil: now, therefore, lest perhaps he put forth his hand, and take also of the tree of life, and eat, and live for ever (*Gen.* iii. 22).

And the Angel of the Lord came again the second time, and touched him, and said to him: Arise, eat: for thou hast yet a great way to go. And he arose, and ate, and drank, and walked in the strength of that food forty days and forty nights, unto the mount of God, Horeb (3 *Kings* xix. 8).

Our fathers did eat manna in the desert, as it is written: He gave them bread from heaven to eat. Then Jesus said to them: Amen, amen, I say to you: Moses gave you not bread from heaven, but My Father giveth you the true bread from heaven. For the bread of God is that which cometh down from heaven,

269. Q. Why has Christ given Himself to us in the Holy Eucharist?

A. Christ has given Himself to us in the Holy Eucharist to be the life and the food of our souls. "He that eateth Me, the same also shall live by Me;" "He that eateth this bread shall live for ever" (*S. John* vi. 58, 59).

and giveth life to the world (*S. John* vi. 31).

Promises.

I am the vine; you the branches: he that abideth in Me, and I in him, the same beareth much fruit: for without Me you can do nothing. If anyone abide not in Me: he shall be cast forth as a branch, and shall wither, and they shall gather him up, and cast him into the fire, and he burneth (*S. John* xv. 5).

He that eateth My flesh, and drinketh My blood, abideth in Me, and I in him. As the living Father hath sent Me, and I live by the Father: so he that eateth Me, the same also shall live by Me. This is the bread that came down from heaven. Not as your fathers did eat manna, and are dead. He that eateth this bread shall live for ever (*S. John* vi. 57).

He that hath an ear, let him hear what the Spirit saith to the churches: To him that overcometh, I will give the hidden manna, and will give him a white counter, and in the counter a new name written, which no man knoweth, but he that receiveth it (*Apoc.* ii. 17).

And He had commanded the clouds from above, and had

opened the doors of heaven. And had rained down manna upon them to eat, and had given them the bread of heaven. Man ate the bread of angels: He sent them provisions in abundance (*Ps.* lxxvii. 23).

Instead of which things thou didst feed thy people with the food of angels, and gavest them bread from heaven prepared without labour; having in it all that is delicious, and the sweetness of every taste. For thy sustenance showed thy sweetness to thy children, and serving every man's will, it was turned to what every man liked (*Wisd.* xvi. 20).

Neither is there any other nation so great, that hath gods so nigh them, as our God is present to all our petitions (*Deut.* iv. 7).

Jesus answered, and said to her: Whosoever drinketh of this water, shall thirst again; but he that shall drink of the water that I will give him, shall not thirst for ever: but the water that I will give him, shall become in him a fountain of water springing up into life everlasting (*S. John* iv. 13).

And they told what things were done in the way: and how they knew Him in the breaking of bread (*S. Luke* xxiv. 35).

270. Q. Is Christ received whole and entire under either kind alone?

A. Christ is received whole and entire under either kind alone.

271. Q. In order to receive the Blessed Sacrament worthily, what is required?

A. In order to receive the Blessed Sacrament worthily, it is required that we be in a state of grace, and fasting from midnight.

272. Q. What is it to be in a state of grace?

A. To be in a state of grace is to be free from mortal sin, and pleasing to God.

Knowing that Christ rising again from the dead dieth now no more, death shall have no more dominion over Him (*Rom.* vi. 9).

The Wedding Garment of Grace.

And the king went in to see the guests: and he saw there a man who had not on a wedding garment. And he saith to him: Friend, how camest thou in hither not having a wedding garment? But he was silent. Then the king said to the waiters: Bind his hands and feet, and cast him into the exterior darkness: there shall be weeping and gnashing of teeth (*S. Matt.* xxii. 11).

Necessity of Preparation.

But let a man prove himself: and so let him eat of that bread, and drink of the chalice (1 *Cor.* xi. 28).

But if we should judge ourselves, we would not be judged (1 *Cor.* xi. 31).

Jesus answered, and said to him: If any man love Me, he will keep My word, and My Father will love him, and we will come to him, and will make our abode with him (*S. John* xiv. 23).

And when Jesus was come to the place, looking up, He saw

273. Q. Is it a great sin to receive Holy Communion in mortal sin?
A. It is a great sin to receive Holy Communion in mortal sin; "For he that eateth and drinketh unworthily eateth and drinketh judgment to himself" (1 *Cor.* xi. 29).

him, and said to him: Zacheus, make haste and come down: for this day I must abide in thy house. And he made haste and came down, and received Him with joy (*S. Luke* xix. 5).

Jesus answered: He it is to whom I shall reach bread dipped. And when He had dipped the bread, He gave it to Judas Iscariot, the son of Simon. And after the morsel, Satan entered into him. And Jesus said to him: That which thou dost, do quickly (*S. John* xiii. 26).

For he that eateth and drinketh unworthily, eateth and drinketh judgment to himself, not discerning the body of the Lord. Therefore are there many infirm and weak among you, and many sleep (1 *Cor.* xi. 29).

Peter saith to Him: Thou shalt never wash my feet. Jesus answered him: If I wash thee not, thou shalt have no part with Me. Simon Peter saith to Him: Lord, not only my feet, but also my hands and my head (*S. John* xiii. 8).

Christ a Continual Sacrifice.

274. Q. Is the Blessed Eucharist a Sacrament only?
A. The Blessed Eucharist is not a Sacra-

And power was given Him over every tribe, and people, and tongue, and nation. And all that dwell upon the earth adored Him, whose names are not

ment only; it is also a sacrifice.

275. Q. What is a sacrifice?

A. A sacrifice is the offering of a victim by a priest to God alone, in testimony of His being the Sovereign Lord of all things.

276. Q. What is the Sacrifice of the New Law?

A. The Sacrifice of the New Law is the Holy Mass.

277. Q. What is the Holy Mass?

A. The Holy Mass is the Sacrifice of the Body and Blood of Jesus Christ, really present on the altar under the appearances of bread and wine, and offered to God for the living and the dead.*

278. Q. Is the Holy Mass one and the same Sacrifice with that of the Cross?

A. The Holy Mass is one and the same Sacrifice with that of the Cross, inasmuch as Christ, Who offered Himself, a bleeding Victim,

written in the book of life of the Lamb, which was slain from the beginning of the world (*Apoc.* xiii. 7).

And I saw: and behold in the midst of the throne and of the four living creatures, and in the midst of the ancients, a Lamb standing as it were slain, having seven horns and seven eyes: which are the seven Spirits of God, sent forth into all the earth (*Apoc.* v. 6).

But Christ, being come an high-priest of the good things to come, by a greater and more perfect tabernacle not made with hand, that is, not of this creation: neither by the blood of goats, or of calves, but by His own blood, entered once into the Holies, having obtained eternal redemption. For if the blood of goats and of oxen, and the ashes of an heifer being sprinkled, sanctify such as are defiled, to the cleansing of the flesh: how much more shall the blood of Christ, Who by the Holy Ghost offered Himself unspotted unto God, cleanse our conscience from dead works, to serve the living God? And therefore He is the Mediator of the new testament: that by means of His death, for the redemption of those transgressions, which were under the

---

° See Note D, the Ancient Liturgies on the Real Presence.

on the Cross to His heavenly Father, continues to offer Himself in an unbloody manner on the altar, through the ministry of His priests.

former testament, they that are called may receive the promise of eternal inheritance (*Heb.* ix. 11).

And they were persevering in the doctrine of the Apostles, and in the communication of the breaking of bread, and in prayers (*Acts* ii. 42).

For he testifieth : Thou art a priest for ever, according to the order of Melchisedech (*Heb.* vii. 17).

And the others indeed were made many priests, because by reason of death they were not suffered to continue : but this, that He continueth for ever, hath an everlasting priesthood. Whereby He is able also to save for ever them that come to God by Him : always living to make intercession for us. For it was fitting that we should have such a high-priest, holy, innocent, undefiled, separated from sinners, and made higher than the heavens : who needeth not daily (as the other priests) to offer sacrifices first for His own sins, and then for the people's : for this He did once, in offering Himself (*Heb.* vii. 23).

Purge out the old leaven, that you may be a new paste, as you are unleavened. For Christ our pasch, is sacrificed (1 *Cor.* v. 7).

279. Q. For what ends is the Sacrifice of the Mass offered?

A. The Sacrifice of the Mass is offered for four ends : first, to give supreme honour and glory to God; secondly, to thank Him for all His benefits; thirdly, to obtain pardon for our sins; and fourthly, to obtain all other graces and blessings through Jesus Christ.

And it came to pass after many days, that Cain offered, of the fruits of the earth, gifts to the Lord. Abel also offered of the firstlings of his flock, and of their fat (*Gen.* iv. 3).

And Noe built an altar unto the Lord : and taking of all cattle and fowls that were clean, offered holocausts upon the altar. And the Lord smelled a sweet savour, and said : I will no more curse the earth for the sake of man : for the imagination and thought of man's heart are prone to evil from his youth: therefore I will no more destroy every living soul as I have done (*Gen.* viii. 20).

But Melchisedech, the king of Salem, bringing forth bread and wine, for he was the priest of the Most High God, blessed him, and said : Blessed be Abram by the Most High God, who created heaven and earth (*Gen.* xiv. 18).

And Abraham said : God will provide Himself a victim for a holocaust, my son. So they went on together. And they came to the place which God had shown him, where he built an altar, and laid the wood in order upon it : and when he had bound Isaac his son, he laid him on the altar upon the pile of wood. And he put forth his hand and took the sword, to sacrifice his son. And behold an Angel of the Lord from heaven called to him, saying: Abraham, Abraham. And he answered: Here I am. And he said to him: Lay not thy hand upon the boy, neither do thou anything to him : Now I know that thou fearest God, and hast not spared thy only begotten son for My sake. Abraham lifted up his eyes, and saw behind his back a ram amongst the briers sticking fast by the horns, which he took and offered for a holocaust instead of his son (*Gen.* xxii. 8).

Sacrifices, and oblations, and holocausts for sin, Thou wouldst not, neither are they pleasing to Thee, which are offered according to the law. Then said I, Behold, I come to do Thy will, O God : He taketh away the first, that He may establish that which followeth. In the which will, we are sanctified by the oblation of the body of Jesus Christ once (*Heb.* x. 8).

For if Thou hadst desired sacrifice, I would indeed have given it : with burnt-offerings Thou wilt not be delighted. A sacrifice to God is an afflicted spirit: a contrite and an humbled heart, O God, Thou wilt not despise. Deal favourably, O Lord, in Thy goodwill with Sion; that the walls of Jerusalem may

A. The Catho[lic]
Church shows great [de]
votion to the Bles[sed]
Virgin because she [is]
the Immaculate Mot[her]
of God.

167. Q. How is [the]
Blessed Virgin Mo[ther]
of God?

A. The Blessed V[irgin]
is Mother of God [be]
cause Jesus Christ [her]
Son, who was bor[n of]
her as man, is not [only]
man, but is also
God.

168. Q. Is the B[lessed]
Virgin our Mothe[r?]

A. The Blessed [Virgin]
is our Mother [be]
cause, being the [Mother]
of Jesus, we [are]
children of Mary

be built up. Then shalt Thou accept the sacrifice of justice, oblations and whole burnt-offerings: then shall they lay calves upon Thy altar (*Ps.* l. 18).

For from the rising of the sun even to the going down, My Name is great among the Gentiles, and in every place there is sacrifice, and there is offered to My Name a clean oblation: for My Name is great among the Gentiles, saith the Lord of Hosts (*Mal.* i. 11).

So also Christ was offered once to take away the sins of many: the second time He shall appear without sin, to them that expect Him unto salvation (*Heb.* ix. 28).

280. Q. Is the Mass also a memorial of the Passion and Death of our Lord?

A. The Mass is also a memorial of the Passion and Death of our Lord, for Christ at His last supper said, "Do this for a commemoration of Me" (*S. Luke* xxii. 19).

And He said to them: With desire I have desired to eat this pasch with you before I suffer. For I say to you, that from this time I will not eat it, till it be fulfilled in the kingdom of God. And having taken the chalice He gave thanks, and said: Take, and divide it among you. For I say to you, that I will not drink of the fruit of the vine, till the kingdom of God come (*S. Luke* xxii. 15).

For as often as you shall eat this bread, and drink the chalice, you shall shew the death of the

IV.

281. Q. What is the Sacrament of Penance?
A. Penance is a Sacrament whereby the sins, whether mortal or venial, which we have committed after Baptism are forgiven.

282. Q. Does the Sacrament of Penance increase the grace of God in the soul?
A. The Sacrament of Penance increases the grace of God in the soul, besides forgiving sin; we should, therefore, often go to confession.

Lord, until He come (1 *Cor.* xi. 26).

He hath made a remembrance of His wonderful works, being a merciful and gracious Lord: He hath given food to them that fear Him (*Ps.* cx. 4).

In that day there shall be a fountain open to the house of David, and to the inhabitants of Jerusalem: for the washing of the sinner, and of the unclean woman (*Zach.* xiii. 1).

Thou shalt sprinkle me with hyssop, and I shall be cleansed: thou shalt wash me, and I shall be made whiter than snow (*Ps.* l. 5).

If your sins be as scarlet, they shall be made as white as snow: and if they be red as crimson, they shall be white as wool (*Isa.* i. 18).

For a just man shall fall seven times, and shall rise again: but the wicked shall fall down into evil (*Prov.* xxiv. 16).

And he that contemneth small things, shall fall by little and little (*Ecclus.* xix. 1).

283. Q. When did our Lord institute the Sacrament of Penance?
A. Our Lord instituted the Sacrament of

And I will give to thee the keys of the kingdom of heaven. And whatsoever thou shalt bind upon earth it shall be bound also in heaven: and whatsoever thou

Penance when He breathed on His Apostles and gave them power to forgive sins, saying, "Whose sins you shall forgive, they are forgiven" (*S. John* xx. 23).

284. Q. How does the priest forgive sins?
A. The priest forgives sins by the power of God, when he pronounces the words of absolution.

shalt loose on earth, it shall be loosed also in heaven (*S. Matt.* xvi. 19).

And when He had said this, He shewed them His hands, and His side. The disciples therefore were glad, when they saw the Lord. He said therefore to them again: Peace be to you. As the Father hath sent Me, I also send you. When He had said this, He breathed on them; and He said to them: Receive ye the Holy Ghost. Whose sins you shall forgive, they are forgiven them; and whose sins you shall retain, they are retained (*S. John* xx. 20).

Now are you clean by reason of the word, which I have spoken to you (*S. John* xv. 33).

And behold they brought to Him one sick of the palsy lying in a bed. And Jesus, seeing their faith, said to the man sick of the palsy: Be of good heart, son, thy sins are forgiven thee. And behold some of the scribes said within themselves: He blasphemeth. And Jesus seeing their thoughts, said: Why do you think evil in your hearts? Whether it is easier to say, Thy sins are forgiven thee: or to say, Arise and walk? But that you may know that the Son of Man hath power on earth to forgive

285. Q. What are the words of absolution?
A. The words of absolution are: "I absolve thee from thy sins, in the name of the Father, and of the Son, and of the Holy Ghost."

286. Q. Are any conditions for forgiveness required on the part of the penitent?
A. Three conditions for forgiveness are required on the part of the penitent: Contrition, Confession, and Satisfaction.

287. Q. What is Contrition?
A. Contrition is a hearty sorrow for our sins, because by them we have offended so good a God, together with a firm purpose of amendment.

288. Q. What is a firm purpose of amendment?
A. A firm purpose of amendment is a resolution to avoid, by the

sins (then said He to the man sick of the palsy), Arise, take up thy bed, and go into thy house (*S. Matt.* ix. 2).

Amen I say to you, whatsoever you shall bind upon earth, shall be bound also in heaven: and whatsoever you shall loose upon earth, shall be loosed also in heaven (*S. Matt.* xviii. 18).

A sacrifice to God is an afflicted spirit: a contrite and humbled heart, O God, thou wilt not despise (*Ps.* l. 19).

The Lord buildeth up Jerusalem: He will gather together the dispersed of Israel. Who healeth the broken of heart, and bindeth up their bruises (*Ps.* cxlvi. 2).

Neither is there at this time prince, or leader, or prophet, or holocaust, or sacrifice, or oblation, or incense, or place of first fruits before Thee, that we may find Thy mercy: nevertheless in a contrite heart and humble spirit let us be accepted (*Dan.* iii. 38).

I have laboured in my groanings, every night I will wash my bed: I will water my couch with my tears (*Ps.* vi. 7).

The Lord is nigh unto them that are of a contrite heart: and He will save the humble of spirit (*Ps.* xxxiii. 9).

grace of God, not only sin, but also the dangerous occasions of sin.

289. Q. How may we obtain a hearty sorrow for our sins?

A. We may obtain a hearty sorrow for our sins by earnestly praying for it, and by making use of such considerations as may lead us to it.

But if the wicked do penance for all his sins, which he hath committed, and keep all My commandments, and do judgment, and justice, living he shall live, and shall not die. I will not remember all his iniquities. that he hath done: in his justice which he hath wrought, he shall live. Is it My will that a sinner should die, saith the Lord God, and not that he should be converted from his ways and live? (*Ezech.* xviii. 21).

And when the wicked turneth himself away from his wickedness, which he hath wrought, and doeth judgment, and justice: he shall save his soul alive. Because he considereth and turneth away himself from all his iniquities which he hath wrought, he shall surely live, and not die (*Ezech.* xviii. 27).

Say not: I have sinned, and what harm hath befallen me? for the Most High is a patient rewarder (*Ecclus.* v. 4).

We fools esteemed their life madness, and their end without honour. Behold how they are numbered among the children of God, and their lot is among the saints. Therefore we have erred from the way of truth, and the light of justice hath not shined unto us, and the sun of understanding hath not risen upon us.

290. Q. What consideration concerning God will lead us to sorrow for our sins?

A. This consideration concerning God will lead us to sorrow for our sins, that by our sins we have offended God, who is infinitely good in Himself, and infinitely good to us.

291. Q. What consideration concerning our Saviour will lead us to sorrow for our sins?

A. This consideration concerning our Saviour will lead us to sorrow for our sins, that our Saviour died for our sins, and that those who sin grievously "crucify again to themselves the Son of God, making Him a mockery" (*Heb.* vi. 8).

292. Q. Is sorrow for our sins, because by

We wearied ourselves in the way of iniquity and destruction, and have walked through hard ways, but the way of the Lord we have not known (*Wisd.* v. 4).

The son honoureth the father and the servant his master: if then I be a father, where is My honour? if I be a master, where is My fear, saith the Lord of hosts (*Mal.* i. 6).

They shall look on Him they pierced (*S. John* xix. 37).
They have dug My hands and My feet, they have numbered all My bones (*Ps.* xxi. 17).
Who His own self bore our sins in His body upon the tree: that we being dead to sins, should live to justice: by Whose stripes you were healed (1 *S. Peter* ii. 24).

Fear ye not them that kill the body and are not able to kill the

them we have lost heaven and deserved hell, sufficient when we go to confession?

A. Sorrow for our sins, because by them we have lost heaven and deserved hell, is sufficient when we go to confession.

293. Q. What is perfect contrition?

A. Perfect contrition is sorrow for sin arising purely from the love of God.

294. Q. What special value has perfect contrition?

A. Perfect contrition has this special value—that by it our sins are forgiven immediately, even before we confess them; but nevertheless, if they are mortal, we are strictly bound to confess them afterwards.

295. Q. What is confession?*

A. Confession is to accuse ourselves of our sins to a priest approved by the Bishop.

296. Q. What if a

soul: but rather fear Him that can destroy both body and soul into hell (*S. Matt.* x. 28).

The fear of the Lord driveth out sin (*Ecclus.* i. 27).

And turning to the woman, He said unto Simon: Dost thou see this woman? I entered into thy house, thou gavest Me no water for My feet; but she with tears hath washed My feet, and with her hairs hath wiped them. Thou gavest Me no kiss; but she, since she came in, hath not ceased to kiss My feet. My head with oil thou didst not anoint; but she with ointment hath anointed My feet. Wherefore I say to thee: Many sins are forgiven her, because she hath loved much (*S. Luke* vii. 44).

If thou perceive that there be among you a hard and doubtful matter in judgment between blood and blood, cause and cause, leprosy and leprosy: and thou shalt see that the words of the judges within thy gates do vary:

* See note E, on Confession.

person wilfully conceal a mortal sin in confession?

A. If a person wilfully conceal a mortal sin in confession he is guilty of a great sacrilege, by telling a lie to the Holy Ghost in making a bad confession.

arise, and go up to the place, which the Lord thy God shall choose. And thou shalt come to the priests of the Levitical race, and to the judge, that shall be at that time: and thou shalt ask of them, and they shall shew thee the truth of the judgment (*Deut.* xvii. 8).

And He charged him that he should tell no man, but, Go, shew thyself to the priest, and offer for thy cleansing according as Moses commanded, for a testimony to them (*S. Luke* v. 14).

And many of them that believed, came confessing and declaring their deeds (*Acts* xix. 18).

Confess therefore your sins one to another: and pray one for another, that you may be saved (*S. James* v. 16).

I will recount to Thee all my years in the bitterness of my soul (*Isa.* xxxviii. 15).

Naaman was angry and went away, saying: I thought he would have come out to me, and standing would have invoked the Name of the Lord his God, and touched with his hand the place of the leprosy, and healed me. Are not the Abana, and the Pharphar, rivers of Damascus, better than all the waters of Israel, that I may wash in them, and be made clean? So as he turned, and was going away with

297. Q. How many things have we to do in order to prepare for confession?

A. We have four things to do in order to prepare for confession: first, we must heartily pray for grace to make a good confession; secondly, we must carefully examine our conscience; thirdly, we must take time and care to make a good act of contrition; and fourthly, we must resolve by the help of God to renounce our sins, and to begin a new life for the future.

298. Q. What is Satisfaction?

A. Satisfaction is doing the penance given us by the priest.

indignation, his servants came to him, and said to him: Father, if the prophet had bid thee do some great thing, surely thou shouldst have done it: how much rather what he now hath said to thee: Wash, and thou shalt be clean? (4 *Kings* v. 11.)

Say not: I have sinned, and what harm hath befallen me? for the Most High is a patient rewarder. Be not without fear about sin forgiven, and add not sin upon sin: and say not: The mercy of the Lord is great, He will have mercy on the multitude of thy sins. For mercy and wrath quickly come from Him, and His wrath looketh upon sinners. Delay not to be converted to the Lord, and defer it not from day to day. For His wrath shall come on a sudden, and in the time of vengeance He will destroy thee (*Ecclus.* v. 4).

Now therefore saith the Lord: Be converted to Me with all your heart, in fasting, and in weeping, and in mourning. And rend your hearts, and not your garments, and turn to the Lord your God: for He is gracious and merciful, patient and rich in mercy, and ready to repent of the evil. Who knoweth but He will return, and forgive, and leave a blessing behind Him, sacrifice and libation to the Lord your God? (*Joel* ii. 12.)

They that fear the Lord, will prepare their hearts, and in His sight will sanctify their souls. They that fear the Lord, keep His commandments, and will have patience even until His visitation, saying: If we do not penance, we shall fall into the hands of the Lord, and not into the hands of men. For according to His greatness, so also is His mercy with Him (*Ecclus.* ii. 20).

Then began He to upbraid the cities wherein were done the most of His miracles, for that they had not done penance. Wo to thee, Corozain, wo to thee, Bethsaida: for if in Tyre and Sidon had been wrought the miracles that have been wrought in you, they had long ago done penance in sackcloth and ashes (*S. Matt.* xi. 20).

299. Q. Does the penance given by the priest always make full satisfaction for our sins?

A. The penance given by the priest does not always make full satisfaction for our sins. We

Be not without fear about sin forgiven, and add not sin upon sin (*Ecclus.* v. 5).

And David said to Nathan: I have sinned against the Lord. And Nathan said to David: The Lord also hath taken away thy sin: thou shalt not die. Never-should therefore add to it other good works and penances, and try to gain Indulgences.

300. Q. What is an Indulgence?

A. An Indulgence is a remission, granted by the Church, of the temporal punishment which often remains due to sin after its guilt has been forgiven.

theless, because thou hast given occasion to the enemies of the Lord to blaspheme, for this thing, the child that is born to thee shall surely die (2 *Kings* xii. 13).

V.

301. Q. What is the Sacrament of Extreme Unction?

A. The Sacrament of Extreme Unction is the anointing of the sick with holy oil, accompanied with prayer.

302. Q. When is Extreme Unction given?

A. Extreme Unction is given when we are in danger of death by sickness.

303. Q. What are the effects of the Sacrament of Extreme Unction?

A. The effects of the Sacrament of Extreme Unction are to comfort and strengthen the soul, to remit sin, and even to restore health, when

And going forth they preached that men should do penance: and they cast out many devils, and anointed with oil many that were sick, and healed them (*S. Mark* vi. 12).

God sees it to be expedient.

304. Q. What authority is there in Scripture for the Sacrament of Extreme Unction?

A. The authority in Scripture for the Sacrament of Extreme Unction is in the fifth chapter of St. James, where it is said: "Is any one sick among you, let him bring in the priests of the Church; and let them pray over him, anointing him with oil in the Name of the Lord. And the prayer of faith shall save the sick man: and the Lord shall raise him up; and if he be in sins they shall be forgiven him" (*S. James* v. 4, 15).

VI.

305. Q. What is the Sacrament of Holy Order?

A. Holy Order is the Sacrament by which Bishops, priests, and other ministers of the Church are ordained, and receive power and grace to perform their sacred duties.

He said therefore to them again: Peace be to you. As the Father hath sent Me, I also send you (*S. John* xx. 21).

And Jesus coming, spoke to them, saying: All power is given to Me in heaven and in earth. Going therefore, teach ye all nations; baptizing them in the Name of the Father, and of the Son, and of the Holy Ghost, teaching them to observe all things whatsoever I have commanded you : and behold I am with you all days, even to the consummation of the world (*S. Matt.* xxviii. 18).

And taking bread, He gave thanks, and brake : and gave to them, saying : This is My body which is given for you. Do this for a commemoration of Me (*S. Luke* xxii. 19).

When He had said this, He breathed on them ; and He said to them : Receive ye the Holy Ghost. Whose sins you shall forgive, they are forgiven them : and whose sins you shall retain, they are retained (*S. John* xx. 22).

These they set before the apostles : and they praying imposed hands upon them (*Acts* vi. 6).

And as they were ministering to the Lord, and fasting, the Holy Ghost said to them : Separate me Saul and Barnabas, for the work whereunto I have taken them. Then they fasting and praying, and imposing their hands upon them, sent them away (*Acts* xiii. 2).

And when they had ordained to them priests in every church, and had prayed with fasting, they commended them to the Lord, in whom they believed (*Acts* xiv. 22).

And the things, which thou hast heard of me by many witnesses, the same commend to faithful men, who shall be fit to teach others also (2 *Tim.* ii. 2).

Let no man despise thy youth: but be thou an example of the faithful, in word, in conversation, in charity, in faith, in chastity. Till I come, attend unto reading, to exhortation, and to doctrine. Neglect not the grace that is in thee, which was given thee by prophecy, with imposition of the hands of the priesthood (1 *Tim.* iv. 12).

Obey your prelates, and be subject to them. For they watch as being to render an account of your souls; that they may do this with joy, and not with grief. For this is not expedient for you (*Heb.* xiii. 17).

Let a man so account of us as of the ministers of Christ, and the dispensers of the mysteries of God. Here now it is required among the dispensers, that a man be found faithful. But to me it is a very small thing to be judged by you, or by man's day: but neither do I judge my own self. For I am not conscious to myself of anything, yet am I not hereby justified: but he that judgeth me, is the Lord (1 *Cor.* iv. 1).

For which cause I admonish thee, that thou stir up the grace of God which is in thee by the imposition of my hands (2 *Tim.* i. 6).

Upon thy walls, O Jerusalem, I have appointed watchmen all the day, and all the night, they shall never hold their peace (*Isa.* lxii. 6).

For the lips of the priest shall keep knowledge, and they shall seek the law at his mouth: because he is the Angel of the Lord of hosts (*Mal.* ii. 7).

The Lord is the portion of my inheritance and of my cup: it is Thou that wilt restore my inheritance to me (*Ps.* xv. 5).

VII.

306. Q. What is the Sacrament of Matrimony?

A. Matrimony is the Sacrament which sanctifies the contract of a Christian marriage, and gives a special grace to those who receive it worthily.

307. Q. What special grace does the Sacrament of Matrimony give to those who receive it worthily?

A. The Sacrament of Matrimony gives to those who receive it worthily a special grace, to enable them to bear the difficulties of their

Let women be subject to their husbands, as to the Lord. Because the husband is the head of the wife: as Christ is the head of the Church. He is the saviour of His body. Therefore as the Church is subject to Christ, so also let the wives be to their husbands in all things. Husbands, love your wives, as Christ also loved the Church, and delivered Himself up for it: that He might sanctify it, cleansing it by the laver of water in the word of life. That He might present it to Himself a glorious Church, not having spot or wrinkle, or any such thing, but that it should be holy and without blemish. So also ought men to love their wives as their own bodies. He

state, to love and be faithful to one another, and to bring up their children in the fear of God.

308. Q. Is it a sacrilege to contract marriage in mortal sin, or in disobedience to the laws of the Church?

A. It is a sacrilege to contract marriage in mortal sin, or in disobedience to the laws of the Church, and, instead of a blessing, the guilty parties draw down upon themselves the anger of God.

309. Q. What is a "mixed marriage"?

A. A "mixed marriage" is a marriage between a Catholic and one who, though baptized, does not profess the Catholic faith.

310. Q. Has the Church always forbidden mixed marriages?

A. The Church has always forbidden mixed marriages, and considered them unlawful and pernicious.

311. Does the Church sometimes permit mixed marriages?

that loveth his wife loveth himself. For no man ever hateth his own flesh: but nourisheth and cherisheth it, as also Christ doth the Church: because we are members of His body, of His flesh, and of His bones. For this cause shall a man leave his father and mother: and shall cleave to his wife, and they shall be two in one flesh. This is a great sacrament; but I speak in Christ and in the Church. Nevertheless let every one of you in particular love his wife as himself; and let the wife fear her husband (*Eph.* v. 22).

Let the husband render the debt to his wife: and the wife also in like manner to the husband. The wife hath not the power of her own body; but the husband. And in like manner the husband also hath not power of his own body; but the wife. Defraud not one another, except, perhaps by consent, for a time, that you may give yourselves to prayer: and return together again, lest Satan tempt you for your incontinency. But I speak this by indulgence, not by commandment (1 *Cor.* vii. 3).

Happy is the husband of a good wife: for the number of his years is double. A virtuous woman rejoiceth her husband, and shall fulfil the years of his

A. The Church sometimes permits mixed marriages, by granting a dispensation, for very grave reasons and under special conditions.

312. Q. Can any human power dissolve the bond of marriage?

A. No human power can dissolve the bond of marriage, because Christ has said, "What God hath joined together let no man put asunder" (*Matt.* xix. 6).

life in peace. A good wife is a good portion, she shall be given in a portion of them that fear God, to a man for his good deeds (*Ecclus.* xxvi. 1).

Every man that passeth beyond his own bed, despising his own soul, and saying: Who seeth me? darkness compasseth me about, and the walls cover me, and no man seeth me: whom do I fear? the Most High will not remember my sins. And he understandeth not that His eye seeth all things, for such a man's fear driveth from him the fear of God, and the eyes of men fearing him: and he knoweth not that the eyes of the Lord are far brighter than the sun, beholding round about all the ways of men, and the bottom of the deep, and looking into the hearts of men, into the most hidden parts. For all things were known to the Lord God, before they were created: so also after they were perfected He beholdeth all things (*Ecclus.* xxiii. 25).

And I say to you, that whosoever shall put away his wife, except it be for fornication, and shall marry another, committeth adultery: and he that shall marry her that is put away, committeth adultery (*S. Matt.* xix. 9).

CHAPTER VII.

OF VIRTUES AND VICES.

313. Q. Which are the Theological Virtues?

A. The Theological Virtues are "Faith, Hope, and Charity" (1 *Cor.* xiii. 13).

314. Q. Why are they called Theological Virtues?

A. They are called Theological Virtues because they relate immediately to God.

315. Q. What are the chief mysteries of Faith which every Christian is bound to know?

A. The chief mysteries of Faith which every Christian is bound to know are the Unity and Trinity of God, and the Incarnation, Death, and Resurrection of our Saviour.

If I should speak with the tongues of men and of angels and have not charity, I am become as a sounding brass and a tinkling cymbal. And if I should have prophecy, and should know all mysteries and all knowledge, and if I should have all faith so that I could remove mountains and have not charity I am nothing. And if I should distribute all my goods to feed the poor, and if I should deliver my body to be burned, and have not charity, it profiteth me nothing ... and now there remain faith, hope, and charity, these three: but the greater of these is charity (1 *Cor.* xiii. 1).

Now faith is the substance of things to be hoped for, the evidence of things that appear not.... But without faith it is impossible to please God. For he that cometh to God must believe that He is, and is a rewarder to them that seek Him (*Heb.* xi. 1—6).

And we have the more firm prophetical word: whereunto you do well to attend as to a

316. Q. Which are the Cardinal Virtues?
A. The Cardinal Virtues are "Prudence, Justice, Fortitude, and Temperance" (*Wisd.* viii. 7).

317. Q. Why are they called Cardinal Virtues?
A. They are called Cardinal Virtues because they are, as it were, the hinges on which all other moral virtues turn.

light shining in a dark place, until the day dawn, and the day star arise in your hearts. Understanding this first, that no prophecy of Scripture is made by private interpretation (2 *S. Peter* i. 19).

For the wisdom of the flesh is death: but the wisdom of the Spirit is life and peace. Because the wisdom of the flesh is an enemy to God: for it is not subject to the law of God, neither can it be (*Rom.* viii. 6).

For I say, through the grace that is given me, to all that are among you, not to be more wise than it behoveth to be wise, but to be wise unto sobriety (*Rom.* xii. 3).

The justice of the upright shall make his way prosperous: and the wicked man shall fall by his own wickedness. The justice of the righteous shall deliver them: and the unjust shall be caught in their own snares (*Prov.* xi. 5).

Behold I send you as sheep in the midst of wolves. Be ye therefore wise as serpents and simple as doves (*S. Matt.* x. 16).

I, I myself will comfort you: who art thou that thou shouldst be afraid of a mortal man, and of the son of man who shall wither away like grass? (*Isa.* li. 12.)

And be not drunk with wine,

The Catechism and Holy Scripture. 179

318. Q. Which are the seven gifts of the Holy Ghost?
A. The seven gifts of the Holy Ghost are:
1. Wisdom.
2. Understanding.
3. Counsel.
4. Fortitude.
5. Knowledge.
6. Piety.
7. The fear of the Lord (*Isa.* xi. 2, 3).

319. Q. Which are the twelve fruits of the Holy Ghost?
A. The twelve fruits of the Holy Ghost are:
1. Charity.
2. Joy.
3. Peace.
4. Patience.
5. Benignity.
6. Goodness.
7. Longanimity.
8. Mildness.
9. Faith.
10. Modesty.
11. Continency.
12. Chastity (*Gal.* v. 22).

wherein is luxury, but be ye filled with the Holy Spirit (*Eph.* v. 18).

And there shall come forth a rod out of the root of Jesse, and a flower shall rise up out of his root. And the Spirit of the Lord shall rest upon him: the Spirit of wisdom and of understanding, the Spirit of counsel and of fortitude, the Spirit of knowledge and of godliness. And he shall be filled with the Spirit of the fear of the Lord (*Isa.* xi. 1).

Now the works of the flesh are manifest, which are fornication, uncleanness, immodesty, luxury, idolatry, witchcraft, enmities, contentions, emulations, wraths, quarrels, dissensions, sects, envies, murders, drunkenness, revellings, and such like: of which I foretell you, as I have foretold to you that they who do such things shall not obtain the kingdom of God. But the fruit of the Spirit is charity, joy, peace, patience, benignity, goodness, longanimity, mildness, faith, modesty, continency, chastity. Against such there is no law. And they that are Christ's have crucified their flesh with the vices and concupiscence (*Gal.* v. 19).

320. Q. Which are the two great precepts of Charity?

A. The two great precepts of Charity are:

1. "Thou shalt love the Lord thy God with thy whole heart, and with thy whole soul, and with thy whole mind, and with thy whole strength."

2. "Thou shalt love thy neighbour as thyself" (S. Mark xii. 30, 31).

321. Q. Which are the seven Corporal Works of Mercy?

A. The seven Corporal Works of Mercy are:

1. To feed the hungry.
2. To give drink to the thirsty.
3. To clothe the naked.
4. To harbour the harbourless.
5. To visit the sick.
6. To visit the imprisoned.
7. To bury the dead (S. Matt. xxv.; Tobias xii.).

And one of them, a doctor of the law, asked Him, tempting Him: Master, which is the great commandment in the law? Jesus said to him: Thou shalt love the Lord thy God with thy whole heart, and with thy whole soul, and with thy whole mind. This is the greatest and the first commandment. And the second is like to this: Thou shalt love thy neighbour as thyself. On these two commandments dependeth the whole law and the prophets (S. Matt. xxii. 35).

Then shall the King say to them that shall be on His right hand: Come, ye blessed of My Father, possess you the kingdom prepared for you from the foundation of the world. For I was hungry, and you gave Me to eat: I was thirsty, and you gave Me to drink: I was a stranger, and you took Me in: naked, and you covered Me: sick, and you visited Me: I was in prison, and you came to Me. Then shall the just answer Him, saying: Lord, when did we see Thee hungry, and fed Thee; thirsty, and gave Thee drink? and when did we see Thee a stranger, and took Thee in? or naked, and covered Thee? or when did we see Thee sick or in prison, and came to Thee? and the King answering, shall say to them: Amen I say to you, as long as you did it to one of these My least brethren, you did it to Me (*S. Matt.* xxv. 34).

And whosoever shall give to drink to one of those little ones a cup of cold water only in the name of a disciple, amen I say to you, he shall not lose his reward (*S. Matt.* x. 42).

And if a brother or sister be naked, and want daily food: and one of you say to them: Go in peace, be you warmed and filled: yet give them not those things that are necessary for the body: what shall it profit? (*S. James* ii. 15).

He that hath the substance of this world, and shall see his brother in need, and shall shut up his bowels from him: how doth the charity of God abide in him? My little children, let us not love in word, nor in tongue, but in deed, and in truth (1 *S. John* iii. 17).

When thou didst pray with tears, and didst bury the dead, and didst leave thy dinner, and hide the dead by day in thy house, and bury them by night, I offered thy prayer to the Lord (*Tobias* xii. 12).

322. Q. Which are the seven Spiritual Works of Mercy?

But they that are learned shall shine as the brightness of the firmament: and they that instruct

A. The seven Spiritual Works of Mercy are:
1. To convert the sinner.
2. To instruct the ignorant.
3. To counsel the doubtful.
4. To comfort the sorrowful.
5. To bear wrongs patiently.
6. To forgive injuries.
7. To pray for the living and the dead.

many to justice, as stars for all eternity (*Dan.* xii. 3).

Brethren, and if a man be overtaken in any fault, you, who are spiritual, instruct such a one in the spirit of meekness, considering thyself, lest thou also be tempted. Bear ye one another's burdens: and so you shall fulfil the law of Christ (*Gal.* vi. 1).

But if thy brother shall offend against thee, go, and rebuke him between thee and him alone. If he shall hear thee, thou shalt gain thy brother. But if he will not hear thee, take with thee one or two more: that in the mouth of two or three witnesses every word may stand (*S. Matt.* xviii. 15).

323. Q. Which are the eight Beatitudes?
A. The eight Beatitudes are:
1. "Blessed are the poor in spirit; for theirs is the kingdom of heaven.
2. "Blessed are the meek; for they shall possess the land.
3. "Blessed are they that mourn; for they shall be comforted.
4. "Blessed are they that hunger and thirst

Then Jesus said to His disciples: Amen I say to you, that a rich man shall hardly enter into the kingdom of heaven. And again I say to you: It is easier for a camel to pass through the eye of a needle, than for a rich man to enter into the kingdom of heaven (*S. Matt.* xix. 23).

He hath filled the hungry with good things: and the rich he hath sent empty away (*S. Luke* i. 53).

And they, indeed, went from the presence of the council, rejoicing that they were accounted

after justice; for they shall have their fill.

5. "Blessed are the merciful; for they shall obtain mercy.

6. "Blessed are the clean of heart; for they shall see God.

7. "Blessed are the peacemakers; for they shall be called the children of God.

8. "Blessed are they that suffer persecution for justice' sake; for theirs is the kingdom of heaven" (*S. Matt.* v. 3-10).

324. Q. Which are the seven capital sins or vices, and their contrary virtues?

A. The seven capital sins or vices and their contrary virtues are:
1. Pride.
2. Covetousness.
3. Lust.
4. Anger.
5. Gluttony.
6. Envy.
7. Sloth.

Contrary Virtues.
1. Humility.
2. Liberality.
3. Chastity.
4. Meekness.
5. Temperance.

worthy to suffer reproach for the name of Jesus (*Acts* v. 41).

For this is thanks-worthy, if for conscience towards God, a man endures sorrows, suffering wrongfully. For what glory is it, if committing sin and being buffeted for it you endure? But if doing well you suffer patiently; this is thanks-worthy before God (1 *S. Peter* ii. 19).

Behold this was the iniquity of Sodom thy sister, pride, fulness of bread, and abundance, and the idleness of her, and of her daughters: and they did not put forth their hand to the needy, and to the poor (*Ezech.* xvi. 49).

For all that is in the world is the concupiscence of the flesh, and the concupiscence of the eyes, and the pride of life, which is not of the Father, but is of the world. And the world passeth away, and the concupiscence thereof. But he that doth the will of God, abideth for ever. (1 *S. John* ii. 16).

In like manner, ye young men, be subject to the ancients. And do you all insinuate humility one

6. Brotherly Love.
7. Diligence.

325. Q. Why are they called capital sins?

A. They are called capital sins because they are the sources from which all other sins take their rise.

to another, for God resisteth the proud, but to the humble He giveth grace. Be you humbled therefore under the mighty hand of God, that He may exalt you in the time of visitation (1 *S. Pet.* v. 5).

And He said: Amen I say to you, unless you be converted, and become as little children you shall not enter into the kingdom of heaven. Whosoever therefore shall humble himself as this little child, he is the greater in the kingdom of heaven (*S. Matt.* xviii. 3).

For know ye this and understand that no fornicator, nor unclean, nor covetous person (which is a serving of idols) hath inheritance in the kingdom of Christ and of God (*Eph.* v. 5).

For to him that is little, mercy is granted: but the mighty shall be mightily tormented. For God will not except any man's person, neither will He stand in awe of any man's greatness: for He made the little and the great, and He hath equally care of all. But a greater punishment is ready for the more mighty (*Wisd.* vi. 7).

326. Q. Which are the six sins against the Holy Ghost?

But he that shall blaspheme against the Holy Ghost, shall never have forgiveness, but shall

A. The six sins against the Holy Ghost are:
1. Presumption.
2. Despair.
3. Resisting the known truth.
4. Envy of another's spiritual good.
5. Obstinacy in sin.
6. Final impenitence.

be guilty of an everlasting sin (*S. Mark* iii. 29).

And Peter answering, said to him: Although all shall be scandalized in Thee, I will never be scandalized. Jesus said to him: Amen I say to thee, that in this night before the cock crow, thou wilt deny me thrice (*S. Matt.* xxvi. 33).

Then Judas, who betrayed Him, seeing that He was condemned, repenting himself, brought back the thirty pieces of silver to the chief priests and ancients. Saying: I have sinned in betraying innocent blood. But they said: What is that to us? look thou to it. And casting down the pieces of silver in the temple, he departed: and went and hanged himself with a halter (*S. Matt.* xxvii. 3).

You stiff-necked and uncircumcised in heart and ears, you always resist the Holy Ghost: as your fathers did, so do you also. Which of the prophets have not your fathers persecuted? and they have slain them who foretold of the coming of the Just One; of whom you have been now the betrayers and murderers (*Acts* vii. 51).

And the Lord had respect to Abel, and to his offerings. But to Cain and his offerings he had no respect: and Cain was exceedingly angry, and his countenance fell. And the Lord said to him: Why art thou angry? and why is thy countenance fallen? if thou do well, shalt thou not receive? but if ill, shall not sin forthwith be present at the door? but the lust thereof shall be under thee, and thou shalt have dominion over it (*Gen.* iv. 4).

And Pharao's heart was hardened, neither did he hear them, as the Lord had commanded. And he turned himself away, and went into his house; neither did he set his heart to it this time also (*Exod.* vii. 22).

Or despisest thou the riches of his goodness, and patience, and long-suffering? knowest thou not that the benignity of God leadeth thee to penance? but according to thy hardness and impenitent heart, thou treasurest up to thyself wrath, against the day of wrath and revelation of the just judgment of God (*Rom.* ii. 4).

327. Q. Which are the four sins crying to heaven for vengeance?

A. The four sins crying to heaven for vengeance are:
1. Wilful murder.
2. The sin of Sodom.

And the Lord said to Cain: Where is thy brother Abel? And he answered, I know not: am I my brother's keeper? and he said to him: What hast thou done? the voice of thy brother's blood crieth to Me from the earth. Now, therefore, cursed shalt thou

3. Oppression of the poor.
4. Defrauding labourers of their wages.

be upon the earth, which hath opened her mouth and received the blood of thy brother at thy hand (*Gen.* iv. 9).

And the Lord said : The cry of Sodom and Gomorrha is multiplied, and their sin is become exceedingly grievous (*Gen.* xviii. 20).

As Sodom and Gomorrha, and the neighbouring cities, in like manner, having given themselves over to fornication, and going after other flesh, were made an example, suffering the punishment of eternal fire. In like manner these men also defile the flesh, and despise dominion, and blaspheme majesty (*S. Jude* 7).

Now, after a long time the King of Egypt died, and the children of Israel groaning, cried because of the works, and their cry went up to God from the works (*Exod.* ii. 23).

Behold the hire of the labourers, who have reaped down your fields, which by fraud have been kept back by you, crieth : and the cry of them hath entered into the ears of the Lord of Sabaoth (*S. James* v. 4).

Wo to him that buildeth up his house by injustice, and his chambers not in judgment : that will oppress his friend without cause, and will not pay him his wages (*Jer.* xxii. 13).

328. Q. When are we answerable for the sins of others?

A. We are answerable for the sins of others whenever we either cause them, or share in them, through our own fault.

329. Q. In how many ways may we either cause or share the guilt of another's sin?

A. We may either cause or share the guilt of another's sin in nine ways:
1. By counsel.
2. By command.
3. By consent.
4. By provocation.
5. By praise or flattery.
6. By concealment.
7. By being a partner in the sin.
8. By silence.
9. By defending the ill done.

330. Q. Which are the three eminent Good Works?

A. The three eminent Good Works are Prayer, Fasting, and Almsdeeds.

Who can understand sins? from my secret ones cleanse me, O Lord: and from those of others spare thy servant (*Ps.* xviii. 13).

And the Lord shall give up Israel for the sins of Jeroboam, who hath sinned and made Israel to sin (3 *Kings* xiv. 16).

Thou shalt not hate thy brother in thy heart, but reprove him openly, lest thou incur sin through him (*Levit.* xix. 17).

I will judge his house for ever for iniquity because he knew that his sons did wickedly and did not chastise them (1 *Kings* iii. 13).

Prayer is good with fasting and alms, more than to lay up treasures of gold: for alms delivereth from death, and the same is that which purgeth away sins, and maketh to find mercy and life everlasting (*Tobias* xii. 8).

And in that day you shall not ask Me anything. Amen, amen

I say to you: if you ask the Father anything in My Name, He will give it you (*S. John* xvi. 23).

Now therefore, saith the Lord: be converted to Me with all your heart, in fasting, and in weeping and in mourning, and rend your hearts and not your garments, and turn to the Lord your God (*Joel* ii. 12).

And whosoever shall give to drink to one of those little ones a cup of cold water only in the name of a disciple, amen I say to you, he shall not lose his reward (*S. Matt.* x. 42).

And He said to him: Thy prayers and thy alms are ascended for a memorial in the sight of God (*Acts* x. 4).

Deal thy bread to the hungry, and bring the needy and the harbourless into thy house: when thou shalt see one naked, cover him, and despise not thy own flesh. Then shall thy light break forth as the morning, and thy health shall speedily arise, and thy justice shall go before thy face, and the glory of the Lord shall gather thee up (*Isa.* lviii. 7).

Poverty.

331. Q. Which are the Evangelical Counsels?

A. The Evangelical

Jesus saith to him: If thou wilt be perfect, go, sell what thou hast, and give to the poor, and thou shalt have treasure in

Counsels are voluntary Poverty, perpetual Chastity, and entire Obedience.

heaven: and come, follow Me. And when the young man had heard this word, he went away sad: for he had great possessions. Then Jesus said to His disciples: Amen I say to you, that a rich man shall hardly enter into the kingdom of heaven (*S. Matt.* xix. 21).

Hearken, my dearest brethren: hath not God chosen the poor in this world, rich in faith, and heirs of the kingdom which God hath promised to them that love Him? (*S. James* ii. 5.)

Chastity.

His disciples say unto Him: If the case of a man with his wife be so, it is not expedient to marry. Who said to them: All men take not this word, but they to whom it is given. For there are eunuchs, who were born so from their mother's womb: and there are eunuchs, who were made so by men: and there are eunuchs who have made themselves eunuchs for the kingdom of heaven. He that can take, let him take it (*S. Matt.* xix. 10).

But I would have you to be without solicitude. He that is without a wife, is solicitous for the things that belong to the Lord how he may please God. But he that is with a wife, is solicitous for the things of the world, how he may please his wife; and he is divided. And the unmarried woman and the virgin thinketh on the things of the Lord: that she may be holy both in body and in spirit. But she that is married thinketh on the things of the world, how she may please her husband (1 *Cor.* vii. 32).

But if any man think that he seemeth dishonoured with regard to his virgin, for that she is above the age, and it must be so: let him do what he will: he sinneth not, if she marry. For he that hath determined being steadfast in his heart, having no necessity, but having power of his own will, and hath judged this in his heart, to keep his virgin, doth well. Therefore both he that giveth his virgin in marriage, doth well: and he that giveth her not, doth better (1 *Cor.* vii. 36).

And I beheld: and lo a Lamb stood upon Mount Sion, and with him an hundred forty-four thousand having His Name, and the Name of His Father written on their foreheads. And I heard a voice from heaven, as the voice of many waters, and as the voice of great thunder: and the voice, which I heard, was as the voice of harpers, harping on their harps. And they sung as it were a new canticle, before the throne, and before the four living creatures, and the ancients: and no man could say the canticle, but those hundred forty-four thousand, who were purchased from the earth. These are they who were not defiled with women: for they are virgins. These follow the Lamb whithersoever He goeth. These were purchased from among men, the first-fruits to God and to the Lamb (*Apoc.* xiv. 1).

Obedience.

Be ye subject therefore to every human creature for God's sake (1 *Pet.* ii. 13).

And Samuel said: Doth the Lord desire holocausts and victims, and not rather that the voice of the Lord should be obeyed? For obedience is better than sacrifices: and to hearken rather than to offer the fat of rams. Because it is like the sin of witchcraft, to rebel: and like the crime of idolatry, to refuse to obey. Forasmuch therefore as thou hast rejected the word of the Lord, the Lord hath also rejected thee from being king (1 *Kings* xv. 22).

332. Q. What are the four last things to be ever remembered?
A. The four last

It is appointed unto men once to die, and, after this, the judgment (*Heb.* ix. 27).

But the end of all is at hand.

things, to be ever remembered, are Death, Judgment, Hell, and Heaven (*Ecclus.* vii.).

Be prudent therefore, and watch in prayers (1 *Pet.* iv. 7).

In all thy works remember thy last end, and thou shalt never sin (*Ecclus.* vii. 40).

For to me, to live is Christ: and to die is gain. And if to live in the flesh, this is to me the fruit of labour, and what I shall choose I know not. But I am straitened between two; having a desire to be dissolved and to be with Christ, a thing by far the better (*Phil.* i. 21).

I beheld till thrones were placed, and the Ancient of days sat: His garment was white as snow, and the hair of His head like clean wool: His throne like flames of fire: the wheels of it like a burning fire. A swift stream of fire issued forth from before Him: thousands of thousands ministered to Him, and ten thousand times a hundred thousand stood before Him: the judgment sat, and the books were opened (*Dan.* vii. 9).

And I saw the dead, great and small, standing in the presence of the throne, and the books were opened: and another book was opened, which is the book of life: and the dead were judged by those things which were written in the books, according to their works (*Apoc.* xx. 12).

Blessed are they that wash

their robes in the blood of the Lamb: that they may have a right to the tree of life, and may enter in by the gates into the city. Without are dogs, and sorcerers, and unchaste, and murderers, and servers of idols, and everyone that loveth and maketh a lie. (*Apoc.* xxii. 14).

CHAPTER VIII.

THE CHRISTIAN'S RULE OF LIFE.

333. Q. What rule of life must we follow if we hope to be saved?

A. If we hope to be saved, we must follow the rule of life taught by Jesus Christ.

Jesus saith to him: I am the way, and the truth, and the life. No man cometh to the Father, but by Me (*S. John* xiv. 6).

I am the door. By Me, if any man enter in, he shall be saved: and he shall go in, and go out, and shall find pastures (*S. John* x. 9).

That was the true light, which enlighteneth every man that cometh into this world (*S. John* i. 9).

334. Q. What are we bound to do by the rule of life taught by Jesus Christ?

A. By the rule of life taught by Jesus Christ we are bound always to hate sin and to love God.

I have hated and abhorred iniquity; but I have loved thy law (*Ps.* cxviii. 163).

Thou hast loved justice, and hated iniquity: therefore God, thy God, hath anointed thee with the oil of gladness above thy fellows (*Ps.* xliv. 8).

Hating that which is evil,

335. Q. How must we hate sin?

A. We must hate sin above all other evils, so as to be resolved never to commit a wilful sin, for the love or fear of anything whatsoever.

cleaving to that which is good (*Rom.* xii. 9).

Flee from sins as from the face of a serpent: for if thou comest near them, they will take hold of thee. The teeth thereof are the teeth of a lion, killing the souls of men. All iniquity is like a two-edged sword, there is no remedy for the wound thereof (*Ecclus.* xxi. 2).

For I am sure that neither death, nor life, nor Angels, nor principalities, nor powers, nor things present, nor things to come, nor might, nor height, nor depth, nor any other creature, shall be able to separate us from the love of God, which is in Christ Jesus our Lord (*Rom.* viii. 38).

And if thy right eye scandalize thee, pluck it out and cast it from thee. For it is expedient for thee that one of thy members should perish, rather than thy whole body be cast into hell. And if thy right hand scandalize thee, cut it off, and cast it from thee; for it is expedient for thee that one of thy members should perish, rather than that thy whole body go into hell (*S. Matt.* v. 29).

336. Q. How must we love God?

And Jesus answered him: The first commandment of all is, Hear,

A. We must love God above all things, and with our whole heart.

337. Q. How must we learn to love God?

A. We must learn to love God by begging of God to teach us to love Him: "O my God, teach me to love Thee."

338. Q. What will the love of God lead us to do?

A. The love of God will lead us often to think how good God is; often to speak to Him in our hearts; and always to seek to please Him.

339. Q. Does Jesus Christ also command us to love one another?

A. Jesus Christ also commands us to love one another—that is, all persons without exception for His sake.

340. Q. How are we to love one another?

A. We are to love one another by wishing well to one another, and praying for one another;

O Israel: the Lord thy God is one God. And thou shalt love the Lord thy God with thy whole heart, and with thy whole soul, and with thy whole mind, and with thy whole strength. This is the first commandment. And the second is like to it: Thou shalt love thy neighbour as thyself. There is no other commandment greater than these. And the scribe said to Him: Well, Master, Thou hast said in truth, that there is one God, and there is no other besides Him. And that He should be loved with the whole heart, and with the whole understanding, and with the whole soul, and with the whole strength: and to love one's neighbour as one's self, is a greater thing than all holocausts and sacrifices (*S. Mark* xii. 29).

But I say to you, Love your enemies: do good to them that hate you: and pray for them that persecute and calumniate you: that you may be the children of your Father who is in heaven, who maketh His sun to rise upon the good and bad, and raineth upon the just and the unjust (*S. Matt.* v. 44).

For all the law is fulfilled in one word: Thou shalt love thy neighbour as thyself (*Gal.* v. 14).

and by never allowing ourselves any thought, word, or deed to the injury of anyone.

341. Q. Are we also bound to love our enemies?
A. We are also bound to love our enemies; not only by forgiving them from our hearts, but also by wishing them well, and praying for them.

For if you love them that love you, what reward shall you have? Do not even the publicans this? And if you salute your brethren only, what do you more? do not also the heathens this? (*S. Matt.* v. 46.)

342. Q. Has Jesus Christ given us another great rule?
A. Jesus Christ has given us another great rule in these words: "If any man will come after Me, let him deny himself, and take up his cross daily, and follow Me" (*S. Luke* ix. 23).

Enter ye in at the narrow gate: for wide is the gate, and broad is the way that leadeth to destruction, and many there are who go in thereat. How narrow is the gate, and strait is the way that leadeth to life: and few there are that find it! (*S. Matt.* vii. 13.)

343. Q. How are we to deny ourselves?
A. We are to deny ourselves by giving up our own will, and by going against our own humours, inclinations, and passions.

Therefore, brethren, we are debtors, not to the flesh, to live according to the flesh. For if you live according to the flesh, you shall die. But if by the spirit you mortify the deeds of the flesh, you shall live. For whosoever are led by the Spirit of God, they are the sons of God (*Rom.* viii. 12).

344. Q. Why are we bound to deny ourselves?
A. We are bound to deny ourselves because our natural inclinations are prone to evil from our very childhood; and, if not corrected by self-denial, they will certainly carry us to hell.

For the flesh lusteth against the spirit: and the spirit against the flesh; for these are contrary one to another: so that you do not the things that you would (*Gal.* v. 17).

I chastise my body and bring it into subjection, lest perhaps, when I have preached to others, I myself should become a castaway (1 *Cor.* ix. 27).

345. Q. How are we to take up our cross daily?
A. We are to take up our cross daily by submitting daily with patience to the labours and sufferings of this short life, and by bearing them willingly for the love of God.

And whosoever doth not carry his cross and come after Me, cannot be My disciple (*S. Luke* xiv. 27).

We glory also in tribulations, knowing that tribulation worketh patience, and patience trial, and trial hope, and hope confoundeth not (*Rom.* v. 3).

346. Q. How are we to follow our Blessed Lord?
A. We are to follow our Blessed Lord by walking in His footsteps and imitating His virtues.

The disciple is not above his Master: but everyone shall be perfect, if he be as his Master (*S. Luke* vi. 40).

Wherefore I beseech you, be ye followers of me, as I also am of Christ (1 *Cor.* iv. 16).

347. Q. What are the principal virtues we are to learn of our Blessed Lord?
A. The principal vir-

Come to Me, all you that labour, and are burdened, and I will refresh you. Take up My yoke upon you, and learn of Me, because I am meek, and humble

tues we are to learn of our Blessed Lord are meekness, humility, and obedience.

348. Q. Which are the enemies we must fight against all the days of our life?
A. The enemies which we must fight against all the days of our life are the devil, the world, and the flesh.

349. Q. What do you mean by the devil?
A. By the devil I mean Satan and all his wicked angels, who are ever seeking to draw us into sin, that we may be damned with them.

of heart: and you shall find rest to your souls. For My yoke is sweet and My burden light (*S. Matt.* xi. 28).

In your patience you shall possess your souls (*S. Luke* xxi. 19).

But I say to you not to resist evil: but if one strike thee on thy right cheek, turn to him the other also (*S. Matt.* v. 39).

Holocausts for sin did not please Thee. Then said I: Behold I come: in the head of the book it is written of me: that I should do Thy will, O God (*Heb.* x. 6).

Put you on the armour of God, that you may be able to stand against the deceits of the devil (*Eph.* vi. 11).

Love not the world, nor the things which are in the world. If any man love the world, the charity of the Father is not in him (1 *S. John* ii. 15).

Be sober and watch: because your adversary the devil, as a roaring lion, goeth about seeking whom he may devour. Whom resist ye, strong in faith (1. *Pet.* v. 8).

And the seventy-two returned with joy, saying: Lord, the devils also are subject to us in Thy name. And He said to them:

350. Q. What do you mean by the world?

A. By the world I mean, the false maxims of the world, and the society of those who love the vanities, riches, and pleasures of this world better than God.

351. Q. Why do you number the devil and the world amongst the enemies of the soul?

A. I number the devil and the world amongst the enemies of the soul, because they are always seeking, by temptation and by word or example, to carry us along with them in the

I saw Satan like lightning falling from heaven (*S. Luke* x. 17).

And lest the greatness of the revelations should lift me up, there was given me a sting of my flesh, an angel of Satan to buffet me (2 *Cor.* xii. 7).

And no wonder: for Satan himself transformeth himself into an angel of light (2 *Cor.* xi. 14).

If the world hate you, know ye that it hated Me before you. If you had been of the world: the world would love its own: but because you are not of the world, but I have chosen you out of the world, therefore the world hateth you (*S. John* xv. 18).

Adulterers, know you not that the friendship of this world is the enemy of God? Whosoever therefore will be a friend of this world, becometh an enemy of God (*S. James* iv. 4).

But wo to you that are rich: for you have your consolation. Wo to you that are filled: for you shall hunger. Wo to you that now laugh: for you shall mourn and weep (*S. Luke* vi. 24).

They have slept their sleep: and all the men of riches have found nothing in their hands (*Ps.* lxxv. 6).

Enter ye in at the narrow gate: for wide is the gate, and broad is the way that leadeth to destruc-

broad road that leads to damnation.

tion, and many there are who go in thereat. How narrow is the gate, and strait is the way that leadeth to life : and few there are that find it ! (*S. Matt.* vii. 13.)

The congregation of sinners is like tow heaped together, and the end of them is a flame of fire. The way of sinners is made plain with stones, and in their end is hell, and darkness, and pains (*Ecclus.* xxi. 10).

352. Q. What do you mean by the flesh ?
A. By the flesh I mean our own corrupt inclinations and passions, which are the most dangerous of all our enemies.

I say then, walk in the spirit, and you shall not fulfil the lusts of the flesh. For the flesh lusteth against the spirit : and the spirit against the flesh ; for these are contrary one to another : so that you do not the things that you would (*Gal.* v. 16).

But I see another law in my members, fighting against the law of my mind, and captivating me in the law of sin that is in my members. Unhappy man that I am, who shall deliver me from the body of this death? (*Rom.* vii. 23.)

353. Q. What must we do to hinder the enemies of our soul from drawing us into sin ?
A. To hinder the enemies of our soul from drawing us into sin, we must watch,

Watch ye, and pray that ye enter not into temptation. The spirit indeed is willing, but the flesh weak (*S. Matt.* xxvi. 41).

Be subject therefore to God, but resist the devil, and he will fly from you. Draw nigh to God, and He will draw nigh to

pray, and fight against all their suggestions and temptations.

354. Q. In the warfare against the devil, the world, and the flesh, on whom must we depend?
A. In the warfare against the devil, the world, and the flesh we must depend not on ourselves, but on God only: "I can do all things in Him who strengtheneth me" (*Phil.* iv. 13).

you. Cleanse your hands, ye sinners: and purify your hearts, ye double minded (*S. James* iv. 7).

Unless the Lord build the house, they labour in vain that build it. Unless the Lord keep the city, he watcheth in vain that keepeth it (*Ps.* cxxvi. 1).

In Thee, O Lord, have I hoped, let me never be confounded: deliver me in Thy justice (*Ps.* xxx. 2).

CHAPTER IX.

THE CHRISTIAN'S DAILY EXERCISE.

355. Q. How should you begin the day?
A. I should begin the day by making the sign of the cross as soon as I awake in the morning, and by saying some short prayer, such as, "O my God, I offer my heart and soul to thee."

356. Q. How should you rise in the morning?

O God my God, to Thee do I watch at break of day. For Thee my soul hath thirsted; for Thee my flesh, O how many ways! In a desert land, and where there is no way, and no water: so in the sanctuary have I come before Thee, to see Thy power and Thy glory (*Ps.* lxii. 2).

The kingdom of heaven is like to a householder, who went out early in the morning to hire

A. I should rise in the morning diligently, dress myself modestly, and then kneel down and say my morning prayers.

357. Q. Should you also hear Mass if you have time and opportunity?

A. I should also hear Mass, if I have time and opportunity, for to hear Mass is by far the best and most profitable of all devotions.

labourers into his vineyard. And having agreed with the labourers for a penny a day, he sent them into his vineyard. And going out about the third hour, he saw others standing in the marketplace idle. And he said to them: Go you also into my vineyard, and I will give you what shall be just. And they went their way. And again he went out about the sixth and the ninth hour: and did in like manner. But about the eleventh hour he went out and found others standing, and he saith to them: Why stand you here all the day idle? They say to him: Because no man hath hired us. He saith to them: Go you also into my vineyard. And when evening was come, the lord of the vineyard saith to his steward: Call the labourers and pay them their hire, beginning from the last even to the first (*S. Matt.* xx. 1).

I must work the works of Him that sent me, whilst it is day: the night cometh when no man can work (*S. John* ix. 4).

And I will say to my soul: Soul, thou hast much goods laid up for many years, take thy rest, eat, drink, make good cheer. But God said to him: Thou fool, this night do they require thy soul of thee; and whose shall those things be which thou hast provided? (*S. Luke* xii. 19.)

358. Q. Is it useful to make daily meditation?

A. It is useful to make daily meditation, for such was the practice of all the Saints.

359. Q. On what ought we to meditate?

A. We ought to meditate especially on the four last things, and the Life and Passion of our Blessed Lord.

360. Q. Ought we frequently to read good books?

A. We ought frequently to read good books, such as the Holy Gospel, the Lives of the Saints, and other spiritual works, which nourish our faith and piety, and arm us against the false maxims of the world.

361. Q. And what should you do as to your eating, drinking, sleeping, and amusements?

A. As to my eating, drinking, sleeping, and

From the morning watch even until night, let Israel hope in the Lord (*Ps.* cxxix. 6).

If I have remembered Thee upon my bed, I will meditate on Thee in the morning: because Thou hast been my helper (*Ps.* lxii. 7).

From the rising of the sun even to the going down, My Name is great among the gentiles, and in every place there is sacrifice, and there is offered to My Name a clean oblation: for My Name is great among the gentiles, saith the Lord of hosts (*Mal.* i. 11).

I will wash my hands among the innocent: and will compass Thy altar, O Lord. That I may hear the voice of Thy praise: and tell of all Thy wondrous works. I have loved, O Lord, the beauty of Thy house: and the place where Thy glory dwelleth (*Ps.* xxv. 6).

I will go in to the altar of God, to God who giveth joy to my youth (*Ps.* lxii. 4).

And the third day there was a marriage in Cana of Galilee: and the mother of Jesus was there. And Jesus also was invited, and His disciples, to the marriage (*S. John* ii. 1).

He that eateth, eateth to the

amusements, I should use all these things with moderation, and with a desire to please God.

262. Q. Say the grace before meals.

A. "Bless us, O Lord, and these Thy gifts, which we are going to receive from Thy bounty, through Christ our Lord. Amen."

363. Q. Say the grace after meals.

A. "We give Thee thanks, Almighty God, for all Thy benefits, who livest and reignest, world without end. Amen. May the souls of the faithful departed, through the mercy of God, rest in peace. Amen."

364. Q. How should you sanctify your ordinary actions and employments of the day?

A. I should sanctify my ordinary actions and employments of the day by often raising up my heart to God whilst I am about them, and saying some short prayer to Him.

Lord: for he giveth thanks to God. And he that eateth not, to the Lord he eateth not, and giveth thanks to God. For none of us liveth to himself, and no man dieth to himself. For whether we live, we live unto the Lord, or whether we die, we die unto the Lord. Therefore, whether we live, or whether we die, we are the Lord's (*Rom.* xiv. 6).

All whatsoever you do in word or work, all things do ye in the Name of the Lord Jesus Christ, giving thanks to God and the Father (*Coloss.* iii. 17).

The Lord appeared to him; and said unto him: I am the Almighty God: walk before Me, and be perfect (*Gen.* xvii. 1).

And the words of my mouth shall be such as may please: and the meditation of my heart always in Thy sight. O Lord, my helper and my redeemer (*Ps.* xviii. 15).

That they should seek God, if haply they may feel after Him or find Him, although He be not far from every one of us: for in Him we live and move and are: as

365. Q. What should you do when you find yourself tempted to sin?

A. When I find myself tempted to sin I should make the sign of the cross on my heart, and call on God as earnestly as I can, saying, "Lord, save me, or I perish."

366. Q. If you have fallen into sin, what should you do?

A. If I have fallen into sin I should cast myself in spirit at the feet of Christ, and humbly beg his pardon by a sincere act of contrition.

some also of your own poets said (*Acts* xvii. 27).

But seeing the wind strong, he was afraid: and when he began to sink, he cried out, saying: Lord, save me. And immediately Jesus stretching forth His hand took hold of him, and said to him: O thou of little faith, why didst thou doubt? (*S. Matt.* xiv. 30.)

And they awaked Him saying: Master, we perish. But He arising rebuked the wind and rage of the water, and it ceased and there was a calm (*S. Luke* viii. 24).

And as Jesus passed from thence, there followed Him two blind men crying out and saying, Have mercy on us, O Son of David (*S. Matt.* ix. 27).

And the publican standing afar off would not so much as lift up his eyes towards heaven; but struck his breast, saying: O God, be merciful to me a sinner (*S. Luke* xviii. 13).

I will arise, and will go to my Father, and say to Him: Father, I have sinned against heaven, and before thee: I am not now worthy to be called Thy son: make me as one of Thy hired servants (*S. Luke* xv. 18).

And there came a leper to Him, beseeching Him, and kneeling down said to Him: If Thou

367. Q. When God sends you any cross, or sickness, or pain, what should you say?
A. When God sends me any cross, or sickness, or pain, I should say, "Lord, Thy will be done; I take this for my sins."

wilt, Thou canst make me clean. And Jesus having compassion on him, stretched forth His hand; and touching him saith to him: I will. Be thou made clean (*S. Mark* i. 40).

And behold a woman that was in the city, a sinner, when she knew that He sat at meat in the Pharisee's house, brought an alabaster box of ointment; and standing behind at His feet, she began to wash His feet with tears, and wiped them with the hairs of her head, and kissed His feet, and anointed them with the ointment (*S. Luke* vii. 37).

Wherefore I say to thee: Many sins are forgiven her, because she hath loved much. But to whom less is forgiven, he loveth less. And He said to her: Thy sins are forgiven thee (*S. Luke* vii. 47).

In those days Ezechias was sick even to death, and Isaias the son of Amos the prophet came unto him, and said to him: Thus saith the Lord: Take order with thy house, for thou shalt die and not live. And Ezechias turned his face toward the wall, and prayed to the Lord, and said: I beseech Thee, O Lord, remember how I have walked before Thee in truth, and with a perfect heart, and have done that which is good in Thy sight.

368. Q. What little indulgenced prayers would you do well to say often to yourself during the day?

A. I should do well to say often to myself during the day such little indulgenced prayers as—

Glory be to the Father, and to the Son, and to the Holy Ghost; as it was in the beginning, is now, and ever shall be, world without end. Amen.

In all things may the most holy, the most just, and the most lovable Will of God be done, praised, and exalted above all for ever.

O Sacrament most holy, O Sacrament divine, all praise and all thanksgiving be every moment thine.

And Ezechias wept with great weeping. And the word of the Lord came to Isaias, saying: Go and say to Ezechias: Thus saith the Lord the God of David thy father: I have heard thy prayer, and I have seen thy tears: Behold I will add to thy days fifteen years (*Isa.* xxxviii. 1).

Hear, O Lord, my prayer; and let my cry come to Thee. Turn not away Thy face from me: in the day when I am in trouble, incline Thy ear to me. In what day soever I shall call upon Thee, hear me speedily (*Ps.* ci. 2).

As the hart panteth after the fountains of water: so my soul panteth after Thee, O God. My soul hath thirsted after the strong living God; when shall I come and appear before the face of God? (*Ps.* xli. 2.)

Praised be Jesus Christ, praised for evermore.

My Jesus, mercy; Mary, help.

369. Q. How should you finish the day?

A. I should finish the day by kneeling down and saying my night prayers.

370. Q. After your night prayers what should you do?

A. After my night prayers I should observe due modesty in going to bed; occupy myself with the thoughts of death; and endeavour to compose myself to rest at the foot of the cross, and give my last thoughts to my crucified Saviour.

Let my prayer be directed as incense in Thy sight; the lifting up of my hands, as evening sacrifice. Set a watch, O Lord, before my mouth: and a door round about my lips. Incline not my heart to evil words; to make excuses in sins (*Ps.* cxl. 2).

Be ye angry, and sin not: the things you say in your hearts, be sorry for them upon your beds (*Ps.* iv. 5).

In peace in the self-same I will sleep, and I will rest: For Thou, O Lord, singularly hast settled me in hope (*Ps.* iv. 9).

Into Thy hands I commend my spirit: Thou hast redeemed me, O Lord, the God of truth (*Ps.* xxx. 6).

APPENDIX.

INDEX OF TEXTS.

The following "Index of Texts" is intended to give a short course of passages illustrating the Catechism which children may easily find out and learn. As far as I have seen, children can easily be led to take an interest in remembering a reasonable number of Scripture passages, appropriate to the Catechism they are learning; and I think that such a practice would be very useful to them, both intellectually and morally. It is arranged in four columns. 1. The different subjects the Catechism treats of, placed in order. 2. Two or three words of the text, chosen so as best to remind them of its bearing. 3. The reference to its place in the Scripture. 4. The page on which it appears in this work.

The texts referred to are all given in full in the earlier part of the book; but I think it well that children should sometimes, at least, try to find them for themselves, so as to know the context in which they occur, and understand the particular part applicable to the subject they are learning. The few words given may sometimes appear rather quaint, standing by themselves; but the object to be considered is, which words will best suggest the passage. Obviously, in many cases, the *first* words would not do so at all.

CHAPTER I.

SUBJECT.		REFERENCE.	PAGE.
Creation	Not we ourselves	Ps. xcix. 3	1
Knowledge of God	Eternal life	S. John xvii. 3	1
Service of God	With trembling	Ps. ii. 11	2
God our reward	Reward exceeding great	Gen. xv. 1	2
Immortality	Destroy both soul and body	S. Matt. x. 28	3
Care of our souls	Seek ye first	S. Matt. vi. 33	3
	For my sake	S. Luke ix. 24	3
	A treasure hidden	S. Matt. xiii. 44	3
	Rust and moth	S. Matt. vi. 19-	3
	Thou fool, this night	S. Luke xii. 20	4

SUBJECT.		REFERENCE.	PAGE.
Faith	Overcometh the world	1 S. John v. 4	6
	Ask in faith	S. James i. 6	6
Truth of God	Not as a man	Num. xxiii. 19	6
Necessity of revelation.	Hid these things	S. Matt. xi. 25	7
	No one knoweth	S. Matt. xi. 27	7
Testimony of the Church.	Shall be witnesses	Acts i. 8	7
Authority of the Church.	He that heareth you	S. Luke x. 16	8

CHAPTER II.

APOSTLES' CREED.

Self-existence of God	I am who I am	Exod. iii. 14	10
	Life in Himself	S. John v. 26	10
	Before Abraham	S. John viii. 58	10
Majesty of God	Nations before Him	Isa. xl. 17	11
	An invincible King	Ecclus. xviii. 1	12
	What is man	Ps. viii. 5	13
God the Creator and Preserver.	He spoke	Ps. xxxii. 9	13
	For Thy will	Apoc. iv. 11	13
	As a vesture	Heb. i. 12	14
	If Thou turn away Thy face	Ps. ciii. 29	15
Eternity of God	Alpha and Omega	Apoc. i. 8	16
	A thousand years	2 S. Pet. iii. 8	16
	Before the mountains	Ps. lxxxix. 2	16
	As a pebble	Ecclus. xviii. 8	16
God is everywhere	If I ascend	Ps. cxxxviii. 7	16
	In Him we live	Acts xvii. 28	17
Wisdom of God	O the depths	Rom. xi. 33	17
	Say not, I shall be hidden	Ecclus. xvi. 16	17
God is a Spirit	Spirit and truth	S. John iv. 24	17
But one God	I alone am	Deut. xxxii. 39	18

SECOND ARTICLE.

Divinity of our Lord	The form of God	Phil. ii. 6	19
	The Word was made flesh	S. John i. 14	20
	Brightness of His glory	Heb. i. 3	20
	King of Israel	S. John i. 49	21
Human nature of our Lord.	In all things like as we are	Heb. iv. 15	23
	Handle and see	S. Luke xxiv. 39	23
	Made of a woman	Gal. iv. 4	24
Christ our Redeemer	By whose stripes you were healed	1 S. Pet. ii. 24	25
	Shall save His people	S. Matt. i. 21	26

14—2

SUBJECT.		REFERENCE.	PAGE.
THIRD ARTICLE.			
Prophecies of the Incarnation.	Crush thy head	Gen. iii. 15	29
	In thy seed	Gen. xxii. 18	29
	The sceptre	Gen. xlix. 10	29
	A virgin shall conceive	Isa. vii. 14	30
	Sixty-two weeks	Dan. ix. 25	31
Birth of Christ·	This day is born	S. Luke ii. 10	32
FOURTH ARTICLE.			
Prophecies of the Passion.	Be betrayed	S. Matt. xx. 18	32
	Lifted up	S. John xii. 32	33
	To the slaughter	Isa. liii. 7	33
The Crucifixion	The veil of the temple	S. Matt. xxvii. 51	35
Sign of the Cross	Sign of the Son of Man	S. Matt. xxiv. 30	36
	God forbid that I should glory	Gal. vi. 14	37
FIFTH ARTICLE.			
Descent of the Lord into Limbo.	Spirits in prison	1 S. Pet. iii. 19	37
	Abraham's bosom	S. Luke xvi. 22	38
The Resurrection	Far as Jonas	S. Matt. xii. 40	38
	Ought not Christ	S. Luke xxiv. 26	40
	Preaching vain	1 Cor. xv. 14	40
	First fruits of the dead	1 Cor. xv. 20	41
SIXTH ARTICLE.			
The Ascension·	He must reign	1 Cor. xv. 25	42
	Right hand of God	Colos. iii. 1	42
SEVENTH ARTICLE.			
Judgment	Taken up from you	Acts i. 11	42
	The sheep from the goats	S. Matt. xxv. 32	43
	They that pierced Him	Apoc. i. 7	43
	Every idle word	S. Matt. xii. 36	43
Hell	The tip of his finger	S. Luke xvi. 24	44
	Pool of fire	Apoc. xx. 15	44
	Smoke of their torments	Apoc. xiv. 11	44
	Their worm shall not die	Isa. lxvi. 24	45
	Torrent of brimstone	Isa. xxx. 33	45
Heaven	Eye hath not seen	1 Cor. ii. 9	45
	God shall wipe away	Apoc. xxi. 4	45
	The lamp thereof	Apoc. xxi. 23	46
EIGHTH ARTICLE.			
The Holy Ghost	Spirit of truth	S. John xvi. 13	47
	Bring back to your minds	S. John xiv. 26	49
	It is not you that speak	S. Matt. x. 20	49

SUBJECT.		REFERENCE.	PAGE.
Ninth Article.			
The whole Church	Mount Sion	Heb. xii. 22	49
	Under His feet	Eph. i. 22	50
Prophecies of the Visible Church.	The top of mountains	Isa. ii. 2	50
	Stone without hands	Dan. ii. 34	51
	Shall stand for ever	Dan. ii. 44	51
Supremacy of S. Peter.	On this rock	S. Matt. xvi. 15	51
	Feed My lambs	S. John xxi. 15	52
	Sift you as wheat	Luke xxii. 31	52
Christ's Church on earth visible.	One fold	S. John x. 16	53
	Net cast into the sea	S. Matt. xiii. 47	54
	One body	Eph. iv. 4	54
Christ's Church an organized body.	The body of Christ	Eph. iv. 11	54
	Placed you bishops	Acts xx. 28	54
	Account of your souls	Heb. xiii. 17	56
Unity of the Church	Keep them in Thy Name	S. John xvii. 11.	56
	Baptized into one body	1 Cor. xii. 12	56
Holiness	Not having spot	Eph. v. 27	57
Catholicity	To every creature	S. Mark xvi. 15	57
	Come from afar	Isa. lx. 1	58
	Tribes, peoples, and tongues	Apoc. vii. 9	59
Apostolicity	I also send you	S. John xx. 21	59
	Unless they be sent	Rom. x. 15	59
Authority of the Church.	Go and teach	S. Matt. xxviii. 19	60
	Heareth Me	S. Luke x. 16	60
	Tell the Church	S. Matt. xviii. 17	60
	Pillar and ground	1 Tim. iii. 15	61
Intercession of Saints	Wrath be kindled	Exod. xxxii. 9	61
	How long, O Lord?	Apoc. vi. 9	63
	Much incense	Apoc. viii. 3	63
Purgatory	The last farthing	S. Matt. v. 25	64
	So as by fire	1 Cor. iii. 12	65
Tenth Article.			
Sin	Deceive ourselves	1 S. John i. 8	66
	An advocate	1 S. John ii. 1	66
Original sin	By one man	Rom. v. 12	67
Actual sin	Reap corruption	Gal. vi. 7	70
	Wages of sin	Rom. vi. 23	70
	A handful of barley	Ezechiel xiii. 19	70
Eleventh Article			
Resurrection of the body.	The dead shall hear	S. John v. 25	72
	At the last trumpet	1 Cor. xv. 51	73
Twelfth Article.			
Life everlasting	Wash their robes	Apoc. xxii. 14	74

HOPE.
CHAPTER III.

SUBJECT.		REFERENCE.	PAGE.
Necessity of faith	Without faith	Heb. xi. 6	76
	Overcometh the world	1 S. John v. 4	76
Good works	Dead in itself	S. James ii. 17	77
	Have all faith	1 Cor. xiii. 2	78
Necessity of grace	No man can say	1 Cor. xii. 3	79
	Am what I am	1 Cor. xv. 10	79
	Except the Father	S. John vi. 44	79
	Without me	S. John xv. 5	80
	Unless the Lord	Ps. cxxvi. 1	80
Sufficiency of grace	Above that which you are able	1 Cor. x. 13	81
	Perfect in infirmity	2 Cor. xii. 9	81
Prayer	Prayer is good	Tobias xii. 8	82
	Before prayer	Ecclus. xviii. 23	82
	Ask amiss	S. James iv. 3	82
Our Father	As a father	Ps. cii. 13	83
	Where is my honour?	Mal. i. 6	84
Hallowed be Thy Name.	How admirable	Ps. viii. 2	84
	Not to us	Ps. cxiii. 9	85
Thy Kingdom come (*Heaven*).	The just shall shine	S. Matt. xiii. 43	85
The Church	A grain of mustard seed	S. Matt. xiii. 31	87
Grace	Within you	S. Luke xvii. 21	88
Thy Will be done	Not as I will	S. Matt. xxvi. 39	88
Daily Bread	The young ravens	Ps. cxlvi. 9	89
Our trespasses	Leave there thy offering	S. Matt. v. 23	90
Temptation	Loveth danger	Ecclus. iii. 27	90
Deliver us from evil	Fall at thy side	Ps. xc. 4	91
Angels	Ministering spirits	Heb. i. 14	91
	Face of My Father	S. Matt. xviii. 10	92
The B. Virgin Mary	All generations	S. Luke i. 48	93

CHARITY.
CHAPTER IV.
ON THE COMMANDMENTS OF GOD.

Charity	First loved us	1 S. John iv. 8	95
Goodness of God	Glory to the Lord	Ps. cv. 1	96
	Everlasting love	Jer. xxxi. 3	96

Appendix.

SUBJECT.		REFERENCE.	PAGE.
Obligation of the Commandments.	A sign on your hands	Deut. xi. 18	98
	Truth is not in him	1 S. John ii. 3	98
	Guilty of all	S. James ii. 10	99
Avoid evil and do good.	Broken cisterns	Jer. ii. 13	99
First Commandment	Greatest and first	S. Matt. xxii. 36	99
Sins against faith	Be anathema	Gal. i. 8	101
	Wind of doctrine	Eph. iv. 14	101
	False prophets	S. Matt. vii. 15	102
Idolatry	Offspring of God	Acts xvii.	103
Images	Cherubim and palm trees	3 Kings vi. 29	104
	Brazen serpent	Num. xxi. 8	104
Dealing with the Devil.	A God in Israel	4 Kings i. 3	105
	Deceived many	Ecclus. xxxiv. 7	107
Sacrilege	Rose a leprosy	2 Paral. xxvi. 16	109
Simony	Perish with thee	Acts viii. 18	111
Honour to saints	To and fro	Wisd. iii. 7	111
	Twelve seats	S. Matt. xix. 27	112
Relics, etc.	Mantle of Elias	4 Kings ii. 13	112
	Bones of Eliseus	4 Kings xiii. 21	112
	Handkerchiefs and aprons	Acts xix. 12	113
Blaspheming, cursing, etc.	Hold him guiltless	Exod. xx. 7	114
	He that blasphemeth	Levit. xxiv. 16	114
	Neither by heaven	S. James v. 12	115
Observance of Sunday.	Keep you My Sabbath	Exod. xxxi. 14	116
	Lord of the Sabbath	S. Matt. xii. 8	116
Duty of children, etc.	Commandment with a promise	Eph. vi. 1	117
	Layeth up a treasure	Ecclus. iii. 5	118
	Well pleasing	Col. iii. 20	118
	Every creature for God's sake	1 S. Pet. ii. 13	118
	Not serving to the eye	Eph. vi. 5	119
	Serve the altar	1 Cor. ix. 13	120
	Account of your souls	Heb. xiii. 17	120
Duty of parents, etc.	Provoke not	Eph. vi. 4	120
	Forbearing threatenings	Eph. vi. 9	121
	A son ill taught	Ecclus. xxii. 3	121
Murder	Thy brother's blood	Gen. iv. 9	122
	His blood shall be shed	Gen. ix. 6	123
Anger, hatred, and revenge.	Angry, and sin not	Eph. iv. 26	123
	Hateth his brother	1 S. John iii. 15	123
	Not revenging yourselves	Rom. xii. 19	123
	Seeketh to revenge	Ecclus xxviii. 1	124

SUBJECT.		REFERENCE.	PAGE.
Scandal	Wo to that man	S. Matt. xviii. 7	125
	Weak brother perish	1 Cor. viii. 11	125
Sixth Commandment	The chaste generation	Wisd. iv. 1	127
	God is not mocked	Gal. vi. 7	127
Stealing, etc.	He that stole	Eph. iv. 28	127
	Let none of you suffer	1 S. Pet. iv. 15	128
Lying	Judge not	S. Luke vi. 37	129
	Lying lips	Prov. xii. 22	130
	Leaven of the Pharisees	S. Luke xii. 1	130
Concupiscence	Every man is tempted	S. James i. 14	131
	Pride of life	1 S. John ii. 16	132

CHAPTER V.

THE COMMANDMENTS OF THE CHURCH.

Fasting	When you fast	S. Matt. vi. 16	135
	Then they shall fast	S. Mark ii. 20	136
	Is not cast out	S. Matt. xvii. 20	136
	Rend your hearts	Joel ii. 13	136
Mortification	Let him deny himself	S. Luke ix. 23	137
	I chastise my body	1 Cor. ix. 25	137
	Suffereth violence	S. Matt. xi. 12	137

CHAPTER VI.

THE SACRAMENTS.

Baptism	Baptizing them	S. Mat. xxviii. 19	143
	One baptism	Eph. iv. 5	144
	Have put on Christ	Gal. iii. 27	144
	Wash away thy sins	Acts xxii. 16	144
Confirmation	The Apostles who were in Jerusalem	Acts viii. 14	147
Holy Eucharist	If any man eat	S. John vi. 51	148
	I have received of the Lord	1 Cor. xi. 23	149
	The chalice of benediction	1 Cor. x. 16	149
	In the strength of that food	3 Kings xix. 8	151
	The hidden manna	Apoc. ii. 17	152
	Nation so great	Deut. iv. 7	153
The Mass	Standing as it were slain	Apoc. v. 6	156
	Priest for ever	Heb. vii. 17	157
	From the rising of the sun	Mal. i. 11	160
	Show the death of the Lord	1 Cor. xi. 26	160

SUBJECT.		REFERENCE.	PAGE.
Penance	Whatsoever thou shalt bind	S. Matt. xvi. 18	161
	Whose sins	S. John xx. 23	162
	Is it easier to say	S. Matt. ix. 5	162
Contrition	An afflicted spirit	Ps. l. 19	163
	If the wicked do penance	Ezec. xviii. 21	164
	Say not, "I have sinned"	Ecclus. v. 4	164
Extreme Unction	Anointed with oil	S. Mark vi. 12	170
Holy Order	Neglect not the grace	1 Tim. iv. 12	173
	Obey your prelates	Heb. xiii. 17	173
	The lips of the priest	Mal. ii. 7	174
Matrimony	Subject to their husbands	Eph. v. 22	174

CHAPTER VII.
VIRTUES AND VICES.

Faith, Hope, and Charity.	Now there remain	1 Cor. xiii. 13	177
	Substance of things	Heb. xi. 1	177
	A light shining in a dark place	2 Pet. i. 19	478
Cardinal Virtues	The wisdom of the flesh	Rom. viii. 6	178
	Not to be more wise	Rom. xii. 3	178
Works of Mercy	Cup of cold water	S. Matt. x. 42	181
	If a brother or sister	S. James ii. 15	181
	In word nor in tongue	1 S. John iii. 17	181
	Hide the dead by day	Tobias xii. 12	181
	Instruct such an one	Gal. vi. 1	182
Eight Beatitudes	Shall hardly enter	S. Matt. xix. 23	182
Deadly Sins	This was the iniquity of Sodom	Ezec. xvi. 49	183
	Be humbled therefore	1 S. Peter v. 5	184
	Crieth to me from the earth	Gen. iv. 10	186
	The hire of the labourers	S. James v. 4	187
	My secret sins.	Ps. xviii. 13	188
Eminent good works	Delivereth from death	Tobias xii. 9	
Four last things	In all thy works	Ecclus. vii. 40	188
	Desire to be dissolved	Phil. i. 21	193
	The dead, great and small	Apoc. xx. 12	193

CHAPTER VIII.
THE CHRISTIAN'S RULE OF LIFE.

Christian's Rule of Life	I am the Way	S. John xiv. 6	194
Hatred of Sin and love of God.	The face of a serpent	Ecclus. xxi. 2	195
	That He should be loved	S. Mark xii. 33	196

SUBJECT.		REFERENCE.	PAGE.
Love of our neighbour	For all the law	Gal. v. 14	196
Self-denial	Wide is the gate	S. Matt. vii. 13	197
	Whosoever doth not carry	S. Luke xiv. 27	198
	My yoke is sweet	S. Matt. xi. 28	199
The Devil	Be sober and watch	1 S. Pet. v. 8	199
The World	The friendship of this world	S. James iv. 4	200
The Flesh	Walk in the Spirit	Gal. v. 16	201
Watching and Prayer	Watch ye and pray	S. Matt. xxvi. 41	201
	Be subject therefore	S. James iv. 7	201
Dependence on God	Unless the Lord	Ps. cxxvi. 1	202

CHAPTER IX.

THE CHRISTIAN'S DAILY EXERCISE.

Christian's Exercise.	Daily	To thee do I watch	Ps. lxii. 2	202
		From the morning watch	Ps. cxxix. 6	204
		If I have remembered	Ps. lxii. 7	204
		All whatsoever you do	Colos. iii. 17	205
		O thou of little faith	Matt. xiv. 30	206
		The Publican standing afar off	S. Luke xviii. 13	206
		Father, I have sinned	S. Luke xv. 18	206
		Many sins are forgiven	S. Luke vii. 47	207
		Let my prayer	Ps. cxl. 2	209
		In peace in the self-same	Ps. iv. 9	209
		Into Thy hands	Ps. xxx. 6	209

NOTES.

NOTE A, page 37.

TESTIMONY OF THE FATHERS TO THE ANCIENT USE OF THE SIGN OF THE CROSS.

THIS "sign of the Son of Man" has always been considered to be the sign of the Cross. The use of this sign has prevailed in the Church from the very beginning of Christianity to the present day.

Tertullian, who was nearly the earliest of the Fathers, and lived in the second century, describes the use of it as a custom then universal and firmly established in the Church. His words are, "In all our travels and movements, in all our coming in and going out, in putting on our clothes and shoes, at the bath, at the table, in lighting our lamps, in lying down, in sitting down, whatever employment occupies us, we mark our foreheads with the sign of the cross. For these and such like rules, if thou requirest the law in the Scriptures, thou shalt find none: tradition will be pleaded to thee as originating, custom as confirming, and faith as observing them."—*De Coron. Mil.* n. 3, 4.

Again, St. Cyril of Jerusalem, in the fourth century, says: 'Let us not, therefore, be ashamed of the Cross of Christ; but even though another hide it, do thou openly seal it on thy brow, that the devils, beholding that royal sign, may flee far away trembling. But make thou this sign when thou eatest and drinkest, sittest or liest down, risest up, speakest, walkest; in a word, on every occasion; for He who was here crucified is above in the heavens.'—*Catech.* iv. n. 14, p. 58.

See "Faith of Catholics attested by the Fathers of the First Five Centuries," by Rev. James Waterworth.*—Vol. iii., pp. 422—438.

NOTE B, page 51.

THE SUPREMACY OF THE POPE IN THE EARLY CHURCH.

In these passages our Lord compares His Church to a house, and makes S. Peter the foundation of it; to a flock, and makes him the shepherd of it; and then, without figure, gives him the

---

* New Edition, published by Pustet (New York), to be had of R. Washbourne, 18 Paternoster Row, London.

office of confirming his brethren, with a distinct guarantee that *his* faith shall not fail.

This antecedent proof of the supremacy of S. Peter and his successors corresponds accurately with the subsequent history of the Church.

1. We find S. Peter, immediately on the ascension of his Master, taking on himself the guidance of the Church. He, on all occasions, speaks for his brethren, and puts the *first hand* to every undertaking.

2. The Popes, from the beginning, assumed a like authority. We find the Popes of the first five centuries using very much the tone which Pope Leo XIII. uses at this day; and we find illustrious Bishops, of the most important sees in the world, acquiescing without a murmur. For instance, Pope S. Julius, in the fourth century, says: 'And why were we not written to concerning the Church, especially of Alexandria? or, are you ignorant that this has been the custom, first to write to us, and thus what is just be decreed from this place? If, therefore, any suspicion fell on the Bishop there, it was befitting to write to this Church.'—*Ep. ad Eusebium*, n. 21, p. 13.

S. Damasus, another Pope in the same century, says: "Although, dearest brethren, the decrees of the Fathers are known to you, yet we cannot wonder at your carefulness as regards the institutes of our forefathers, that you cease not, as custom has ever been, to refer all those things which can admit of any doubt to us, as to the head, that thence you may derive answers whence you received the institution, and rule of living rightly. . . . . Not that you are in any way deficient in knowledge of the law of the Church; but that, supported by the authority of the Apostolic See, you may not deviate in anything from its regulations. . . . . It does with reason concern us, who ought to hold the chief government in the Church, if we by our silence favour error.'—*Epis.* v. *Prospero Numid. et aliis*.

S. Innocent I., Pope in the fifth century, says: "After having caused your letter to be several times read to me, I noticed that a kind of injury was done to the Apostolic See, unto which, as unto the head of the Churches, that statement was sent—the sentence of that See being still treated as doubtful. The renewed questioning contained in your report compels me, therefore, to repeat in plainer terms the subjects concerning which I remember having written to you."—*Ep.* xvii., n. 1.

Pope S. Boniface, also in the fifth century, says: "The institution of the Universal Church took its beginning from the honour bestowed on Blessed Peter, in whom its government and headship reside. For from him, as its source, did ecclesiastical discipline flow over all the Churches when the culture of religion had begun to make progress. The precepts of the Synod of Nicæa bear no other testimony; insomuch that that Synod did not attempt to make any regulations in his regard, as it saw that nothing could be conferred that was superior to his own dignity: it knew, in fine, that everything had been bestowed on him by the word of the Lord. It is, therefore, certain that this Church is, to the Churches spread over the whole world, as the head is to its members; from which Church whoso has cast himself off, becomes an alien from the Christian religion, whereas he has begun not to be in the same bonds of fellowship."—*Ep.*, xiv. *Epis. Thess.*

Could the present Pope assert his right with less ceremony or more conclusiveness?

3. Not only did the Popes assert their authority, but the Church admitted it.

S. Irenæus, in the second century, says: "To this Church [Rome], on account of a more powerful principality, it is necessary that every Church, that is, those who are on every side faithful, resort, in which [Church] always by those, who are on every side, has been preserved the tradition which is from Apostles."—*Adv. hæres.*

S. Ambrose, Archbishop of Milan in the fourth century, says: "We have recognised in the letter of your Holiness the watchfulness of the good shepherd, who dost faithfully keep the gate entrusted to thee; and with pious solicitude dost guard the fold of Christ, worthy, indeed, that the Lord's sheep should hear and follow thee. . . . . Those, therefore, whom your Holiness has condemned, know that, amongst us also, they have been, according to your judgment, condemned."—*Ep.* xcii., *Siricio.*

S. Jerome says (fourth century): "Following no chief but Christ, I am joined in communion with your Holiness, that is, with the chair of Peter. Upon that rock I know that the Church is built. Whosoever eats the Lamb out of this house is profane. If any be not in the ark of Noah, he will perish whilst the deluge prevaileth." Again he says: "The Church here is rent into three parts, each of which is eager to drag me to itself. . . . Meanwhile I cry aloud: 'If anyone is united to the chair of S. Peter, he is mine.' Meletius, Vitalis, and Paulinus, all assert that they adhere to thee. I might assent if only one of them declared this: as it is, either two or all of them are liars. Wherefore, I beseech your Holiness, by the cross of our Lord, that—as you follow the Apostles in honour, you may follow them also in merit—you would, by your letter, make known to me with whom I ought to hold communion in Syria."—*Ep.* xv., xvi., *ad Damas. Papam.*

S. John Chrysostom, Patriarch of Constantinople, also in the fourth century, says: "Christ, speaking to the leader of the Apostles, says: 'Peter, lovest thou Me?' and upon his affirming that he did, He replies, 'If thou lovest Me, feed My sheep.' . . . . Why did Christ shed His blood? That He might obtain possession of those very sheep which He entrusted to Peter and to his successors."—*De Sacerd.*

S. Augustin, Bishop of Hippo in the fifth century, says: "That city [Carthage] had a Bishop of no slight authority, who was able not to heed the multitude of enemies conspiring against him, when he saw himself united by letters of communion, both with the Roman Church, in which the primacy of the Apostolic Chair has always been in force, and with other lands."—*Ep.* xliii.

He also says: "In the Catholic Church . . . . the succession of priests, from the very Chair of the Apostle Peter—to whom the Lord, after His resurrection, committed His sheep to be fed—down even to the present Bishop, keeps me."—*Contr. Ep. Fund. Manich.*

We may add the words addressed by the Pope's legate to the Council of Ephesus in the fifth century: "It is a matter of doubt to none, yea, rather it is a thing known to all ages, that the holy and most blessed Peter, the prince and head of the Apostles, the pillar of the faith, the foundation of the Catholic Church, received the keys of the kingdom from Jesus Christ, our Lord and Saviour and Redeemer of mankind. And to him was given authority to bind and loose sins: who even till this present, and always, both lives and judges in his successors. Our holy and most blessed Pope Celestin, the Bishop, the canonical successor, and vicegerent of this Peter, has sent us as representatives of his person."—*Concil. Eph. Act.* iii.

When we consider that the Fathers who speak thus of the Pope's authority were themselves men of the greatest weight in their day, from position and talents, we may reasonably conclude that the Church then accepted the assertion of the Pope's authority in much the same way in which she accepts it now—that is, with the respect and obedience due to an authority established by God.

These passages may be found respectively at pp. 67, 71, 77, 85, 61, 73, 75, 76, 81, of Waterworth's "Faith of Catholics" (vol. ii.), where a great number of similar ones may be read.

NOTE C, page 148.
ON THE REAL PRESENCE.

There are very few subjects on which the Holy Scriptures speak with such clearness as they do about the Real Presence of our Lord in the Holy Eucharist.

We have, first, the promise of our Lord whilst He was yet with His Apostles (S. John vi.). Second, the words of Institution when this promise was fulfilled. Third, the reference made to it by S. Paul years after, when the Holy Eucharist had become the daily practice of the Church, in which he repeats these same words of Institution, and draws from them consequences which could only follow from the doctrine of the Real Presence. "He that eateth and drinketh unworthily, eateth and drinketh judgment to himself, not *discerning the Body of the Lord*." In all these places the same truth is declared in the very plainest of words, without the remotest hint at any figurative explanation. If these words do not express it, let us ask what words would? Is it *possible* for words to convey the Catholic doctrine more clearly than these do?—at least, putting aside those words which have since acquired a technical and controversial sense.

The Fathers, too, abound in the clearest possible passages on this subject. I will give one specimen of their language from S. Ambrose. He says : "Now if a human benediction availed so much to change nature, what shall we say concerning the Divine Consecration itself, where the very words of the Lord, the Saviour, operate? For this sacrament, which thou receivest, is affected by the word of Christ. Now if the word of Elias so availed as to draw down fire from heaven, shall not the word of Christ be of avail to change the natures of elements? Concerning the works of the whole world, you have read that ' He spoke and they were made, He commanded and they were created.' The word, therefore, of Christ, which could out of nothing make that which was not—cannot it change those things which are into that which they were not? For to give new natures to things is not less than to change their natures. . . . . The Lord Jesus himself cries out, ' This is My body.' Before the benediction of heavenly words, another species is named ; after the consecration His Body is signified. Himself declares it His own Blood. Before the consecration it is called another thing ; after consecration it is called blood. And thou sayest, Amen ; that is, it is true. What the mouth speaks, let the inward mind confess: what language expresses, let thought feel.'—See Waterworth's "Faith of Catholics" (vol. ii., pp. 289, 290).

Perhaps, however, the most striking testimony to the faith of the early Church comes from the ancient Liturgies, of which mention will be made in the Note on the Mass.

NOTE D, page 156.
THE ANCIENT LITURGIES ON THE REAL PRESENCE.

Besides the Latin "Mass," there are, both in the Church and in schismatical bodies out of the Church, a number of other "Liturgies,' or forms, in which the Eucharistic Sacrifice is offered up. These present, perhaps, the most remarkable proof of the Doctrine of the Real Presence.

They are of the highest antiquity, going up, as far as can be traced, to the times of the Apostles. They vary very considerably in ritual; that is, they are celebrated in different languages, and use different forms of words. The ceremonies employed, and the vestments worn, are also widely different. Nevertheless in substance they perfectly agree. Their testimony to the faith of the early Church about the Real Presence is unanimous, and is set forth, for the most part, in language far more striking than that employed by the Roman Mass.

It will be interesting to quote the account of the origin of these Liturgies given by S. Proclus, a father of the fifth century.

He says: "Many other individuals, and they divine pastors and teachers of the Church, who have succeeded the Sacred Apostles, have left in writing, and delivered to the Church, the exposition of the mystic liturgy. Of these, the first and most celebrated are blessed Clement, the disciple and successor of the Coryphæus of the Apostles, the Apostles themselves dictating to him" [he then mentions S. James of Jerusalem and S. Basil, who, he says, abbreviated the former Liturgy]. "After our Saviour was taken up into heaven, the Apostles, before being scattered over the whole world, being together in oneness of mind, passed whole days in prayer; and having found the mystic Sacrifice of the Lord's Body a great consolation, they sang it at very great length; for this, and teaching, they considered preferable to anything else. With very great gladness and much joy were they instant in this Divine Sacrifice, ever bearing in mind the Lord's words, which He says: '*This is My body;*' and '*Do this in memory of me;*' and '*He that eateth My flesh and drinketh My Blood, abideth in Me and I in him.*' For

this cause, too, with a contrite heart, they sang many prayers, earnestly imploring the Divine aid. . . . . Through those prayers they expected the advent of the Holy Ghost, that by His own Divine Presence He might make and exhibit the bread that lay there for a sacrifice, and the wine mixed with water, that very same Body and Blood of our Lord Jesus Christ; which is no less done even to this day, and will be done even to the consummation of the world." [He adds that S. John Chrysostom, to meet the degeneracy of the times, also abridged the Liturgy.] "For this cause he also omitted much, and arranged it to be celebrated in a conciser form, for fear lest, by degrees, men who are specially fond of a kind of liberty and ease, deluded by the deceitful reasonings of the enemy, might keep aloof from so great an Apostolical and Divine tradition."
—*Tract. de Traditione Divinæ Missæ.*

It appears that the Liturgies were generally committed to writing about the middle of the fourth century. Up till that time, that is, in the days of persecution, they had been handed down by unwritten tradition, on account of that fear in which the early Church lived lest holy things should fall into the hands of the pagans.

There are three great sources from which are derived the numerous Liturgies in use in the Christian Church :—

1. That of S. James the Apostle, the first Bishop of Jerusalem, which is chiefly followed by the Oriental Churches.
2. That of S. Mark the Evangelist. S. Mark was the disciple of S. Peter, and Bishop of Alexandria. This is followed by the Ethiopian Liturgy used in Africa.
3. That of S. Peter, used in the Latin Churches.

These Liturgies all contain,—
1. Prayers for the dead.
2. A narrative of the institution of the Holy Eucharist— which is almost word for word the same in every Liturgy, except the Ethiopian, and yet is not taken from any of the Scripture accounts.
3. A prayer that God will make, or change, the bread and wine into the Body and Blood of Christ.
4. They declare that a mystery and sacrifice are celebrated, and they contain an actual sacrificial oblation.
5. Generally they mention the mixture of water with the wine.
6. The sign of the cross.

I will quote now a few expressions from some of these Liturgies to show how vivid a belief in the Real Presence is expressed in them.

In the Alexandrian Liturgy of S. Basil the priest elevates the larger part of the consecrated Host, and says: "The Holy body and precious true Blood of Jesus Christ the Son of God." The people answer, "Amen." *Priest.*—"The Holy Precious Body and true Blood of Jesus Christ the Son of God." *People.*—"Amen." *Priest.*—"Body and Blood of Emmanuel our God, this is truly. Amen." *People.*—"Amen. I believe, I believe and confess, till my last breath, that it is the very life-giving flesh of Thine only-begotten Son, but our Lord and God and Saviour Jesus Christ.'—*Waterworth*, vol. ii., p. 179.

In the Alexandrian Liturgy of S. Gregory the Illuminator we find: "Thou hast granted unto us, lowly men and sinners, and Thine unworthy servants, confidence to stand at Thy holy altar, and to offer up to Thee the awful and unbloody sacrifice, for our own sins, and the ignorances of Thy people, for the pardon and rest of our fathers and brethren who have already fallen asleep." —*Ib.*, p. 182.

The Æthiopian Liturgy, called that of the Apostles, says: "Have mercy, O Lord, on the souls of Thy servants, who have eaten Thy Body, and drunk Thy Blood, and received rest in Thy faith."—*Ib.*, p. 184.

The same Liturgy has also the following testimony to the *worship* due to our Lord in the Holy Sacrament:—

"Hosts of Angels stand before the Saviour of the world, and surround the Body and Blood of our Lord and Saviour Jesus Christ: let us approach before His presence and venerate Christ with faith."—*Ib.*, p. 184.

Also it says: "The holy, precious, living, and true Body of our Lord and Saviour Jesus Christ, which is given for remission of sins, and everlasting life to those who receive it with faith. Amen. . . .

"This is, in real truth, the Body and Blood of Emmanuel. Amen. I believe, I believe, I believe, from this time forth, now, and for evermore. Amen. This is the Body and Blood of our Lord and Saviour Jesus Christ, which He received of the Lady of us all, the holy and pure Virgin Mary."—*Ib.*, p. 184.

Quotations in the same strain might be continued to a great length. They may be found in the book already mentioned, "Faith of Catholics" (vol. ii.), pp. 171-190.

May we not then say, if the faith of the Catholic Church *now* about the Holy Eucharist and the Mass was *not* that of the Apostles, let us hear how it is that the same faith is so vividly impressed on every line of the earliest Christian liturgical records in all parts of the world, and breathes, if we may so say, from the very heart of the early Church?

NOTE E, page 166.

CONFESSION.

The testimony of the Fathers to the practice of confession is singularly full and clear. It begins, too, with almost the earliest Fathers of both East and West.

Tertullian, in the second century, says: "Brave art thou in thy modesty, truly! bearing an open front in sinning, and a bashful one in praying for pardon! .... Is it better to be damned in secret than absolved openly? It is a miserable thing thus to come to confession. .... It is a miserable thing to be cut and to be burnt with the cautery. .... Nevertheless, those things which heal by unpleasant means excuse likewise, by the benefit of the cure, their own offensiveness. ...."—*Faith of Catholics*, vol. iii., p. 41.

"If thou drawest back from confession, consider in thine heart that hell-fire which confession shall quench for thee. ....

"When, therefore, thou knowest that, against hell-fire, after that first protection of baptism ordained by the Lord, there is yet in confession a second aid, why dost thou abandon thy salvation? ...."—*Ib.*, p. 43.

In the third century Origen, the great doctor of the early Greek Church, says: "So also they who have sinned, if they conceal and retain the sin within them, they are oppressed within and almost suffocated. .... But if a man becomes his own accuser, while he accuses himself and confesses, he at the same time ejects the sin, and digests the whole cause of the disease. Only look diligently round to whom thou oughtest to confess thy sin. Prove first the physician .... who knows how to be weak with the weak. .... If he shall have understood and foresee, that thy sickness is such as ought to be set forth and cured in the assembly of the whole Church, and, thereby, perhaps, others be edified, and thou thyself easily cured, this must be prescribed with much deliberation, and on the very experienced advice of that physician."—*Ib.*, p. 47.

This quotation clearly proves that the confession referred to was not *necessarily* a *public* confession, but *private* confession, such as it is now the discipline of the Church to employ.

The following shows that confession was not confined to notorious or even grievous sins. S. Cyprian, in the fourth century, says: "How much loftier in faith, and in fear of God superior, are they who, though implicated in no crime of sacrifice or of accepting a certificate,* yet, because they have only had thought thereof, this very thing sorrowingly and honestly confessing before the priests of God, make a confession of their conscience, expose the burthen of the soul, seek out a salutary cure even for light and little wounds."—*Faith of Catholics*, vol. iii., p. 51.

I must again refer the reader to the "Faith of Catholics" (vol. iii.), where testimonies of the Fathers breathing the same spirit are quoted at great length.

* Referring to those who had fallen away in time of persecution, and either sacrificed to idols or pretended to do so, and saved themselves by receiving certificates from the pagan authorities that they had sacrificed.

FINIS.

Extract from the **NEW YORK CATHOLIC BOOK NEWS**, May, 1879:

"*No publisher does more than Mr. Washbourne to produce a variety of excellent books, and to spread Catholic literature far and wide.*"

ROBERT WASHBOURNE'S
CATALOGUE OF BOOKS,
18 PATERNOSTER ROW, LONDON.

PRAYER BOOKS (385) **SEE PAGE 30**

Mary Foreshadowed. A new book for every day in the Month of May. By Rev. Fr. Thaddeus, O.S.F. 3s.

Catholic Controversial Letters. By Rev. P. Sweeny, D.D. [*In the Press.*

The Maid of Limerick, and other Tales, Essays and Sketches (Catholic Progress for 1884). Handsomely bound in cloth. 2s. 6d.

Cardinal Manning on Divine Faith. 6d. (by post 6½d.)

The Revolt of the Netherlands. By Wilfred C. Robinson. 3s.

The Valley of Chiomonte, and other Tales. 3s.

Contemplations and Meditations on the Public Life of Our Lord, according to the Method of St. Ignatius, translated from the French, by a Sister of Mercy. Revised by a Priest S.J. [*In the Press.*

The Catechism and Holy Scripture, a new editon of the Catechism illustrated by Examples. By Rev. J. B. Bagshawe, D.D., author of "The Threshold of the Catholic Church," "Credentials of the Catholic Church." [*In the Press.*

The Brides of Kensington. By Miss Bridges, author of "Sir Thomas Maxwell and his Ward." 1s. 6d.

A Village Beauty and other Tales. With 10 Illustrations. [*In the Press.*

Corpus Christi. A Story for First Communion. By Rev. Francis Drew. 1s. [*In the Press.*

Catechism of Christian Doctrine. The *revised* edition. 1d.

*** *All other Books not mentioned in this Catalogue supplied.*

Catalogue of American Catholic Books supplied.
Catalogues of Medals, Crucifixes, Scapulars, Rosaries, Incense, Candlesticks, Vases, &c., &c., supplied. FOREIGN BOOKS supplied.

R. Washbourne, Paternoster Row, London.

Snowflakes and other Tales. By M. Sinclair Allison. 1s.

Father Placid; or, the Custodian of the Blessed Sacrament. By Lætitia Oliver. 1s.

Rose Fortescue; or, the Devout Client of Our Lady of Dolours. By Lætitia Oliver. 1s.

A Friendly Voice; or, The Daily Monitor, and Visits to the Blessed Sacrament. By the author of "Golden Sands." 6d.

Little Books of St. Nicholas. By Rev. F. Drew. 1s. each.

- Corpus Christi. A Story for First Communion.
- Ora Pro Nobis; or, Tristram's Friends.
- Ave Maria; or, Catesby's Story.
- Credo; or, Justin's Martyrdom.
- Veni Creator; or, Ulrich's Money.
- Per Jesum Christum; or, Two Good Fridays.
- Pater Noster; or, an Orphan Boy.
- Dominus Vobiscum; or, The Sailor Boy.
- Oremus; or, Little Mildred.

The Gamekeeper's Little Son, and other Tales for Children. By F. I. M. Kershaw, author of "Bobbie and Birdie." 2s. 6d.

Bobbie and Birdie; or, Our Lady's Picture. A story for the very little ones. By Frances J. M. Kershaw. 2s. 6d.

True Wayside Tales. By Lady Herbert. Foolscap 8vo., 3s.; or cheap edition, in 5 vols., in pretty binding, price 6d. each.

Second Series of True Wayside Tales. By Lady Herbert. 3s.

- Moothoosawmy; or, Natural Uprightness Supernaturally Rewarded. Saveriammal; or, the Story of a Snake-bite and its Cure. Father Koblyowicz; or, the Martyr to Sacramental Silence. 1s.
- Emily; Nancy; the Efficacy of Prayer; and the White Necktie, a Story of First Communion. 1s.
- The Two Cousins; The Result of a Mother's Prayers; and The Two School-boys. 1s.

For Better, *not* for Worse. A tale of our own Times. By Rev. Langton George Vere. 3s.

Catholic Hymn Book. By Rev. Langton George Vere. 20 pages, price 2d.; in cloth, 4d. This is the best and cheapest Hymn book printed. *An Abridged Edition is now ready.* Price 1d, or in cloth, 2d.

R. Washbourne, Paternoster Row, London.

The Office of Holy Week, according to the Roman Rite. This edition gives (including the Ordinary of the Mass, and the Services generally included in Holy Week Books) the Vespers and Complin for every day of Holy Week; the Blessing of the Holy Oils on Maundy Thursday; and the Matins, Lauds, Mass, Vespers, and Complin of Easter Sunday. Cloth, 1s. Soft morocco, 2s. 6d.

Little Office of the Immaculate Conception. Latin and English: with Imprimatur of the Cardinal Archbishop of Westminster. Cloth 6d. Soft morocco, 1s. 6d.
This edition has the great advantage over most English and other prayer-books, of reproducing the only Latin text which has the approval of the Congregation of Sacred Rites (17 May, 1876), and to which the Indulgence is attached. Provost Husenbeth's English Version has, where necessary, been revised to agree with this text.

Portiuncula. The Indulgence of Portiuncula. A short account of its Origin, Development, and Conditions. 1d.

The Most Beautiful among the Children of Men. Meditations upon the Life of Our Lord Jesus Christ. By Mrs. Abel Ram. With a Preface by the Cardinal Archbishop of Westminster. 3s.

Cheap Edition of **The Threshold of the Catholic Church.** A Course of Plain Instructions for those entering her Communion. By Rev. J. B. Bagshawe, D.D. 1s. *nett*, (post 3d.), or 12 copies for 10s. (post 1s. 6d.)

Cheap Edition of **Bishop Luck's Short Meditations for every day in the year.** For the Religious. 6s.

Tempora Mutantur; or, the Return of St. Chad and Archbishop Langton to the Cathedral of Lichfield. 6d.

Solid Virtue. By Father Bellécius, S.J. Translated by a Religious of the Ursuline Community at Thurles. New edition, 7s. 6d.

OREMUS, A Liturgical Prayer Book: with the Imprimatur of the Cardinal Archbishop of Westminster. 32mo., 452 pages, cloth, 2s.; French morocco, 3s. 6d; calf or morocco, 5s.; extra gilt, 6s. 6d.; Russia, 7s. 6d. Also in superior and more expensive bindings.

A Smaller Oremus; an abridgment of the above. Cloth, 6d.; French morocco, 1s. 6d.; calf or morocco, 2s. 6d.; extra gilt, 4s.; russia, 5s. Also in superior and more expensive bindings.

The Child of Mary's Manual. Compiled from the French. Third Edition, with Imprimatur. 9d.

Child's Picture Prayer Book. Sixteen coloured Illustrations, cloth, 1s.; stronger bound, 1s. 6d.; prettier bound, 2s.; full gilt, 2s. 6d.

Lives of the Saints. From Alban Butler, selected and edited by Rt. Rev. Mgr. Goddard. 5s.

For Dramas, *see* page 11.

ADELSTAN'S (Countess), Life and Letters. From the French of the Rev. Père Marquigny, S.J., 2s.

Adolphus; or, the Good Son. 18mo., 6d.

Adventures of a Protestant in Search of a Religion. By Iota. 12mo., 2s. and 3s. 6d.

Agnes Wilmott's History, and the Lessons it Taught. By the author of "Bertram Eldon," "Nellie Gordon," &c. 1s. 6d.

A'KEMPIS—Following of Christ. Dr. Challoner's Edition, 32mo., 1s.; red edges, 1s. 6d.; French morocco. 2s.; calf or morocco, 4s.; gilt, 5s.; russia, 7s. 6d., 9s. and 12s.; ivory, with rims and clasp, 15s., 16s., 18s.; mor. antique, with corners and clasps, 17s. 6d.; russia, ditto, ditto, 16s. 20s. With Reflections, 1s.; soft morocco, 3s. 6d.; with red borders round pages, cloth, 3s. 6d.; soft morocco, 7s. 6d.; calf, 10s. 6d.; antique morocco, 15s.

Albertus Magnus, Life of. By Rev. Fr. Dixon. 8vo. 6s.

Allah Akbar—God is Great. An Arab Legend of the Siege and Conquest of Granada. From the Spanish. By Mariana Monteiro. 12mo., 3s.

ALLISON (M. Sinclair), Snowflakes and other Tales. 1s.

AMHERST (Rt. Rev. Dr.), Lenten Thoughts. 1s.; stronger bound, 2s.

ANDERDON (Rev. W. H., S.J.), To Rome and Back. Fly-Leaves from a Flying Tour. 12mo., 2s.

ANDERSEN (Carl), Three Sketches of Life in Iceland. Translated by Myfanwy Fenton. 1s. 6d.

Angela Merici (S.) Her Life, her Virtues, and her Institute. From the French of the Abbé G. Beetemé. 12mo., 3s.

Angels (The) and the Sacraments. Fcap 8vo., 1s.

——— Month of the Holy Angels. By Abbé Ricard. 1s.

Anglicanism, Harmony of. By T. W. M. Marshall. 2s. 6d.

Annals of the Society of the Holy Childhood. 3d.

ARNOLD (Miss M. J.), Personal Recollections of Cardinal Wiseman, with other Memories. 12mo., 2s.

ARRAS (Madame d') The Two Friends; or Marie's Self-Denial. 12mo., 1s.

Aunt Margaret's Little Neighbours; or, Chats about the Rosary. By Miss Plues. 12mo., 3s.

Ave Maria; or Catesby's Story. By Rev. F. Drew. 1s.

R. Washbourne, Paternoster Row, London.

BAGSHAWE (Rev. J. B.), The Credentials of the Catholic Church. 12mo., 4s.

——— The Catechism and Holy Scripture. A new edition of The Catechism illustrated by Examples.

——— Threshold of the Catholic Church. A Course of Plain Instructions for those entering her Communion. 1s. *nett*, (postage 3d.), 12 copies for 10s. (postage 1s. 6d.)

Baker's Boy; or, Life of General Drouot. 18mo., 6d.

BALDESCHI. Ceremonial according to the Roman Rite. Translated by Rev. J. D. Hilarius Dale. 12mo., 6s. 6d.

Bambozzi (Fr. Benvenuto, O.M.C.), of the Conventual Friars Minor, Life of, from the Italian (2nd edition) of Fr. Nicholas Treggiari, D.D. 3s. 6d.

BAMPFIELD (Rev. G.), Sir Ælfric and other Tales. 18mo., 6d.; cloth, 1s.

Battista Varani (B.), *see* Veronica (S.). 12mo., 5s.

Battle of Connemara. By Kathleen O'Meara. 2s 6d.

BELLECIUS (Fr.), Solid Virtue. New edition. 12mo., 7s. 6d.

Bellevue and its Owners. A Tale for Boys. By C. Pilley. 1s. 6d.

BELLINGHAM (Lady Constance) The Duties of Christian Parents. Conferences by Père Matignon. Translated. 3s. 6d.

Bells of the Sanctuary,—A Daughter of St. Dominick. By Grace Ramsay. 1s. 6d.

Benedict's (S.) Manual. 3s.

——— Life and Miracles. By S. Gregory the Great. From an old English version. By P. W. (Paris, 1608). Edited by Bishop Luck, O.S.B. 1s.; or in stronger binding, 2s.

——— Explanation of the Medal. 1d.

Bernardine (St.) of Siena, Life of. 5s.

Bertram Eldon, and how he found a Home. By M. A. Pennell, author of "Nellie Gordon" (6d) "Agnes Wilmott's History" (1s. 6d.). 12mo., 1s.

Bessy; or, the Fatal Consequence of Telling Lies. By Miss K. M. Weld. 1s.

BESTE (J. R. Digby), Holy Readings. 2s.

BETHELL (Rev. A.), Our Lady's Month; or, Short Lessons for the Month of May, and the Feasts of Our Lady. 18mo., 1s.

R. Washbourne, Paternoster Row, London.

Bible. Douay Version. 12mo., 3s.; Persian, 8s.; morocco, 12s. 18mo., 2s. 6d.; Persian, 5s.; calf or morocco, 7s.; gilt, 8s. 6d. 4to. Illustrated, morocco, £5 5s.; superior, £6 6s.

Blessed Sacrament, Meditations on. 1s. 6d.

Blessed Virgin, Devotions to. From Ancient Sources. 2s.

——— History of. By Orsini. Translated by Dr. Husenbeth. 3s. 6d.

——— Life of. Proposed as a model to Christian women. 12mo., 1s.

——— *See* Our Lady, p. 22; Leaflets, p. 17; May, p. 19.

BLOSIUS, Spiritual Works of :—The Rule of the Spiritual Life; The Spiritual Mirror; String of Spiritual Jewels. Edited by Rev. Fr. John Bowden. 3s. 6d.

Bluebeard; or, the Key of the Cellar. A Drama in 3 Acts. 6d.

Blue Scapular, Origin of. 18mo., 1d.

BLYTH (Rev. Fr.), Devout Paraphrase on the Seven Penitential Psalms. To which is added "Necessity of Purifying the Soul," by S. Francis de Sales. 18mo., 6d.

Bobbie and Birdie; or, Our Lady's Picture. A Story for the very little ones. By Frances J. M. Kershaw. 2s. 6d.

BONA (Cardinal), Easy Way to God. Translated by Father Collins. 12mo., 3s.

BONAVENTURE (S.), Life of St. Francis of Assisi. From the Italian by the author of "The Life of St. Teresa." 3s. 6d.

Boniface (S.), Life of. By Mrs. Hope. 12mo., 6s.

BOWDEN (Rev. Fr. John), Spiritual Works of Louis of Blois. 12mo., 3s. 6d.

———Oratorian Lives of the Saints. (Page 22).

BOWDEN (Mrs.), Lives of the First Religious of the Visitation of Holy Mary. 2 vols., 12mo., 10s.

BOWLES (Emily), Eagle and Dove. Translated from the French of Mdlle. Zénaïde Fleuriot. 5s.

BRADBURY (Rev. Fr.), Sophia and Eulalie. (The Catholic Pilgrim's Progress). 2s. 6d.

BRIDGES (Miss), Sir Thomas Maxwell and his Ward. 1s. 6d.

——— The Brides of Kensington. 1s. 6d.

R. Washbourne, Paternoster Row, London.

R. Washbourne's List of Books. 7

Bridget (S.), Life of, and other Saints of Ireland. 12mo., 1s.

Brigit (S.) Life of, &c. By M. F. Cusack. 8vo., 6s.

Broken Chain. A Tale. 18mo., 6d.

BROWNLOW (Rev. Canon), "Vitis Mystica"; or, the True Vine: a Treatise on the Passion of our Lord. 2s. 6d.

BURDER (Abbot), Confidence in the Mercy of God. By Mgr. Languet. 12mo., 3s.

——— The Consoler; or, Pious Readings addressed to the Sick and all who are afflicted. By Père Lambilotte. 3s. 6d.

——— Souls in Purgatory. 32mo., 2d.

Burial of the Dead. For Children and Adults. (Latin and English.) Clear type edition, 32mo., 6d.; roan, 1s. 6d.

BURKE (Rev. Fr.), Lectures and Sermons. 3 vols., 32s. 6d.

BUTLER (Alban), Lives of the Saints. 2 vols., 8vo., 28s.; gilt, 34s.; 4 vols., 8vo., 36s.; gilt, 42s.

CALIXTE—Life of the Ven. Anna Maria Taigi. Translated by A. V. Smith Sligo. 8vo., 3s. 6d.

Callista. Dramatised by Dr. Husenbeth. 1s.

CAMERON (Marie), The Golden Thought, and other Stories. 1s. 6d.; or cheap edition, separately, 6d. each.

   1. The Golden Thought, and The Brother's Grave.

   2. The Rod that bore Blossoms, and Patience and Impatience.

CARAHER (Hugh), A Month at Lourdes and its Neighbourhood. Two Illustrations. 12mo., 2s.

Catechisms — The Catechism of Christian Doctrine. *Revised edition*, 1d.

——— *Cardinal Wiseman's edition offered at Half Price*, ½d.

——— Dr. Bagshawe's edition. "The Catechism and Holy Scripture."

——— Bishop Challoner's Grounds of Catholic Doctrine. 4d.

——— Frassinetti's Dogmatic. 12mo., 3s.

——— Keenan's Controversial. 2s.

——— for First Confession. By Rev. R. G. Davis, 1d.

——— of Confirmation. A very complete book. 72 pages, 3d.

——— of Perseverance. By Gaume. 4 vols., 30s.; abridged, 2s.

R. Washbourne, Paternoster Row, London.

Catherine Hamilton. By M. F. S. 1s. 6d.; }
Catherine Grown Older. By M. F. S. 2s.; } in one vol., 3s.

Catholic Church Calendar for England. 6d.; Almanack, 1d.

Catholic Directory for Scotland. 1s.

Catholic Piety. *See* Prayer Books, page 30.

Catholic Pilgrim's Progress—The Journey of Sophia and Eulalie to the Palace of True Happiness. 2s. 6d.

Catholic Progress. A Quarterly Magazine. Price 2s.

CHALLONER (Dr.), Grounds of Catholic Doctrine. 4d.

———— Memoirs of Missionary Priests. 8vo., illustrated, 8s.

———— Think Well on't. 18mo., 2d.; cloth, 6d.

Chats about the Commandments. By Miss Plues. 3s.

Chats about the Rosary. By Miss Plues. 3s.

CHAUGY (Mother Frances Magdalen de), Lives of the First Religious of the Visitation. 2 vols., 12mo., 10s.

Child (The) of Mary's Manual. Third edition, 32mo. 9d.

Child's Book of the Passion of Our Lord. 32mo., 6d.

Child's Picture Prayer Book. With 16 Illustrations. Cloth, 1s.; stronger bound, 1s. 6d.; prettier binding, 2s.; gilt, 2s. 6d.

Children of Mary Card of Enrolment. Folio, 9d., post free on a roller, 1s.

Children of Mary in the World, Rules of. 32mo., 1d.

CHRISTOPHER (S.) The Rose of Venice. A Tale. 3s. 6d.

Church Defence. By T. W. M. Marshall. 2s. 6d.

Cistercian Legends of the XIII. Century. 3s.

Clare's Sacrifice. By C. M. O'Hara. A Tale for First Communicants. 6d.

COBBETT'S History of the Protestant Reformation. 4s. 6d.

COLLINS (Rev. Fr.), Legends of the XIII. Century. 3s.

———— Easy Way to God. From the Latin of Cardinal Bona. 3s.

R. Washbourne, Paternoster Row, London.

COLLINS (Rev. Fr.), Spiritual Conferences on the Mysteries of Faith and the Interior Life. 12mo., 5s.

COLOMBIERE (Father Claude de la), The Sufferings of Our Lord. Sermons preached in the Chapel Royal, St. James' in the year 1677. Preface by Fr. Doyotte, S.J. 18mo., 1s.

Colombini (B. Giovanni), Life of. By Belcari. Translated from the editions of 1541 and 1832. 3s. 6d.

Comedy of Convocation in the English Church. Edited by Archdeacon Chasuble. 8vo., 2s. 6d.

Communion, Prayers for, for Children. Preparation, Mass before Communion, Thanksgiving. 32mo. 1d.

Conferences. *See* Collins, Lacordaire, Mermillod, Matignon, Ravignan.

Confession and Holy Communion : Young Catholic's Guide. By Dr. Kenny. 32mo., 4d.

Confidence in the Mercy of God. By Mgr. Languet. Translated by Abbot Burder. 12mo., 3s.

Confirmation, Instructions for the Sacrament of. A very complete book. 72 pages, 3d.

Consoler (The) ; or, Pious Readings addressed to the Sick and all who are afflicted. By Abbot Burder. 3s. 6d.

Contemplations on the Most Holy Sacrament of the Altar ; or Devout Meditations to serve as Preparations for, and Thanksgiving after, Communion. 1s. 6d.

Continental Fish Cook ; or, a Few Hints on Maigre Dinners. By M. J. N. de Frederic. Third edition, with additions, 1s.

Convert Martyr; or, "Callista," by the Rev. Dr. Newman, Dramatised by the Rev. Dr. Husenbeth. 1s.

Convocation, Comedy of. By Arthur Marshall. 8vo. 2s. 6d.

Corpus Christi. A Story for First Communion. By Rev. F. Drew. 1s.

Credentials of the Catholic Church. By Rev. J. B. Bagshawe, author of "The Threshold of the Catholic Church." 12mo., 4s.

CUSACK (M. F.):—Sister Mary Francis Clare.

    Book of the Blessed Ones. 12mo., 4s. 6d.
    Case of Ireland Stated. 7s. 6d.
    Father Mathew, Life of. 2s. 6d.
    Good Reading for Sundays and Festivals. 2s. 6d.

R. Washbourne, Paternoster Row, London.

CUSACK (M. F.) Knock ; Apparitions, &c. 1s.
    Ireland, History of. 18mo., 2s.
    Jesus and Jerusalem. 4s. 6d.
    Knock : Three Visits to. 2s.
    Knock: Devotions for Pilgrims. 4d. Souvenir, 8 views, 1s. 6d.
    Life of the Blessed Virgin, 12s.
    Life of Most Rev. Dr. Dixon. 7s. 6d.
    Life of Mother Mary O'Hagan. 6s.
    Lives of St. Columba and St. Brigit. 8vo., 6s.
    Meditations for Advent and Easter. 3s. 6d.
    Nun's Advice to her Girls. 12mo., 2s. 6d.
    Pilgrim's Way to Heaven. 12mo., 4s. 6d.
    Prayers for Times of Public Calamity or Pestilence. 4d.
    Retreat for the Three Last Days of the Year. 1s.
    Tim O'Halloran's Choice. 12mo., 3s. 6d.
    Tronson's Conferences. 12mo., 4s. 6d.

Dark Shadow (The). A Tale. 12mo., 2s. 6d.

Daughter (A) of S. Dominick : (Bells of the Sanctuary). By Grace Ramsay. 1s. 6d.

DAVIS (Rev. R. G.) Garden of the Soul. *See* pages 30 and 32.

——— Catechism for First Confession. 1d.

DEHAM (Rev. F.) Sacred Heart of Jesus, offered to the Piety of the Young engaged in Study. 32mo., 9d.

Diary of a Confessor of the Faith. 12mo., 1s.

Directorium Asceticum. By Scaramelli. 4 vols., 12mo., 24s.

DIXON (Fr., O.P.) Albertus Magnus: his Life and Scholastic Labours. From original documents. By Dr. Sighart. 8vo. 6s.

——— Life of St. Vincent Ferrer. From the French of Rev. Fr. Pradel. 12mo., 5s.

Dominus Vobiscum ; or, the Sailor Boy. By Rev. F. Drew. 1s.

DOYLE (Canon, O.S.B.), Life of Gregory Lopez, the Hermit. 12mo., 3s. 6d.

——— Lectures for Boys. 2 vols. 10s. 6d. ; or sold separately, The Sundays of the Year, 3s. 6d. ; Our Lady's Festivals, etc., 2s. 6d. ; The Passion of Our Lord, 3s. ; and The Sacred Heart, 3s.

DOYOTTE (Fr., S.J.), Elevations to the Heart of Jesus. 2s.

DRAMAS. Bluebeard; or, the Key of the Cellar. A Drama in 3 Acts. Mixed. 6d.

—————— **Convert Martyr**; or, "Callista" dramatised. 1s.

—————— **The Duchess Transformed** (Girls, 1 Act). Comedy. 6d.

—————— **The Enchanted Violin** (Boys, 2 Acts). Comedy. 6d.

—————— **Ernscliff Hall** (Girls, 3 Acts). Drama. 6d.

—————— **Filiola** (Girls, 4 Acts). Drama. 6d.

—————— **He would be a Lord** (Boys, 3 Acts), a Comedy. 2s.

—————— **Mary Queen of Scots.** (Mixed, 3 Acts) Tragedy, 6d.

—————— **Reverse of the Medal** (Girls, 4 Acts). Drama. 6d.

—————— **The Secret** (Girls, 1 Act). Drama. 6d.

—————— **Shandy Maguire** (Boys, 2 Acts), a Farce. 6d.

—————— **St. Eustace** (Boys, 5 Acts). Drama. 6d.

—————— **St. William of York** (Boys, 2 Acts). Drama. 6d.

—————— **The Violet Sellers** (3 Acts). Drama for Children. 6d.

—————— **Whittington and his Cat.** Drama for Children. 9 Scenes. By Henrietta Fairfield. 6d.

—————— *See* R. Washbourne's **American List.**

DRANE (Augusta Theodosia), Inner Life of Pere Lacordaire. Translated from the French of Père Chocarne. 6s. 6d.

DREW (Rev. F.), Little Books of St. Nicholas. 1s. each. 1 to 8 now ready. 1. Oremus; 2. Dominus Vobiscum; 3. Pater Noster. 4. Per Jesum Christum; 5. Veni Creator; 6. Credo; 7. Ave Maria; 8. Ora pro nobis: 9. Corpus Christi; 10. Dei Genitrix; 11. Requiem; 12. Miserere; 13. Deo Gratias; 14. Angelus Domini.

Duchess (The), Transformed. By W. H. A. A Comedy. 6d.

Dusseldorf Society for the Distribution of Good Religious Pictures. Subscription, 9s. a year.

Duties of Christian Parents. Conferences by Père Matignon. Translated from the French by Lady Constance Bellingham. 3s. 6d.

Eagle and Dove. Translated by Emily Bowles. 5s.

Easy Way to God. By Cardinal Bona. 12mo., 3s.

Electricity and Magnetism; an Enquiry into the Nature and Results of. By Amyclanus. Illustrated. 12mo., 6s. 6d.

Enchanted Violin, The. A Comedy in 2 Acts (Boys), 6d.

R. Washbourne, Paternoster Row, London.

Epistles and Gospels. Good clear type edition, 4d.; roan, 1s. This edition is more complete than any other one.

———, **Explanation of.** By Rev. F. Goffine. Illustrated, 8vo., 9s.

Ernscliff Hall. A Drama in Three Acts, for Girls. 12mo., 6d.

Eucharist (The) and the Christian Life. 3s. 6d.

Eustace (St.). A Drama in 5 Acts for Boys. 6d.

FAIRFIELD (Henrietta), Whittington and his Cat. A Drama, in 9 Scenes, for Children. 12mo., 6d.

Fairy Ching (The); or, the Chinese Fairies' Visit to England. By Henrica Frederic. 12mo., 1s.

Faith of our Fathers. By Most Rev. Archbishop Gibbons. 4s.

Fardel (Sister Claude Simplicienne), Life of. With the Lives of others of the First Religious of the Visitation. 6s.

Father Placid; or, the Custodian of the Blessed Sacrament. By Lætitia Oliver. 1s.

FAVRE (Abbe), Heaven Opened by the Practice of Frequent Confession and Communion. 2s. 6d.

Favre (Mother Marie Jacqueline), Life of. With the Lives of others of the First Religious of the Visitation. 6s.

Feasts (The) of Camelot, with the Tales that were told there. By Mrs. E. L. Hervey. 3s.

Filiola. A Drama in Four Acts, for Girls. 12mo., 6d.

First Communion and Confirmation Memorial. Beautifully printed in gold and colours, folio. New edition, 6d. each.

First Communion; or, Clare's Sacrifice. By Miss O'Hara. 6d.

First Communion, Emily, Nancy, etc. By Lady Herbert. 1s.

First Religious of the Visitation of Holy Mary, Lives of. Translated, with a Preface, by Mrs. Bowden. 2 vols., 10s.

FLEURIOT (Mlle. Zenaide), Eagle and Dove. Translated by Emily Bowles. 5s.

Flowers of Christian Wisdom. By Henry Lucien. 1s. 6d.

Fluffy. A Tale for Boys. By M. F. S. 12mo., 3s.

Following of Christ. *See* A'Kempis.

For Better, not for Worse. By Rev. Langton George Vere. 3s.

Foreign Books, obtained from America, France, Germany, Italy, etc., without delay.

Francis of Assisi (S.) Life of. By S. Bonaventure. Translated by Miss Lockhart. 12mo., 3s. 6d.

Francis of Assisi (St.) Works of. Translated by a Religious of the Order. 4s.

FRANCIS OF SALES (S.), Consoling Thoughts. 18mo., 2s.

———— **Necessity of Purifying the Soul.** 6d.

———— **Sweetness of Holy Living.** 1s.

FRASSINETTI—Dogmatic Catechism. 12mo., 3s.

FREDERIC (Henrica), The Fairy Ching; or, the Chinese Fairies' Visit to England. 1s.

———— **Story of a Paper Knife.** 1s.

FREDERIC (M. J. N. de) Continental Fish Cook; or, a Few Hints on Maigre Dinners. 3rd edition, 1s.

Friendly Voice; or, the Daily Monitor. Red border, cloth, 6d.

GAHAN (Rev. W.), Sermons. 8vo., 8s.

Gamekeeper's Little Son, and other Tales for Children. By F. I. M. Kershaw. 2s. 6d.

Garden of the Soul. *See* page 32.

Gathered Gems from Spanish Authors. By M. Monteiro. 3s.

GAUME (Abbe), Catechism of Perseverance. 4 vols., 30s. Abridged in 1 vol., 2s.

GAYRARD (Mme. Paul) Harmony of the Passion. Compiled from the four Gospels, in Latin and French. 18mo., 1s. 6d.

George Lawson; or, the Dark Shadow. A Tale. 2s. 6d.

GIBBONS (Most Rev. Archbishop), The Faith of our Fathers; Being a Plain Exposition and Vindication of the Church Founded by our Lord Jesus Christ. 4s.; paper covers, 2s. *nett.*

GODDARD (Rt. Rev. Mgr.), Selection from Alban Butler's Lives of the Saints. 5s.

GOFFINE (Rev. F.), Explanation of the Epistles and Gospels. Illustrated. 8vo., 9s.

Golden Thought of Queen Beryl, and other Stories. By Marie Cameron. 1s. 6d.; or cheap edition, in 2 vols. 6d. each.

GRACE RAMSAY. *See* O'Meara (Kathleen).

Grains of Gold. Series 1 and 2, cloth, 2s. 6d., separately, 1s. each.

GRANT (Bishop), Pastoral on St. Joseph. 32mo., 3d. & 4d.

Gregory Lopez, the Hermit, Life of. By Canon Doyle, O.S.B. 3s. 6d.

Grounds of the Catholic Doctrine. By Bishop Challoner. Large type edition, 18mo., 4d.

Harmony of Anglicanism. By T. W. Marshall. 8vo., 2s. 6d.

HAY (Bishop), Devout Christian. 18mo., 2s.

HAY (Bishop), Sincere Christian. 18mo., 2s.

He would be a Lord. A Comedy in 3 Acts. (Boys.) 12mo., 2s.

Heaven Opened by the Practice of frequent Confession and Holy Communion. By the Abbé Favre. 2s. 6d.

HEIGHAM (John), A Devout Exposition of the Holy Mass. Edited by Austin John Rowley, Priest. 3s.

HENRY (Lucien), Flowers of Christian Wisdom. 1s. 6d.

HERBERT (Lady), True Wayside Tales. 12mo., 3s. ; or in 5 vols., cheap edition, 6d. each.

1. The Brigand Chief, and other Tales. 2. Now is the Accepted Time, and other Tales. 3. What a Child can do, and other Tales. 4. Sowing Wild Oats, and other Tales. 5. The Two Hosts, and other Tales.

—— **Second Series of True Wayside Tales.** 3s., or separately

—— **Moothoosawmy, & other Indian Tales.** 1s. **Emily, &c.** 1s. **The Two Cousins, &c.** 1s.

HERBERT (Wallace), My Dream and other Verses. 1s.

—— **The Angels and the Sacraments.** 1s.

Hermann, Fr. (Carmelite), Life of. From the French of Abbé Sylvain. 8vo., 3s. 6d. ; better bound, 4s. 6d.

HERVEY (E. L.), Stories from many Lands. 12mo., 3s. 6d.

—— **Rest, on the Cross.** 12mo., 3s. 6d.

—— **The Feasts of Camelot, with the Tales that were told there.** 3s.

HOFFMAN (Franz), Industry and Laziness. 2s. 6d.

Holy Family Card of Membership. A beautiful design. Folio. Price 6d., or 8d., on a roller, post free ; 4s. 6d. a dozen, or post free 5s.

Holy Isle ; or, Lives of some Saints of Ireland. 1s.

Holy Places : their Sanctity and Authenticity. 3s. 6d.

Holy Readings. By J. R. Digby Beste, Esq. 2s.

Holy Week Book. New edition, with Ordinary of the Mass, Vespers and Complin, Blessing of the Holy Oils, &c. Edited by Mr. Seager. 1s., soft morocco, 2s. 6d.

Horace. Literally translated by Smart, 2s. Latin and English, 3s. 6d.

HUMPHREY (Rev. W., S.J.), The Panegyrics of Fr. Segneri, S.J. Translated from the orignal Italian. With a Preface by the Rev. W. Humphrey, S.J. 12mo., 6s.

HUSENBETH (Rev. Dr.), Convert Martyr. 1s.

——— **History of the Blessed Virgin.** Translated from Orsini. Illustrated. 12mo., 3s. 6d.

——— **Life and Sufferings of Our Lord.** By Rev. H. Rutter. Illustrated. 12mo., 3s. 6d.

——— **Little Office of the Immaculate Conception.** In Latin and English. 32mo., cloth, 6d.; soft morocco 1s. 6d. Please refer to page 3 for particulars of this edition.

——— **Our Blessed Lady of Lourdes.** Paper cover, 6d. with the Novena, cloth, 1s.; Novena, separately, 3d.; Litany, 1d.

Hymn Book (The Catholic). Edited by Rev. G. Langton Vere. 32mo., 1d.; larger edition, 204 pages, 2d.; cloth, 4d.

Iceland (Three Sketches of Life in). By Carl Andersen. 1s. 6d.

Imitation of Christ. *See* A'Kempis.

Indian Tales, edited by Lady Herbert. 1s.

Industry and Laziness. By Franz Hoffman. From the German, by James King. 12mo., 2s. 6d.

IOTA. The Adventures of a Protestant in Search of a Religion: being the Story of a late Student of Divinity at Bunyan Baptist College; a Nonconformist Minister, who seceded to the Catholic Church. 12mo., 3s. 6d.; cheap edition, 2s.

Italian Revolution (The History of). The History of the Barricades. By Keyes O'Clery, M.P. 8vo., 4s.

Jack's Boy. By M. F. S., author of "Fluffy." 12mo, 3s.

John of God (S.), Life of. 5s.

Joseph (S.). Novena to, with a Pastoral by the late Bishop Grant. 32mo., 3d.; cloth, 4d.

——— *See* Leaflets.

Journey of Sophia and Eulalie to the Palace of True Happiness. (The Catholic Pilgrim's Progress.) From the French by Rev. Fr. Bradbury. 2s. 6d.

R. Washbourne, Paternoster Row, London.

Kainer; or, the Usurer's Doom. By James King. 1s.

KEENAN (Rev. S.), Controversial Catechism. 12mo., 2s.

KENNY (Dr.), Young Catholic's Guide to Confession and Holy Communion. 32mo., 4d.

KERSHAW (Frances I. M.), Bobbie and Birdie; or, Our Lady's Picture. A Story for the very little ones. 2s. 6d.

———— Gamekeeper's Little Son, and other Tales for Children. 2s. 6d.

Key of Heaven. *See* Prayers, page 31.

Killed at Sedan. By Samuel Richardson, A.B., B.L. 5s.

KINANE (Rev. T. H.), Angel of the Altar; or, the Love of the Most Adorable and Most Sacred Heart of Jesus. 2s. 6d.

———— Dove of the Tabernacle. 1s. 6d.

———— Lamb of God. 18mo., 2s.

———— Mary Immaculate. 2s.

———— St. Joseph. A month of March in his honour. 2s.

KING (James). Industry and Laziness. 2s. 6d.

———— Kainer; or, the Usurer's Doom. 1s.

LA BOUILLERIE (Mgr. de), The Eucharist and the Christian Life. Translated by L. C. 12mo., 3s. 6d.

Lacordaire. The Inner Life of Pere Lacordaire. From the French of Père Chocarne. By Augusta Theodosia Drane. 6s. 6d.

LAING (Rev. Dr.), Knight of the Faith.
        Absurd Protestant Opinions concerning *Intention*. 4d.
        Catholic, not Roman Catholic. 4d.
        Challenge to the Churches. 1d.
        Descriptive Guide to the Mass. 1s. and 1s. 6d.
        Favourite Fallacy about Private Judgment and Inquiry. 1d.
        Protestantism against the Natural Moral Law. 1d.
        What is Christianity? 6d.
        Whence does the Monarch get his right to Rule? 2s. 6d.

LAMBILOTTE (Pere), The Consoler. Translated by Abbot Burder. 3s. 6d.

LANE-CLARKE (T. M. L.) The Violet Sellers. A Drama for Children in 3 Acts. 6d.

LANGUET (Mgr.), Confidence in the Mercy of God. Translated by Abbot Burder. 12mo., 3s.

Leaflets. 1d. each, or 1s. 2d. per 100 post free, (a single dozen 4d.)

One of each (as sample) post free, 1s.

Act of Reparation to the Sacred Heart.
Archconfraternity of the Agonising Heart of Jesus and the Compassionate Heart of Mary: Prayers for the Dying.
Archconfraternity of Our Lady of Angels. Ditto, Rules.
Christmas Offering (or 7s. 6d. per 1000).
Devotions to S. Joseph.
New Indulgenced Prayer to St. Joseph.
Divine Praises.
Gospel according to S. John, *in Latin.* 1s. 6d. per 100.
Indulgenced Prayers for Souls in Purgatory.
Indulgences attached to Medals, Crosses, Statues, &c.
Intentions for Indulgences.
Litany of Our Lady of Angels.
Litany of Resignation.
Miraculous Prayer—August Queen of Angels.
Prayer for One's Confessor.
Prayers for the Holy Souls in Purgatory. By St. Ligouri.
Union of our Life with the Passion of our Lord.
Visits to the Blessed Sacrament.

Leaflets. 1d. each, or 4s. per 100, (a single dozen 10d.).

Act of Consecration to the Holy Angels.
Act of Consecration to the Sacred Heart.
Concise Portrait of the Blessed Virgin.
Explanation of the Medal or Cross of St. Benedict. 6s. per 100.
Indulgenced Prayers for the Rosary of the Holy Souls.
Indulgenced Prayer before a Crucifix. 6s. per 100.
Litany of Our Lady of Lourdes. 6s. per 100.
Litany of the Seven Dolours.
Office of the Sacred Heart. 6s. per 100.
Prayer to S. Philip Neri.
Prayer to the Wounded Shoulder of Our Lord.
Prayers for Three Days before and after Holy Communion.

Lectures for Boys. By Canon Doyle. 2 vols., 12mo., 10s. 6d.
Legends of the Saints. By M. F. S. 3s. 6d.

R. Washbourne, Paternoster Row, London.

Legends of the Thirteenth Century. By Rev. H. Collins. 3s.

Lenten Thoughts. By Bishop Amherst. 18mo., 1s.; stronger bound, 2s.

LIGUORI (S.), Selva; or, a Collection of Matter for Sermons. 12mo., 6s.

——— **Way of Salvation.** 32mo., 1s.

Lily of S. Joseph: A little Manual of Prayers and Hymns for Mass. 2d.; cloth, 4d. Larger edition with Fr. Vere's Hymns. 8d.

LINGARD (Dr.), Anglo-Saxon Church. 2 vols., 12mo., 10s.

Links with the Absent; or, Chapters on Correspondence. By a Member of the Ursuline Community, Thurles. 1s. 6d.

Little Mildred, or Oremus. By F. B. Bickerstaffe Drew. 1s.

Little Office of the Immaculate Conception. By Rev. Dr. Husenbeth. Cloth, 6d.; soft morocco, 1s. 6d.

Little Prayer Book for ordinary Catholic Devotions. 3d.

Lives of the First Religious of the Visitation of Holy Mary. By Mother Frances Magdalen de Chaugy. 2 vols., 10s.

Lost Children of Mount St. Bernard. 18mo., 6d.

Lourdes, Our Blessed Lady of. By Rev. Dr. Husenbeth. 18mo., 6d.; with the Novena, cloth, 1s.

——— **Novena to,** for the use of the Sick. 3d.

——— **Litany of.** 1d. each.

——— **Month at Lourdes.** By H. Caraher. 2s.

LUCK (Bishop, O.S.B.), Short Meditations for every Day in the Year. For the Regular Clergy. From the Italian. 6s. Edition for the Secular Clergy and others, 2 vols., 9s.

——— **S. Gregory's Life and Miracles of St. Benedict.** 1s.; stronger bound, 2s.

MACDANIEL (M. A.), Novena to S. Joseph. 3d.; cloth, 4d.

Manual of Catholic Devotions. *See* Prayers, page 31.

Manual of Devotions in honour of Our Lady of Sorrows. Compiled by the Clergy at St. Patrick's, Soho. 18mo., 1s. & 1s. 6d.

Margarethe Verflassen. Translated from the German by Mrs. Smith Sligo. 2s. 6d.

MARQUIGNY (Pere), Life and Letters of Countess Adelstan. 2s.

MARSHALL (Arthur), Comedy of Convocation in the English Church. 8vo., 2s. 6d.

────── **Oxford Undergraduate of Twenty Years Ago.** 8vo., 2s. 6d.

MARSHALL (Rev. W., D.D.), Doctrine of Purgatory. 1s.

MARSHALL (T. W. M.), Harmony of Anglicanism— Church Defence. 8vo., 2s. 6d.

Mary Queen of Scots. A Tragedy in 3 Acts (mixed). 6d.

Mary Venerated in all Ages—Regina Sæculorum. 2s.

Mass, A Devout Exposition of. By Rev. A. J. Rowley. 3s.

Mass, Ordinary of. 2d.

MATIGNON (Pere) The Duties of Christian Parents. 3s. 6d.

Maxims of the Kingdom of Heaven. The Bible arranged under subjects. With Prefatory Notice, by J. H. N. 5s.

May Readings for every day. By Rev. Fr. Thaddeus. 3s.

May Readings for the Feasts of Our Lady. By Rev. A. P. Bethell. 18mo., 1s.

May Templeton; a Tale of Faith and Love. 12mo., 5s.

Meditations on the Blessed Sacrament. 1s. 6d.

Meditations on the Life of Our Lord. By Mrs. Abel Ram. 3s.

Meditations for every Day in the Year. By Bishop Luck. Secular, 2 vols., 9s. Regular, 2 vols. in one, 6s.

MERMILLOD (Mgr.), The Supernatural Life. Translated from the French, with a Preface by Lady Herbert. 12mo., 5s.

MEYRICK (Rev. T.), Life of St. Wenefred. 12mo., 2s.

────── **The Early Popes.** St. Peter to Charlemagne. 6s.

────── **St. Eustace.** A Drama (5 Acts) for Boys. 6d.

M. F. S., Catherine Hamilton. 1s. 6d. ; } in one vol., 3s.
────── **Catherine Grown Older.** 2s. }

────── **Fluffy.** A Tale for Boys. 3s.

────── **Jack's Boy.** 3s.

────── **Legends of the Saints.** 3s. 6d.

────── **My Golden Days.** 2s. 6d. ; or in 3 vols., 1s. each.
    Yellow Holly, and other Tales.
    Tableaux Vivants, and other Tales.
    Wet Days, and other Tales.

R. Washbourne, Paternoster Row, London.

M. F. S., Our Esther. 2s. 6d.

———— Out in the Cold World. 3s.

———— Stories of Holy Lives. 3s. 6d.

———— Stories of Martyr Priests. 3s. 6d.

———— Stories of the Saints. Five Series, 3s. 6d. each.

———— Story of the Life of S. Paul. 2s.

———— The Three Wishes. A Tale. 2s.

———— Tom's Crucifix, and other Tales. 3s. 6d., or in 5 vols. 1s. each.

    Tom's Crucifix, and Pat's Rosary.

    Good for Evil, and Joe Ryan's Repentance.

    The Old Prayer Book, and Charlie Pearson's Medal.

    Catherine's Promise, and Norah's Temptation.

    Annie's First Prayer, and Only a Picture.

Mildred (St.) Abbess of Minster, Life of. By a Lay-Tertiary of St. Francis. 2s.

Missal. *See* Prayers, page 31.

Mission Cross. By Mrs. Bartle Teeling. 1s. 6d.

MOEHLER (Dr.), Symbolism. By Professor Robertson. 8s.

Monk of the Monastery of Yuste. By Mariana Monteiro. 2s.

MONTEIRO (Mariana), Allah Akbar—God is Great. An Arab Legend of the Siege and Conquest of Granada. 12mo., 3s.

———— Monk of the Monastery of Yuste; or, The Last Days of the Emperor Charles V. An Historical Legend of the 16th Century. 12mo., 2s.

———— Gathered Gems from Spanish Authors. 12mo., 3s.

MOORE'S Irish Melodies. Music and words, 4to., 3s. 6d.

Mora (Ven. Elizabeth Canori), Life of. Translated from the Italian, with Preface by Lady Herbert. 3s. 6d.

R. Washbourne, Paternoster Row, London.

Most Beautiful among the Children of Men. Meditations on the Life of Our Lord. By Mrs. Abel Ram. 3s.

Music: Antiphons (9) of the Blessed Virgin. 3s. 6d.
    Catholic Hymnal. By Leopold de Prins. 2s.; bound, 3s.
    Litanies (36) and Benediction Service. By W. Schulthes. 6s. Second Series (Corona Lauretana). 2s.
    Litanies (6). By E. Leslie. 6d.
    Litany of the B.V.M. By Baronesse Emma Freemantle. 6d.
    Mass of the Holy Child Jesus. By W. Schulthes. The vocal part only, 4d.; or 3s. per doz. Cloth, 6d.; or 4s. 6d. per doz.
    Mass in honour of S. Patrick. Three equal voices By Schaller. 3s. 6d.
    Mass "Jesu Bona Pastor." Four Voices. By Schaller. 3s. 6d.
    Motetts (5). Four Voices. By Benz and Santner. 3s. 6d.
    Oratory Hymns. By W. Schulthes. 2 vols., 8s.
    Vespers and Benediction Service. Four Voices or Unison. By Leopold de Prins. 3s. 6d.

    * *All the above (music) prices are nett.*

My Conversion and Vocation. By Rev. Father Schouvaloff, 5s.

My Golden Days. By M. F. S. 2s. 6d., or in 3 vols., 1s. each.

My Lady, at Last. A Tale, by M. Taunton. 3s. 6d.

Nellie Gordon, the Factory Girl; or, Lost and Saved. By M. A. Pennell. 18mo., 6d.

New Testament. 12mo., 1s., large type, 2s. 6d. Persian calf, 7s. 6d., morocco, 10s.

Nicholas; or, the Reward of a Good Action. 18mo., 6d.

Nina and Pippo, the Lost Children of Mt. St. Bernard. 6d.

Novena to Our Blessed Lady of Lourdes for the use of the Sick. 18mo., 3d.

Novena to St. Joseph, with a Pastoral by Bishop Grant. 3d.; cloth, 4d.

O'CLERY (Keyes, K.S.G.), The History of the Italian Revolution. First Period—The Revolution of the Barricades (1796-1849). 8vo., 4s.

R. Washbourne, Paternoster Row, London.

Office of the Dead, with Meditations for every day in November. 1s.

O'HARA (C. M.), Clare's Sacrifice. An impressive little Tale for First Communicants. 6d.

OLIVER (Lætitia), Father Placid; or, the Custodian of the Blessed Sacrament. 1s.

—— Rose Fortescue; or, the Devout Client of Our Lady of Dolours. 1s.

O'MEARA (Kathleen), The Battle of Connemara. 2s. 6d.

—— A Daughter of S. Dominick. 1s. 6d.

Ora Pro Nobis; or, Tristram's Friends. By Rev. F. Drew. 1s.

Oratorian Lives of the Saints. Second series, 5s. a vol.

   I. S. Bernardine of Siena, Minor Observatine.

   II. S. Philip Benizi, Fifth General of the Servites.

   III. S. Veronica Giuliani, and B. Battista Varani.

   IV. S. John of God. By Canon Cianfogni.

Oremus; or, Little Mildred. By Rev. F. Drew. 1s.

Oremus, A Liturgical Prayer Book. *See* page 31.

Our Esther. By M.F.S., author of "Out in the Cold World." 2s. 6d.

Our Lady's Month. By Rev. A. P. Bethell. 18mo., 1s. and 1s. 6d.

—— Festivals—Lectures for Boys. By Very Rev. Canon Doyle, O.S.B. 2s. 6d.

Our Lord's Life, Passion, Death, and Resurrection. 1s.

Out in the Cold World. By M. F. S., Author of "Fluffy." 3s.

Oxford Undergraduate of Twenty Years Ago. By Arthur Marshall. 8vo., 2s. 6d.

Panegyrics of Fr. Segneri, S.J. Translated from the original Italian. With a Preface, by Rev. W. Humphrey, S.J. 12mo., 6s.

Passion of Our Lord, Harmony of. By Gayrard, 1s. 6d.

—— Lectures for Boys. By Very Rev. Canon Doyle, O.S.B. 3s.

Pater Noster; or, an Orphan Boy. By Rev. F. Drew. 1s.

Path to Paradise. *See* Prayers, page 31.

R. Washbourne, Paternoster Row, London.

Patrick (S.), Life of. 1s.

Penitential Psalms Paraphrased. By Rev. F. Blyth. 1s.

PENNELL (M. A.), Agnes Wilmott. 1s. 6d.

—————— Bertram Eldon. 12mo., 1s.

—————— Nellie Gordon, the Factory Girl. 18mo., 6d.

Pens, Washbourne's Free and Easy. Fine, or Middle, or Broad Points, 1s. per gross.

Per Jesum Christum; or, Two Good Fridays. By Rev. F. Drew. 1s.

Philip Benizi (S.), Life of. 5s.

PHILPIN (Rev. F.), Holy Places; their sanctity and authenticity. With three Maps. 3s. 6d.; cheap edition, 2s. 6d.

PILLEY (C.), Walter Ferrers' School Days; or, Bellevue and its Owners. 1s. 6d.

PLAYS. *See* Dramas, page 11.

PLUES (Margaret), Chats about the Commandments. 3s.

—————— Chats about the Rosary. 3s.

Popes, Lives of the Early. By Rev. T. Meyrick. 6s.

Portiuncula, Indulgence of. 1d.; 100 for 6d.

PRADEL (Fr., O. P.), Life of St. Vincent Ferrer. Translated by Rev. Fr. Dixon. 5s.

PRAYER BOOKS. *See* page 30.

PRAYERS, a Short Form of. 1d.

PRICE (Rev. E.), Sick Calls. 12mo., 3s. 6d.

Purgatory, Doctrine of. By Rev. W. Marshall, D.D. 1s.

Purgatory, Indulgenced Prayers for Souls in. 1s. per 100.

Purgatory, Month of the Souls in Purgatory. By Ricard, 1s.

Purgatory, Prayers for Holy Souls in. By St. Liguori. 1s. per 100.

Purgatory, Souls in. By Abbot Burder. 32mo., 2d.

PYE (Henry John, M.A.), Revelation. Being the substance of several conversations on First Principles. 6d.

R. Washbourne, Paternoster Row, London.

PYE (H. J. M.A.), The Religion of Common Sense. 1s.

QUINN (Mary), Mary Queen of Scots. A Tragedy in 3 Acts (Mixed) 6d.

RAM (Mrs. Abel), Meditations on the Life of Our Lord. With a Preface by the Cardinal Archbishop of Westminster. 3s.

RAVIGNAN (Pere), The Spiritual Life, Conferences Translated by Mrs. Abel Ram. 12mo., 5s.

RAYMOND-BARKER (Mrs. F.) Life and Letters of the Countess Adelstan. 2s.

—— Fr. Hermann (Carmelite). 3s. 6d. and 4s. 6d.

—— Paul Seigneret (Seminarist and Martyr). 1s. 6d.

—— Regina Sæculorum. 2s.

—— Rosalie ; or, Memoir of a French Child. 1s. 6d.

—— Science and Faith upon the Sacred Heart. 2s.

REEVES' History of the Bible. 12mo., 3s. 18mo., 1s.

Regina Sæculorum ; or, Mary Venerated in all Ages. Devotions to the Blessed Virgin from Ancient Sources. 2s.

Religion of Common Sense. By H. J. Pye, M.A. 12mo., 1s.

Rest, on the Cross. By Eleanora Louisa Hervey. 12mo., 3s. 6d.

Revelation. By Henry John Pye, Esq. 6d.

Reverse of the Medal. A Drama for Girls. 12mo., 6d.

Revolt of the Netherlands. By W. C. Robinson. 3s.

RIBADENEIRA—Life of Our Lord. 12mo., 1s.

RICARD (Abbe), Month of the Holy Angels. 18mo., 1s.

—— Month of the Souls in Purgatory. 18mo., 1s.

RICHARDSON (Rev. Fr.), Lily of St. Joseph. A little Manual of Prayers and Hymns for Mass. 64mo., 1s. roan, 1s. 6d. soft morocco, 2s. calf or morocco, 2s. 6d. extra gilt. 32mo. cloth, with Fr. Vere's Hymns, 8d.

RICHARDSON (Samuel, A.B., B.L., of the Middle Temple), Killed at Sedan. A Novel. Crown 8vo., 5s.

RICHE (Abbé A.), Agreement of Science and Faith upon the Sacred Heart of Jesus. 2s.

R. Washbourne, Paternoster Row, London.

Ritus Servandus in Expositione et Benedictione. Red morocco, 10s., gilt, 12s. 6d.

Road to Heaven. A game. 1s., with the Rules bound, 2s.

ROBINSON (W. C.), The Revolt of the Netherlands. 3s.

Rome (To) and Back. Fly-Leaves from a Flying Tour. Edited by Rev. W. H. Anderdon, S.J., 12mo., 2s.

Rosalie ; or, the Memoir of a French Child, told by herself. By Mrs. F. Raymond-Barker. 1s. 6d.

Rosary, Fifteen Mysteries of, and Fourteen Stations of the Cross. In One Volume, 32 Illustrations. 16mo., 2s.

Rosary for the Souls in Purgatory, with Indulgenced Prayer. 4d., 6d. and 9d. Medals separately, 1d. each, or 9d. a dozen. Prayers separately, ½d. each, 4d. a dozen, or 4s. for 100.

Rosary, Chats about the; Aunt Margaret's Little Neighbours. 3s.

Rose Fortescue ; or, the Devout Client of Our Lady of Dolours. By Lætitia Oliver. 1s.

Rose of Venice. A Tale. By S. Christopher. Crown 8vo., 3s. 6d.

ROWLEY (Rev. Austin John), A Devout Exposition of the Holy Mass. Composed by John Heigham. 3s.

RUSSELL (Rev. M.), Emmanuel : Eucharistic Verses. 2s.

——————— **Erin : Verses Irish and Catholic.** 2s.

——————— **Madonna.** Verses on Our Lady and the Saints, 2s.

RYAN (Bishop). What Catholics do not Believe. 12mo., 1s.

Sacred Heart. Act of Consecration to. 1d.; or 4s. per 100.

——————————, **Act of Reparation to.** 1s. 2d. per 100.

——————————, **Elevations to the.** By Rev. Fr. Doyotte, S.J. 2s.

——————————, **Lectures for Boys.** By Very Rev. Canon Doyle, O.S.B. 3s.

—————————— **offered to the Piety of the Young engaged in Study.** By Rev. F. Deham. 32mo., 9d.

———————————, **Office.** 1d.

———————————, **Treasury of.** 32mo., 1s. 6d.; French morocco, 2s.; calf or morocco, 5s. 18mo., 2s. 6d.; roan, 3s. ; soft morocco, 5s.

Saints, Lives of, from Alban Butler. Selected and edited by the Rt. Rev. Mgr. Goddard. 5s.

R. Washbourne, Paternoster Row, London.

SCARAMELLI—Directorium Asceticum; or, Guide to the Spiritual Life. 4 vols. 12mo., 24s.

SCHMID (Canon), Tales. Illustrated. 12mo., 3s. 6d. Separately:—The Canary Bird, The Dove, The Inundation, The Rose Tree, The Water Jug, The Wooden Cross. 6d. each; gilt, 1s.

School of Jesus Crucified. By Fr. Ignatius, Cong. Pass. 2s. 6d.

SCHOUVALOFF (Rev. Father, Barnabite), My Conversion and Vocation. Translated from the French, with an Appendix, by Fr. C. Tondini. 12mo., 5s.

SCHULTHES (William). *See* Music.

SEAMER (Mrs.), *See* M. F. S., page 19.

SEBASTIAN (Fr.), Manual of the Infant Jesus. 2s. 6d.

——————— ——— Cross and Passion. 2s. 6d.

——————————————— Seven Dolours. 2s. 6d.

————————————— a Happy Eternity. 2s. 6d.

Secret, The. A Drama for Girls in 1 Act. By Mrs. Sadlier. 6d.

SEGNERI (Fr., S.J.), Panegyrics. Translated from the original Italian. With a Preface, by Rev. W. Humphrey. 12mo., 6s.

SEGUR (Mgr.), Books for Little Children. Translated. 32mo., 3d. each. Confession, Holy Communion, Child Jesus, Piety, Prayer, Temptation and Sin. In one volume, cloth, 1s. 6d.

Seigneret (Paul), Seminarist and Martyr, Life of. 1s. 6d.

Selva; a Collection of Matter for Sermons. By St. Liguori. 12mo., 6s.

Sermons. *See* Doyle, 2 vols., 10s. 6d.; Scaramelli, 4 vols., 24s.; Segneri, 6s.; Gahan, 8s.; Perry, 2 vols., 7s.

Serving Boy's Manual, and Book of Public Devotions. Containing all those prayers and devotions for Sundays and Holydays, usually divided in their recitation between the Priest and the Congregation. Compiled from approved sources, and adapted to Churches, served either by the Secular or Regular Clergy. 32mo., embossed, 1s.; French morocco, 2s.; calf, 4s.; with Epistles and Gospels, 6d. extra.

Shandy Maguire. A Farce for Boys. 2 Acts. 6d.

SIGHART (Dr.), Life of Albertus Magnus. 6s.

Sinner's Guide. 3s. 6d.

Sir Ælfric and other Tales. By Rev. G. Bampfield. 6d. and 1s.

Sir Thomas Maxwell and his Ward. By Miss Bridges. 1s. 6d

SMITH-SLIGO (A. V., Esq.), Life of the Ven. Anna Maria Taigi. Translated from French of Calixte. 3s. 6d.

———— (Mrs.) Margarethe Verflassen. 12mo., 2s. 6d.

Snowflakes and other Tales. By M. Sinclair Allison. 1s.

Solid Virtue. By Father Bellécius, S.J. With a Preface by Dr. Croke, Archbishop of Cashel and Emly. New edition, revised and corrected. Crown 8vo., 7s. 6d.

Sophia and Eulalie. (The Catholic Pilgrim's Progress.) From the French by Rev. Fr. Bradbury. 12mo., 2s. 6d.

Spiritual Conferences on the Mysteries of Faith and the Interior Life. By Father Collins. 12mo., 5s.

Spiritual Life. Conferences by Père Ravignan. Translated by Mrs. Abel Ram. 12mo., 5s.

Spiritual Life of Rev. Fr. Schouvaloff. 12mo., 5s.

Spiritual Works of Louis of Blois. Edited by Rev. F. John Bowden. 12mo., 3s. 6d.

Stations, and Mysteries of the Rosary. Illustrated 2s.

Stories for my Children. Angels and the Sacraments. 1s.

Stories of Holy Lives. By M. F. S. 12mo., 3s. 6d.

Stories of Martyr Priests. By M. F. S. 12mo., 3s. 6d.

Stories of the Saints. By M. F. S. Five Series, each 3s. 6d.

Stories from many Lands. Compiled by E. L. Hervey. 3s. 6d.

Story of a Paper Knife. 12mo., 1s.

Story of Marie and other Tales. 12mo., 2s. 6d.

Story of the Life of St. Paul. By M. F. S., author of "Stories of the Saints." 12mo., 2s.

Sufferings of Our Lord. Sermons preached by Father Claude de la Colombière, S.J., in the Chapel Royal, St. James's, in the year 1677. 18mo., 1s.

Supernatural Life, The. By Mgr. Mermillod. Translated from the French, with a Preface by Lady Herbert. 12mo., 5s.

Sure Way to Heaven. A Little Manual for Confession and Holy Communion. 32mo., 6d.; persian, 2s. 6d.; calf or morocco, 3s. 6d.

Tales of the Jewish Church. By Charles Walker. 1s. 6d., **2s.**
TANDY (Rev. Dr.), Terry O'Flinn. 1s.
TAUNTON (M.), My Lady, at Last. A Tale. 3s. 6d.
TEELING (Mrs. Bartle), The Mission Cross. 1s. 6d.
TERESA (S.), Book of the Foundations. Translated by Canon Dalton. 12mo., 3s. 6d.
———— Letters of. Translated by Canon Dalton. 12mo., 3s. **6d.**
———— Way of Perfection. 12mo., 3s. 6d.
———— The Interior Castle. 12mo., 3s. 6d.
Terry O'Flinn. By Rev. Dr. Tandy. 1s.
Three Wishes. A Tale. By M. F. S. 2s.
Threshold of the Catholic Church. By Dr. Bagshawe. 1s. *nett*, (postage 3d.), 12 copies for 10s. (postage 1s. 6d.).
Tom's Crucifix, and other Tales. By M. F. S. 12mo., 3s. 6d., or in 5 vols., 1s. each.
True Wayside Tales. By Lady Herbert. 3s., or in 5 vols., 6d. each.
———— Second Series. 3s., or separately in 3 vols., 1s. each.
Two Friends; or Marie's Self-Denial. By Madame d'Arras. 1s.
Ursuline Manual. *See* Prayers, page 31.
Vatican and the Quirinal. By A. Wood. 1s. 6d.
Veni Creator; or, Ulrich's Money. By Rev. F. Drew. 1s.
VERE (Rev. G. L.), The Catholic Hymn Book. 32mo., 2d.; cloth, 4d.; abridged edition, 1d., cloth, 2d.
———— For Better, not for Worse. A Tale. 3s.
Veronica Giuliani (S.), Life of, and B. Battista Varani 12mo., 5s.
Village Beauty, and other Tales. 10 Illustrations.
[*In the Press..*
Village Lily. A Tale. 12mo., 1s.
Vincent Ferrer (S.), of the Order of Friar Preachers; his Life, Spiritual Teaching, and Practical Devotion. By Rev. Fr. Andrew Pradel, O.P. Translated from the French by the Rev. Fr. T. A. Dixon, O. P. 5s.

R. Washbourne, Paternoster Row, London.

Violet Sellers, The ; a Drama in 3 Acts, for Children. 6d.

VIRGIL. Literally translated by Davidson. 12mo., 2s. 6d.

"Vitis Mystica"; or, the True Vine. By Canon Brownlow. 2s. 6d.

WALKER (Charles), Tales of the Jewish Church. 1s. 6d., 2s.

Walter Ferrers' School Days; or, Bellevue and its Owners. By C. Pilley. 1s. 6d.

WELD (Miss K. M.), Bessy ; or, the Fatal Consequences of Telling Lies. 1s.

Wenefred (St.), Life of. By Rev. T. Meyrick. 12mo., 2s.

What Catholics do not Believe. By Bishop Ryan. 12mo., 1s.

William (St.), of York. A Drama in Two Acts. (Boys.) 12mo., 6d.

WISEMAN (Cardinal), Doctrines and Practices of the Catholic Church. 12mo., 3s. 6d.

——— Science and Religion. 12mo., 5s.

Wiseman (Cardinal), Recollections of. By M. J. Arnold. 2s.

WOOD (Alexander), The Vatican and the Quirinal. 1s. 6d.

Young Catholic's Guide to Confession and Holy Communion. By Dr. Kenny. 4d.

R. WASHBOURNE'S

Catalogue of

CATHOLIC BOOKS

IMPORTED FROM

AMERICA,

SENT POST FREE ON APPLICATION.

R. Washbourne, Paternoster Row, London.

Garden, Little, of the Soul. Edited by the Rev. R. G. Davis. *With Imprimatur of the Cardinal Archbishop of Westminster.* This book, as its name imports, contains a selection from the "Garden of the Soul" of the Prayers and Devotions of most general use. Whilst it will serve as a *Pocket Prayer Book* for all, it is, by its low price, *par excellence*, the Prayer Book for children and for the very poor. In it are to be found the old familiar Devotions of the "Garden of the Soul," as well as many important additions, such as the Devotions to the Sacred Heart, to Saint Joseph, to the Guardian Angels, and others. The omissions are mainly the Forms of administering the Sacraments, and Devotions that are not of very general use. It is printed in a clear type, on a good paper, both especially selected, for the purpose of obviating the disagreeableness of small type and inferior paper. Twentieth Thousand.

32mo., price, cloth, 6d.; with Epistles and Gospels, 6d.; stronger bound, 8d., with clasp, 1s.; blue cloth, 1s.; with clasp, 1s. 6d. Roan, 1s.; with E. and G. 1s. 6d.; with rims and clasp, 1s 6d. and 2s. French morocco, 1s. 6d.; with E. and G., 2s.; with rims and clasp, 2s. and 2s. 6d. French morocco extra gilt, 2s.; with E. and G., 2s. 6d.; with rims and clasp, 2s. 6d. and 3s. Calf or morocco, 3s.; with E. and G., 3s. 6d.; with clasp, 4s. and 4s. 6d. Calf or morocco, extra gilt, 4s.; with E. and G., 4s. 6d.; with clasp, 5s. and 5s. 6d. Russia, 5s., 5s. 6d., 6s., 6s. 6d., 7s. 6d., 8s. Russia antique, 17s. 6d. Ivory, with rims and clasp, 10s. 6d., 13s., 15s., 17s. 6d. Imitation ivory, with rims and clasp, 2s. 6d. Calf or morocco tuck (as a pocket book), 5s. 6d.

Illustrated edition, cloth, 1s.; with clasp, 1s. 6d.; roan, 1s 6d.; French mor., 2s.; extra gilt, 2s. 6d.; calf or morocco, 3s. 6d.; extra gilt, 4s. 6d.

Catholic Piety; or, Key of Heaven, with Epistles and Gospels. Large 32mo., roan, 1s. 6d. and 2s.; French morocco, with rims and clasp, 2s. 6d.; extra gilt, 3s.; with rims and clasp, 3s. 6d.

Catholic Piety. 32mo., 6d.; rims and clasp, 1s.; French morocco, 1s.; velvet, with rims and clasp, 2s. 6d. With Epistles and Gospels, roan, 1s.; French morocco, 1s. 6d.; with rims and clasp, 2s.; extra gilt, 2s.; Persian, 2s. 6d.; morocco, 3s. 6d.

Key of Heaven, same prices as above.

Crown of Jesus. Soft morocco, 5s. 6d. Persian calf, 6s. Calf or morocco, 8s.; with clasp, 10s. 6d. Calf or morocco, extra gilt, 10s. 6d.; with clasp, 12s. 6d; morocco, with turn-over edges, 10s. 6d.

Garden of the Soul. Very large Type. 18mo., cloth, 1s.; with Epistles and Gospels, 1s. 6d.; French morocco, 2s. 6d.; Morocco circuit, 7s. 6d.; calf antique, with clasp, 8s. French morocco, antique, with clasp, 6s. 6d.

Little Prayer Book for ordinary Catholic Devotions. 3d.

Child's Picture Prayer Book. 16 coloured Illustrations. Cloth, 1s.; stronger bound, 1s. 6d.; prettier bound, 2s.; gilt, 2s. 6d.

R. Washbourne, Paternoster Row, London.

R. Washbourne's List of Prayer Books. 31

Holy Week Book. New edition, with Ordinary of the Mass, Vespers and Complin, Blessing of the Holy Oils, &c. Cloth, 1s.; soft morocco, 2s. 6d.

Holy Childhood. 6d., 1s. and 1s. 6d.

Key of Heaven. *Very large type.* 18mo., 1s.; leather, 2s. 6d.

Lily of St. Joseph, The; a little Manual of Prayers and Hymns for Mass. 64mo., 2d.; roan, 1s.; French morocco, 1s. 6d.; calf or morocco, 2s.; gilt, 2s. 6d. 32mo., with Fr. Vere's Hymns, 8d.

Manual of Catholic Devotions. Small, for the waistcoat pocket. 64mo., 4d.; with Epistles and Gospels, cloth, 6d.; with rims, 1s.; roan, 1s.; calf or morocco, 2s. 6d.; ivorine, 2s. 6d.

Manual of Devotions in Honour of Our Lady of Sorrows. 18mo., 1s. 6d.; cheaper binding, 1s.

Missal (Complete). 18mo., roan, 5s.; Persian, 7s. 6d.; calf or morocco, 10s. 6d.; with rims and clasp, 13s. 6d.; calf or mor., extra gilt, 12s. 6d., with rims and clasp, 15s. 6d.; morocco, with turn-over edges, 13s. 6d.; morocco antique, 15s.; velvet, 20s.; Russia, 20s.; ivory, with rims and clasp, 31s. 6d. and 35s.

Missal and Vesper Book, in one vol. morocco, 6s. 6d.

Ordinary of the Mass. 32mo., 2d.

Oremus, A Liturgical Prayer Book: with the Imprimatur of the Cardinal Archbishop of Westminster. An adaptation of the Church Offices: containing Morning and Evening Devotions; Devotion for Mass, Confession, and Communion, and various other Devotions; Common and Proper, Hymns, Lessons, Collects, Epistles and Gospels for Sundays, Feasts, and Week Days; and short notices of over 200 Saints' Days. 32mo., 452 pages, cloth, 2s.; French morocco, 3s. 6d.; calf or morocco, 5s.; extra gilt, 6s. 6d.; Russia, 7s. 6d., &c., &c., &c.

A Smaller Oremus. An abridgment of the above. Cloth, 6d., French morocco, 1s. 6d.; calf or morocco, 2s. 6d.; extra gilt, 4s.; Russia, 5s.

A Short Form of Prayers. 1d.

Path to Paradise. 32 full-page Illustrations. 32mo., cloth, 3d. With 50 Illustrations, cloth, 4d. Superior edition, 6d. and 1s.

Public Devotions, and Serving Boy's Manual. Containing all those Prayers and Devotions for Sundays and Holidays, usually divided in their recitation between the Priest and the Congregation. Compiled from approved sources, and adapted to Churches served either by the Secular or the Regular Clergy, 32mo., Embossed, 1s.; with Epistles and Gospels, 1s. 6d.; French morocco, 2s., with Epistles and Gospels, 2s. 6d.; calf, 4s., with Epistles and Gospels, 4s. 6d.

Sure Way to Heaven. Cloth, 6d.; Persian, 2s. 6d.; morocco, 3s. 6d.

Treasury of the Sacred Heart. 18mo., 2s. 6d.; roan, 3s.; Soft morocco, 5s. 32mo., 1s. 6d.; leather, 2s.; calf or mor., 5s.

Ursuline Manual. 18mo., 4s.; Persian calf, 7s. 6d.; morocco, 10s.

R. Washbourne, Paternoster Row, London.

Garden of the Soul. (WASHBOURNE'S EDITION.) Edited by Rev R. G. Davis. *With Imprimatur of the Cardinal Abp. of W[minster.* Twenty-third Thousand. This Edition retains all the [de]votions that have made the GARDEN OF THE SOUL, now for n[any] generations, the well-known Prayer-book for English Cathc[lics.] During many years various Devotions have been introduced, [which,] in the form of appendices, have been added to other edit[ions.] These have now been incorporated into the body of the work, together with the Devotions to the Sacred Heart, to Saint Jos[eph,] to the Guardian Angels, the Itinerarium, and other important [ad]ditions, render this edition pre-eminently the Manual of Prayer, [for] both public and private use. The version of the Psalms has [been] carefully revised, and strictly conformed to the Douay transla[tion] of the Bible, published with the approbation of the LATE CARDI[NAL] WISEMAN. The Forms of administering the Sacraments have b[een] carefully translated, *as also the rubrical airections*, from the O[rdo] Administrandi Sacramenta. To enable all present, either at b[ap]tisms or other public administrations of the Sacraments, to pay d[ue] attention to the sacred rites, the Forms are inserted without a[ny] curtailment, both in Latin and English. The Devotions at M[ass] have been carefully revised, and enriched by copious adaptatio[ns] from the prayers of the Missal. The preparation for the Sacr[a]ments of Penance and the Holy Eucharist have been the objects [of] especial care, to adapt them to the wants of those whose religio[us] instruction may be deficient. Great attention has been paid to t[he] quality of the paper and to the size of type used in the printing, [to] obviate that weariness so distressing to the eyes, caused by the u[se] of books printed in small close type and on inferior paper.

32mo. Embossed, 1s.; with rims and clasp, 1s. 6d.; wi[th] Epistles and Gospels, 1s. 6d.; with rims and clasp, 2s. Frenc[h] morocco, 2s.; with rims and clasp, 2s. 6d.; with E. and G., 2s. 6d[.,] with rims and clasp, 3s. French morocco extra gilt, 2s. 6d.; wi[th] rims and clasp, 3s.; with E. and G., 3s.; with rims and clas[p,] 3s. 6d. Calf, or morocco 4s.; with best gilt clasp, 5s. 6d.; wit[h] E. and G., 4s. 6d., with best gilt clasp, 6s. Calf or morocco ext[ra] gilt, 5s.; with best gilt clasp, 6s. 6d.; with E. and G., 5s. 6[d.,] with best gilt clasp, 7s. Morocco antique, 8s. 6d. 9s. an[d] 12s. 6d.; morocco, with turn-over edges, 7s. 6d.; with E. an[d] G., 8s. Russia, antique, with clasp, 8s. 6d., 10s., 12s. 6d. [,] with E. and G., 9s., 10s. 6d.. 13s. Ivory 14s., 16s., 18s., and 20[s.,] with E. and G., 14s. 6d., 16s. 6d., 18s. 6d., and 20s. 6d.

The Epistles and Gospels. *Complete,* cloth, 4d.; roan, 1s.

"This is one of the best editions we have seen of one of the best of all our Praye[r] Books. It is well printed in clear, large type, on good paper."—*Catholic Opinion.*
A very complete arrangement of this which is emphatically the Prayer Book c[f] every Catholic household. It is as cheap as it is good, and we heartily recommen[d] it."—*Universe.* "Two striking features are the admirable order displayed through[
out the book, and the insertion of the Indulgences in small type above Indulgence[d] Prayers. In the Devotions for Mass, the editor has, with great discrimination, draw[n] largely on the Church's Prayers, as given us in the Missal."—*Weekly Register.*

R. Washbourne, Paternoster Row, London.

www.ingramcontent.com/pod-product-compliance
Lightning Source LLC
Chambersburg PA
CBHW031941230426
43672CB00010B/2011